RIGHTEOUS LIVES

RIGHTEOUS LIVES

*Narratives of the New Orleans
Civil Rights Movement*

KIM LACY ROGERS

NEW YORK UNIVERSITY PRESS
NEW YORK & LONDON

NEW YORK UNIVERSITY PRESS
New York and London

Copyright © 1993 by New York University
All rights reserved

Library of Congress Cataloging-in-Publication Data

Rogers, Kim Lacy.
Righteous lives : narratives of the New Orleans civil rights movement /
Kim Lacy Rogers.
p.   cm.
Includes bibliographical references and index.
ISBN 0-8147-7431-8 (cloth)
1. Afro-Americans—Civil rights—Louisiana—New Orleans.   2. Civil
rights movements—Louisiana—New Orleans—History—20th century.
3. New Orleans (La.)—Race relations.   I. Title.
F379.N59N4 1992   92-24735
976.3'35—dc20   CIP

New York University Press books are printed on acid-free paper, and
their binding materials are chosen for strength and durability.

Manufactured in the United States of America

c 10 9 8 7 6 5 4 3 2 1

For Andrea Hinding, John Lankford,
and Monte Piliawsky,
who saw me through, and saw this through.

Contents

Acknowledgments

*T*HIS book is the product of many voices and lives. I would first like to acknowledge my debt to the women and men of New Orleans, who patiently told me their stories, and graciously consented to see me on more than one occasion. I would especially like to thank Tom Dent, Lolis Elie, John P. Nelson, Jr., and Rosa Keller for many long hours of their time, and their generous explanation of their experiences.

Dr. Clifton Johnson and his staff at the Amistad Research Center have been exceptionally helpful and gracious over the many years in which I have returned to New Orleans to conduct interviews, acquire photographs, and accumulate the information necessary to make a book. I owe a special debt to Dr. Johnson and his staff, particularly archivists Lester Sullivan and Andy Simons. It was always a pleasure to do business with Amistad.

Dickinson College has also been very supportive of the years of research and exploration that went into this project. A 1988 Board of Advisors Grant allowed me to return to the city and re-interview many of the people with whom I'd spoken in 1978 and 1979. I must also thank Dickinson for other support in the form of research and development grants and publications grants. I must also thank Mrs. Gladys Cashman for her very patient editorial work on the manuscript, and for her marvelous ability to unscramble the mysteries of computer programs.

Finally, I would like to particularly thank my close friends and colleagues who have read the manuscript, exchanged ideas, and improved my analysis and writing over the years. The greatest debt is to Andrea Hinding, John Lankford, and Monte Piliawsky—three friends who have seen this work progress through many stages and lives. Also appreciated are the advice, comfort and wisdom of Eva McMahan and Steve Brouwer, who also read and critiqued the manuscript. Finally, I would like to thank the friends and colleagues who have valiantly endured my sometimes chaotic states as I have thought through and struggled with this work—especially Susan Rose, Lonna Malmsheimer, and Ann Hill of Dickinson College, and Major Joseph Burroughs, USMC. The flaws of this work are, needless to say, mine alone.

I would also like to extend a special thanks to the readers and critics who have helped to improve this work. Michael Frisch, Don Ritchie, George Lipsitz, and Charles Payne suggested important improvements; my editor Niko Pfund at New York University Press has been interested, helpful and supportive throughout the travail of editing and rewriting.

Abbreviations

ACLU	American Civil Liberties Association
CCC	Civilian Conservation Corps
CCGNO	Coordinating Council of Greater New Orleans
CD & E	Collins, Douglas, and Elie (lawyers)
CIC	Commission on Interracial Co-operation
COFO	Council of Federated Organizations
CORE	Congress of Racial Equality
COUP	Community Organization for Urban Politics
CRA	Civil Rights Act
CRC	Community Relations Council
FAMU	Florida A & M University
FST	Free Southern Theater
HUAC	House Un-American Activities Committee
HUD	Department of Housing and Urban Development
IMA	Interdenominational Ministerial Alliance
Inc. Fund	NAACP Legal Defense Fund
IWO	Independent Women's Organization
LCDC	Lawyers' Constitutional Defense Committee
LSU	Louisiana State University

LUAC	Louisiana Un-American Activities Committee
LWV	League of Women Voters
MAC	Metropolitan Area Committee
MFDP	Mississippi Freedom Democratic Party
NAACP	National Association for the Advancement of Colored People
NLG	National Lawyers' Guild
OPPVL	Orleans Parish Progressive Voters' League
OPSB	Orleans Parish School Board
PAC	Political Action Committee
PTAs	Parent Teach Associations
SCEF	Southern Conference Educational Fund
SCHW	Southern Conference for Human Welfare
SCLC	Southern Christian Leadership Conference
SISS	Senate Internal Security Subcommittee
SNCC	Student Non-Violent Coordinating Committee
SOS	Save our Schools
SOUL	Southern Organization for United Leadership
SRC	Southern Regional Council
SUNO	Southern University of New Orleans
TCA	Total Community Action
YMBC	Young Men's Business Club
VEP	Voter Education Project

RIGHTEOUS LIVES

ONE

Introduction

NEW ORLEANS was a peculiarly segregated city in the 1950s. An old, colorful port at the mouth of the Mississippi River, it was famous for its French and Spanish heritage, distinctive architecture, fine restaurants, jazz, and an aura of steamy sexuality and vice. The city had long inflamed the fantasies of American writers and artists, who were intrigued by its bohemianism, decayed gentility, and langorous sensuality. New Orleans always seemed more Caribbean than Southern, more open about its corruption and frivolity than places in the historically Protestant South. Awash with tropical colors and smells, comfortably mixing decadence and piety, it was a heavily Catholic port city, a mecca for gamblers, sailors, and adventurers, and home to an ethnically and racially diverse population. Musicians like Jelly Roll Morton began their careers in New Orleans—the birthplace of jazz—playing music in the bordellos of the notorious Storyville district. Morton and his colleagues were part of a long tradition of Creole and African-American musicians who fused African, Southern, and Caribbean rhythms into an indigenous American art form. Long after Storyville was closed by reformers who tried to cleanse the city of vice, New Orleans remained a sensualist's delight—the home of clubs, music, food, and pleasure.

The romance of the city was a product of the syncretic fusion of African-American, Caribbean, European, and white Southern cultures. Even in the late twentieth century, the influence of these diverse traditions remains evident in the city's music, food, architecture, and rituals. Jazz funerals, the "second-lines" of revelers that follow jazz bands, the many festivals that dot the community's calendar, and the Caribbean spices and sauces that have become part of the city's traditional foods are all products of a cultural syncretism that make New Orleans distinctive in the South. While other Deep South cities were dominated by black and white Southern Protestant traditions, New Orleans has a rich and complex religious history: Southern Protestant, European Catholic, and African beliefs are part of its recent and distant past. This mixture of diverse peoples and cultures gave the city an ambiguous and complicated racial and ethnic identity.

Righteous Lives tells the story of black and white civil rights activists who worked to end racial segregation and discrimination in their city in the 1950s and 1960s. It is a collective biography of explicitly political lives, but it is also a chronicle of individual and collective responses to segregation in a very distinctive place: a highly cultured, European- and Latin-influenced city in the Deep South. The history of New Orleans shaped the context of its civil rights struggle. The historic complexity of race relations promoted different perceptions of African-American liberation and possibility than existed elsewhere in the South. These perceptions were rooted in the strength and diversity of the city's black and white Creole cultures, in its African-American and Caribbean traditions, and in a mythology of "harmonious" race relations based on both widespread miscegenation and less intimate forms of race mixing.

New Orleans was founded in 1718, as a French port. It was ceded to Spain in 1767, but was returned to France in 1800. With the Louisiana Purchase of 1803, the city became an American port. Due to the frontier conditions that prevailed in Louisiana during its first century of settlement, few European women voluntarily undertook the hardships of colonization. As in other Caribbean colonies, unions between European men and African or Indian women soon produced a "third caste" between whites and African slaves. These became Louisiana's "free people of color"—or "colored Creoles." Often the manumitted children of European men and African or African-American women, this "third caste" made an early appearance and assumed a distinctive place in New Orleans' history. In 1810, the city contained 5,727 free blacks, 8,000 whites, and 10,824 African and African-American slaves.[1]

The white and black Creoles of New Orleans maintained an ambivalent relationship to the Americans and German and Irish immigrants who came to the city after 1803. The "white" Creoles sought to preserve their social and ethnic status by claiming an aristocratic lineage in the Spanish and French adventurers whom they counted as ancestors. They tried to maintain their European culture, language, and religious traditions in the face of the sprawling expansionism of the cotton and sugar frontiers of the Old Southwest—the nineteenth-century term for the Deep South states of Louisiana, Mississippi, and Alabama. As in other Southern territories, the rush for fortunes in slaves, sugar, and cotton brought quick wealth, speculators, "cotton snobs," and additional slave traders and their captives to New Orleans. Such expansion also generated opportunities for independent, skilled craftsmen and professionals—many of whom were colored Creoles.[2]

Prior to the Civil War, free people of color were well represented among New Orleans' slaveowners, property holders, and skilled craftsmen. In 1830, 41 percent of the 1,834 free Negro heads of household in the city owned at least one slave. Free people of color also owned substantial amounts of property—one estimate placed the real estate value of free black heads of household between $1,000 and $3,000 in 1830. This was a substantial figure for that period. Additionally, 80 to 85 percent of black Creole men possessed enough education or skill to be classified as skilled workers, clerks, teachers, and medical doctors in 1850. Black Creoles dominated the trades of cabinetmaking, carpentry, cigar manufacturing, masonry, and plastering. They were also well represented as merchants, mechanics, shoemakers, and tailors in the 1850 census. Black Creoles thus established a tradition of economic independence from white control and from manual labor. They also developed a distinctive religious, cultural, and status system that identified them as colored or "mixed" rather than black, and emphasized their European roots and Catholic heritage. In the nineteenth and twentieth centuries, colored or black Creoles prized fair skin, "good" or straight hair, Latin or European features, economic independence, social propriety, and education.[3]

The free people of color distanced themselves from the African and African-American slave culture in the antebellum era. The continuing infusion of slaves from other regions of the slave South, from the Caribbean, and Africa meant that many aspects of West African cultures flourished in the local slave community. The "ring shout" religious ritual, African burial practices, and African drumming and dancing at Congo Square slave festivities reinforced the native traditions of newly arrived and seasoned slaves. Additionally, African religious traditions, enriched with Caribbean practices, produced a lively African-American version of Christianity. Many slaves continued to honor African deities through hoodoo or voodoo religious rites, which were devoted to the worship of Damballa, the snake god.[4]

The widespread miscegenation that had created the colored Creoles in the eighteenth century continued through the nineteenth. Transients, sailors, and respectable gentlemen frequented the hundreds of black and white prostitutes who worked in the city; slave women were often hired as concubines. The *placage* system, which institutionalized miscegenation as a form of common-law marriage, allowed wealthy white men to set up housekeeping with a "quadroon," a light-skinned and well-bred young woman of mixed ancestry. Placage arrangements often lasted for many years, and produced children who could claim an intimate relationship to the city's upper-class white families. Frequently, the white fathers freed and educated the children of these relationships, who entered adult life as members of the colored Creole elite.[5]

Following the Civil War, many leaders of Louisiana's black Creole community became important state political leaders. With the end of Reconstruction in 1877, black Creoles saw their own prospects collapse into the system of oppression that came to dominate all African-Americans in the Southern states. Following Mississippi, Southern states enacted measures to disenfranchise and segregate all freedmen, and to return blacks to a condition of economic bondage. Creole blacks found that their education and skills did not prevent them from suffering the same humiliations as those placed upon African-American freedmen. Because they were *part* African, they were consigned to the same subordinate status as were the freedmen. In successive generations, the Creoles became a color-conscious, and status-conscious leadership group in New Orleans' black community.

Although white supremacists struggled to enforce norms of racial purity in the years after Reconstruction, interracial sexual relationships continued in many neighborhoods of the city. New Orleans' population included large numbers of foreign-born whites who had fewer prejudices against interracial unions than did Anglo-Saxon Southerners. Thus, French, Latin, and Caribbean immigrant men were frequently listed as partners in mixed marriages. Smaller numbers of white women married black men, but openly interracial marriages persisted despite anti-miscegenation statutes. Throughout the grim years of the 1880s, when Southern whites consolidated political power through open violence, New Orleans' racial relations remained complex, and racial identity was frequently an ambiguous matter. Many light-skinned Creoles and African-Americans responded to the increasingly oppressive atmosphere by passing for white. One scholar has estimated that between 100 and 500 blacks "became 'white' every year from 1875 to the 1890s."[6]

In 1950, roughly a third of the city's population of 570,445 was African-American. Some 40 percent of the total population, and approximately a third of New Orleans' blacks were Catholic.[7] Unlike many Southern cities, New Orleans had not developed large black ghettoes in the 1950s. Instead, many neighborhoods were characterized by "salt-and-pepper" housing patterns, with blacks and whites living in close proximity. These included the Ninth Ward, the heavily black Creole Seventh Ward, the downtown Creole Treme neighborhood of the Sixth Ward, and the Uptown neighborhoods of Carrollton. Although blacks and whites did not mix socially, or attend school together, neither were they as isolated or estranged as in more rigidly segregated areas in the South. Suburbanization and white flight from the old city of the 1940s occurred rather slowly during the 1950s, but accelerated in the early and mid-1960s as the swamplands of surrounding parishes were drained and developed.[8]

In the 1950s, New Orleans' population contained a mixture of blacks, white Creoles, people of Irish, German, and Italian descent, people from numerous parts of Latin America, and the descendants of Louisiana's "gens de couleur."[9] The intermarriages and mixtures of these populations produced an astonishing variety of skin colors and features among the nominally "white" and "black" populations. Black and white Creoles both claimed to possess Mediterranean looks: dark hair and eyes, fair or olive complexions, Anglo or Spanish features. Many of the city's Hispanic citizens shared these looks; so did many "blacks" and "whites." In newspaper photographs from the 1950s, it is often impossible to tell the race of an ostensibly black or white community leader.

The sheer variety of skin color among blacks and whites in the city made passing for white a common experience for some African-Americans. Leontine Luke, an NAACP leader of the 1950s and 1960s, remembered passing for white when her fair-skinned grandmother took her shopping as a child. Virginia Collins, another black leader of the 1950s and 1960s, had a family that contained both very light and very dark blacks—and knew that a number of her relatives had "become" white in order to work at jobs that were closed to those who were obviously black. And Matt Suarez, an activist with the Congress of Racial Equality (CORE) of the 1960s, recalled humorous incidents of passing in his own Creole family—like the light-skinned uncle who confessed to his bride that he was black, only to find out that his new wife had also been passing for white. Suarez had his own memories: as a teenager, he had been light enough to pass in whites-only clubs and bars in the French Quarter.

New Orleans' racial mixture and its ethnic diversity had created a rich local culture in the 1950s. The black community had a number of educational and religious institutions, and a self-conscious, educated elite. While Tulane University, Loyola University of the South, and St. Mary's Dominican College served white students in the city, Dillard University and the Catholic Xavier University served blacks. Several black private and Catholic schools provided superior educational opportunities to talented black students. Xavier Prep and Gilbert Academy, especially, promoted hard work, constant striving, and racial uplift. These schools educated a number of the city's leaders of the 1950s and 1960s. Gilbert Academy embodied a kind of racial upward mobility, according to writer Tom Dent. Dent remembered the school's principal admonishing her students to work hard to uplift the race. She also "warned us in a voice drenched in acid: 'Stay away from South Rampart Street, or you'll end up there. A *hint* to the wise is sufficient.' "[10]

Rampart Street represented the other side of black New Orleans—"the commercial center of the struggling black nation within the city we had all emerged from," according to Dent.[11] Rampart Street had black businesses, clubs, and was a center of black night life and music. It also represented the reality of black laboring and social life to the black middle class, which by 1960 constituted only 10 percent of the black population.[12] The music, the festivity, the vice, and the folk culture of Rampart Street and the "blues people" were anathema to many of the blacks who treasured their upward mobility and newly won status. For Rampart Street and the blues people represented a series of racial stereotypes that middle-class blacks longed to escape.

Civil rights lawyer Lolis Elie remembered that the divisions between the "blues people" and the more respectable blacks of his uptown neighborhood were symbolized by quarrels about the area's name. Respectable blacks referred to the area as "Carrollton." These women and men considered the blues people to be "niggers." The latter, Elie wrote in 1977, were "people who did not attend church, who lived together without benefit of ceremony, who joined in second lines, who did not work, who enjoyed the blues, who frequented the bars, who cursed in front of women." They also called the neighborhood "Niggertown."[13]

Between the blues people and the tight respectability of the black middle class were the hard-working, striving blacks whom Elie remembered as important to his childhood. Elie recalled the women of Carrollton who "worked three days in one": who fed their children, sent them to school, then spent a full workday minding children and cleaning white folks' houses, and then "returned to their own houses and their own children where they again cooked, cleaned, served and loved and grew flowers and prayed. Three days of work in one."[14] In 1960, about 85 percent of the city's black workers were classified as blue-collar workers; half of them were considered menial laborers. Most employed black women worked as domestics.[15]

If the black middle class disdained the stereotypes of frivolity and sensuality that Rampart Street seemed to symbolize, many blacks in New Orleans celebrated African-American and Caribbean traditions that had developed over centuries in the city. One tradition was second-lining, that is marching and dancing after a jazz band during a parade or funeral. Other traditions involved Mardi Gras, the mid winter carnival season that celebrates the return of spring. In New Orleans, men from black neighborhoods created distinctive "Indian" krewes that marched on Carnival Day and on St. Joseph's Day, March 19. The Mardi Gras Indians made and wore elaborate costumes that outglittered the white krewes in finery, feathers, and glory. The Indians were highly competitive, based in very localized neighborhoods. On Carnival Day, Indians were not "supposed to give way to anyone because you represented the pride of your tribe and your neighborhood," said Toudy Montana, chief of the Yellow Pocohantas tribe. On Carnival Night, rival tribes often fought among themselves, or clashed with police, which brought many wounded Indians into the emergency room of Charity Hospital in years past. Indian traditions, like the parades and music of black New Orleans, were highly developed cultural expressions that enriched the lives of many African-Americans in the city.[16]

The 1950s were years of growing black protests throughout the South. Ministers and community leaders had organized transit boycotts in Baton Rouge, Montgomery, and Tallahassee. Southern state legislatures had responded to the Supreme Court decision of *Brown vs. Board of Education* by launching the furious reaction known as "Massive Resistance." In New Orleans, public libraries and buses and streetcars desegregated quietly, and the black community mobilized for three important boycotts—the McDonogh Day Boycotts of 1954 and 1955, the Carnival Blackouts of 1957 and 1960, and the Dryades Street Boycott of 1959–1960.

As in other Southern cities, the black leadership of New Orleans changed in the 1950s. Accommodating black leaders who had begged for favors from segregationist white elites were being displaced by racial diplomats, who were usually urbane, college-educated professionals. The diplomats, in turn, were increasingly challenged by race men, who impatiently demanded their full rights as citizens. The race men were often ministers who could mobilize hundreds of blacks for boycotts, marches, or other protests. Race men, in turn, were pushed by militant student and student-aged protestors who swept into direct-action protests in 1960.

Styles and strategies of racial leadership varied with the age, class, and religious affiliations of black elites. Black Creoles tended to be racial diplomats, most comfortable when acting as negotiators with white men of power. They were frequently professionals—doctors, lawyers, and teachers—and few identified strongly with the masses of black folk. The Creole leaders differed sharply from the black ministers, who were the most effective mass leaders in the city. The ministers, in turn, often found the student activists of CORE and the NAACP Youth Council too independent, too impatient, and too willing to take dangerous risks.[17]

The diverse groups of leaders performed different roles. Racial diplomats interacted well with white men of power, and personally demonstrated that blacks deserved the rights guaranteed to them by the Constitution. They also protected moderate and liberal whites from the rage of other blacks—particularly those with less formal education, or more strident demands. Alternately, race men mobilized voters and congregations, and could threaten demonstrations if their demands were not met. The students could, and did, push both groups of their elders into more adamant positions on the pace and extent of racial change. Within all three groups, women and men came to activism from a variety of perspectives and goals; they were inspired by visions as divergent as black nationalism, Christian brotherhood, working-class political autonomy, racial uplift, and personal and collective empowerment.

In the 1950s and 1960s, these women and men worked with a small but principled group of white liberals and radicals. Like the black leadership, these people came to interracial activism from an array of backgrounds and perspectives. Christian concepts of social justice, horrified responses to Nazi Germany and the Holocaust, Depression-nurtured liberalism and radicalism, and a devotion to national principles of law and justice led a small, but significant number of white Southerners to openly oppose segregation and racial discrimination.

Righteous Lives relates the stories of twenty-five of these black and white leaders of the 1950s and 1960s (see Table 1).

The individuals in this book tell personal and collective stories of social change. They recount careers as interracial leaders, women and men who walked an often ambivalent line during a volatile period of racial change. Few blacks and fewer whites emerged as civil rights activists in the South of the 1950s and 1950s. Those who became activists often risked their economic standing, their positions within a community, and their lives in the tumultuous years after 1954. While New Orleans' black leaders and their few white allies obtained significant victories without violence or bloodshed, many experienced terror and harassment during their political crusades. Black activists were sometimes threatened and attacked by white mobs, or by the Ku Klux Klan—particularly if they left the city to work in a neighboring community. Frequently, blacks and whites were fired for activism, or found their careers ruined. White leaders were often ostracized by former friends and neighbors; some were threatened, or were treated to the colorful signature of the Klan—the flaming cross, blazing on a lawn at night. Even in a city known for peaceful race relations, activism was personally draining, as well as empowering, and came at considerable individual sacrifice, frequently placing great strains on marriages and other personal relationships.

Righteous Lives examines the personal territory of civil rights activism. In this book, activists describe the subjective experience of interracial leadership. They tell of the developmental processes that led them to work for a different racial future than that dictated by Southern tradition. Leaders also describe the powerful bonds that they developed with fellow activists who encouraged and supported their efforts. They recount their victories, and moments of triumph, as well as their often grave disappointments with

Table 1

First-Generation Leaders

Black	*White*
Leontine Luke (b. 1909)	Rosa Keller (1911)
Virginia Y. Collins (1915)	Helen Mervis (1917)
A. L. Davis (1914)	Albert D'Orlando (1915)
Albert Dent (1905)	James Dombrowski (1897)
Revius Ortique (1924)	
Dr. Leonard Burns (1922)	

Second-Generation Leaders

Black	*White*
Lolis Elie (1930)	John P. Nelson, Jr.(1921)
Robert Collins (1931)	Moon Landrieu (1930)
Ernest ("Dutch") Morial (1929)	Ann Dlugos (1927)
	Betty Wisdom (1930)
	Peggy Murison (1917)

Third-Generation Leaders

Black
Rudy Lombard (1939)
Richard Haley (ca. 1925)
Tom Dent (1932)
Jerome Smith (ca. 1938)
Matt Suarez (1938)
Oretha Castle (1940)
Doris Jean Castle (1942)

more recent political history. Finally, activists explore the meaning of their experiences from the distance of the present. In the late 1970s and in 1988, New Orleans' former activists ranged in age between the forties and eighties. Twenty and thirty years had given them perspectives on their political lives, and most were anxious to discuss the meaning of their experiences in history. In this book, many describe the importance of interracial leadership in their lives. Their stories—and their lives—give flesh and voice to the process of racial change.

In *Righteous Lives*, an array of racial diplomats, race men, white liberals, black and white radicals, and once-militant black students tell the stories of their lives as activists. Most describe their families and childhoods as sources of strength and self-confidence, and relate their growing convictions that the social system in which they lived was morally wrong and inhumane. And all describe the processes that led them to act—to become makers and molders of history, rather than its victims.

New Orleans' leaders fall into roughly three generations. The first generation was born between 1897 and 1924; the second between 1925 and 1935; the third between 1935 and 1945. While these age-groups do not fall within the classic definition of a generation as a twenty- or thirty-year entity, New Orleans' leaders seem to function as generation units—as individuals who shared a specific collective historical experience, developed a distinctive set of perceptions, and chose a characteristic plan of action.

Generation units incorporate individual and collective experiences of history. Sociologist Karl Mannheim believed that generation units develop an "identity of responses" to their common historical and social experiences within a more formal generational span. Members of a generation unit come to share a similar consciousness of their historical and political experience; they do this within mutually stimulating, closely bonded groups that enable them "to develop integrative attitudes which do justice to their common 'location.'" When such generation units cohere within social movements, they realize their potential as self-conscious collective historical actors. A common collective consciousness, historical understanding, and vision of necessary social change distinguish activist generation units from other temporally related groups that do not realize themselves in public action.[18]

A variety of factors place individuals in specific generation units as shown in Table 1. Individual age and the historical timing of activism are important variables, though not exclusionary. The personal timing of activism in the life of the individual, and the type or style of activism are also important indicators of a leader's location in a generation unit. Thus, although Revius Ortique and Dr. Leonard Burns would seem to share their biological age and the personal timing of their activism with Dutch Morial, Lolis Elie, and Robert Collins, they are considered to be members of the Integrationist generation because they entered activism in the 1950s, and they engaged in a style of activism that was prominent among the black leadership of that decade. Both were racial diplomats who were active in the Urban League, and developed strong ties with white liberals like Rosa Keller and Helen Mervis. More critically, both led major boycotts of the decade: Ortique emerged as a leader of the McDonogh Day Boycott in

1954, and Burns led the United Clubs to call successful boycotts of Mardi Gras festivities in 1957 and 1960. Similarly, Tom Dent might appear to be of the same generation as Lolis Elie and Dutch Morial—he was born in 1932. Dent, however, emerged as a cultural nationalist and "culture worker" in the early 1960s—first with the Umbra writers in New York City, then with the Free Southern Theater, an eventually all-black troupe that settled in New Orleans in 1964. Dent's political sensibilities, his style of activism, and his sense of the meaning of the civil rights movement, mirrored those of the CORE leaders, rather than those of men closer to his age.

Individually and collectively, the narratives of this book form stories of political careers. They document the experience of making history, and of creating and living political lives. Because these stories are rooted in one community, they reveal the broken and enduring relationships that social movement participation often provokes. Above all, the narratives describe a movement across and through time, from a segregated city and region to a politically integrated community. Because the narratives describe lives, they bring the past and present together in dramatic contrasts of consciousness.

Like any collective biography, this book reflects intentional emphases and omissions. It is not a comprehensive community study, nor should it be regarded as a definitive examination of race relations in New Orleans in the 1950s and 1960s. Time, age, and life-changes made several important actors impossible to interview: one black minister died in 1978, another was occupied in the legislature in 1988, and a number of other leaders had either died, moved, or were unable to recall much about their pasts when I attempted to contact them. Moreover, I chose to relate what seemed to be the generic experiences of each generation—those shared efforts that bound individuals together as a collectivity. This choice resulted in several deliberate inclusions and omissions. Although Bruce Waltzer and Jack Peebles did important legal work for the movement in the early 1960s, I chose to focus on the experiences of those whites who were directly involved in local struggles in New Orleans. Activists like Moon Landrieu, Jack Nelson, Ann Dlugos, Peggy Murison, and Betty Wisdom were deeply involved in the school crisis of 1960–1961, and in local political campaigns. Similarly, I chose to examine the mix of local activity and "field work" common to many of the young blacks in CORE in the early and mid-1960s, and thus did not detail the experiences of the young women and men of the NAACP Youth Council. Further, since few whites remained in the local CORE chapter after 1962, I chose to focus on the black CORE experience exclusively, because this particular trajectory of political life has not received as extensive a treatment in recent literature as has that of the white activists of the Student Non-Violent Coordinating Committee, Freedom Summer, and the New Left.[19]

The stories of *Righteous Lives* are drawn from interviews taped between 1978 and 1980, and in 1988. In both sets of interviews, I asked former activists how and why they had become civil rights and community leaders. I hoped to discover the origins of activism in family relationships, educational experiences, and mentorship relations. The timing of activism interested me, because narrators of different ages seemed to have become active at different junctures of their lives, and had developed distinctive, age-specific political careers. The type of activism chosen seemed important: the experiences of a racial negotiator were far different from those of an "actionist" or a "field-worker" of CORE. I expected that differing political experiences would have had divergent effects on the lives and subsequent choices of activists.

I sought to determine how the collective historical experiences of each generation had affected its perceptions of race and segregation. Did historical location give individuals characteristic models of activism, and of possible social change? How did perceptions of race, activism, and the movement change between the 1950s and 1960s, and what were the sources of changing perceptions? My interviews provided a conduit to both individual perceptions and to their collective impact. I asked questions that directly addressed the timing, formation, and content of each individual's political career.

Interviews revealed the creation and shaping of activists' political lives. Specific types of career patterns emerged within generations, and these were created and sustained by networks of mentors, colleagues, and family members. In their political careers, activists attempted to fulfill and embody their dreams of change—which often involved nothing less than personal and collective transformation.

As retrospective documents, interview narratives chronicle the subjective meanings of civil rights activism. Interviews indicate the function that activism played in an individual's life—whether interracial leadership was part of a constellation of community leadership roles, or whether activism became a transformative experience of growth and personal development. Interviews also reveal the relationship between the timing of activism and its function in a leader's life: whether activism became part of an occupational career, or the basis of a way of life, as it did for many of the young militants of the black student movement. Additionally, oral narratives describe a varied class and racial geography among activists: the meaning of the political experience varied according to race, class, and the type of activism chosen.

Interviews provide answers to these questions because they are retrospective, and grounded in memory. Personal narratives relate meaningful incidents in individuals' lives, incidents which cumulatively recall a career. The passage of time tends to erase the trivial or repetitive moments in a life, but leaves the dramatic scenes of self-definition or self-testing favored in recollection. Subjectively important events remain fixed in memory, and also those moments in which personal history is joined to public, acknowledged historical change. People retain the meaning of these moments of self-definition and personal efficacy because they function as transitional experiences in their lives—as moments of growth, revelation, and transformation. The meaning of such narratives is, in fact, the individual meaning of a collective effort, in which the individual is the agent of social change.[20]

Interview narratives also reveal the social context of activism, as people describe the networks of friends and colleagues who gave them support, encouragement, and hope. New Orleans' activists gave a highly relational account of their political careers. They recalled parents who gave them confidence and a sense of self-worth, mentors who opened doors, and friends and colleagues who sustained them in their vision of a new world. They also described their perceptions of the opponents of change: from segregationist elites like Leander Perez, who led local Citizens' Councils in opposition to integration in any form, to the mobs of working-class whites who attacked demonstrators and organizers, to the more subtle opponents of black liberation—the elites who sanctioned the worst excesses of racism by openly advocating resistance to *Brown* and other federal mandates.

Interview narratives provide answers to biographical and political questions in ways that reveal the structure, experience, and meaning of an activist career. By structure, I refer to the collective historical experience of each activist, the timing and nature of activism, and its duration in a leader's life. The experience of activism is each individual's personal history of significant political events. The meaning of activism is derived from the function that leadership played in an individual's life, as revealed by retrospective assessments of the experience. Most activists felt their efforts affirmed by a mixture of internal and external rewards. Most also recalled varying levels of optimism and hope in their political lives. And most remembered very vividly the periods in which they experienced their greatest sense of political efficacy—those moments when their own efforts seemed to affect the course of historical change. To these moments, activists attributed the greatest meaning of their political lives, for such moments remained in memory as epiphanies of understanding, victory, and an almost transcendent sense of personal connection. Interviews, then, connect the structure of human experience to the action of civil rights leadership, as mediated by the meaning imposed at mid-life and late-life by the former negotiators, politicians, strategists, and "field-workers" of New Orleans' civil rights leadership.

The activists' stories are contemporary dramas of self-creation through collective action. These women and men changed their own lives, and local and national history. In many of their recollections, a dialectical relationship exists between the act of changing one's own life—one's story—and altering the narrative of public history in the process. The personal and the political become fused in these interpretive acts, and the movement from oppression to freedom becomes a metaphor for the opening, the connecting, and the transforming of lives.

The process of making freedom was a journey of self-discovery and collective creation. Often, this process released enormous creativity and hope, as personal ambitions became joined to revolutionary possibilities. For many men and women, this efflorescence proved costly. As the 1960s ended, many experienced disillusionment with the political and social system they had tried to change. And yet, their stories reveal the consistency of their beliefs and desires, even in the discouraging years of the 1980s, when the political career of David Duke, an ex-Klansman, seemed to symbolize the conservative politics and racial polarization of American voters.

These stories of personal and historical change are all the more important because they are told by ordinary women and men, whose lives have not been memorialized by national holidays or glamorized by celebrity status. Their struggles have often been quiet dramas that have demanded a patient persistence over the years. And yet, in these ordinary lives we may find the most important chronicles of personal and historical change. Their stories reveal a continuing faith in human possibility—an ongoing commitment that connects them to the human community that they sought to transform and to save.

Two

Overcoming Massive Resistance: Integrationists, 1954–1959

*T*HE decade of the 1950s was a frightening period for black activists and their few white allies, as the convulsion known as Massive Resistance swept the South in the wake of the *Brown* decision. By 1954, New Orleans' civil rights leaders had lived through two decades of extremes. The Depression of the 1930s had deepened the South's agricultural crisis, and World War II had brought population shifts, increased prosperity, and the beginnings of the region's economic integration into the national system. The war had also heightened the aspirations of Southern blacks who served in the military, or enjoyed higher wages as a result of the heightened demand for labor. These changes produced an increased militancy among many blacks, and an explosive anger among the region's old agricultural elite, which controlled much of the Democratic Party in the one-party South. In 1954, the U.S. Supreme Court sanctioned black aspirations with the *Brown* decision, which declared segregated school systems unconstitutional. Immediately afterwards, the Southern right swung into a campaign of Massive Resistance. Regional and state elites used legal maneuvers, quasi-legal tactics, and outright terrorism to evade

and subvert federal court orders, crush black political initiatives, and in-
timidate black and white civil rights activists.

New Orleans' civil rights elite of the 1950s included women and men
who traditionally acted as leaders of Southern black communities, and a
smattering of white liberals. Most were integrationists who used religious
doctrines to justify their racial politics. These women and men were acutely
conscious of the potential for change that the New Deal and World War
II had released. They saw in those experiences both a promise and a
warning—the promise of an integrated and economically transformed
South, and the threatening model of Nazi Germany as a consequence of
unbridled racism.

These leaders were members of the black middle and upper classes, and
affluent white liberals and middle-class "progressives."[1] They were economically independent of segregationist control, which was a necessity
during a decade of emerging black protest and white reprisals. And they
devoted most of their energies to the triumvirate of issues that dominated
the black crusade of the 1950s—equal access to public accommodations,
equal and integrated education, and voting rights.

Black activists came to politics from a variety of backgrounds, but most
had strong roots in black Protestant churches. Their families had stressed
education, hard work, and achievement. The activists of the 1950s were
consequently ambitious and upwardly mobile. Most envisioned a society
of racial equality, and, as individuals, hoped for personal success and recognition in the black and white communities of New Orleans. In the late
1970s and 1980s, almost all felt their lives validated by the social changes
they had worked to bring about.[2]

Mrs. Virginia Young Collins and Mrs. Leontine Goins Luke led neigh-
borhood-based organizations, voter-registration drives, and black PTA
groups in the 1950s and 1960s. Both were daughters of ministers who had
campaigned against the poll tax, and both were politically socialized by
their fathers. Both women also witnessed the arbitrary nature of racial
designation in their own families, as light-skinned relatives passed for white
in the complex racial and ethnic milieu of New Orleans.

Leontine Goins Luke was born in 1909. Her father, the Reverend Bur-
nell Goins, was a contractor as well as a minister at Grace Spiritual Church.
Her mother was a missionary, and mother of the church. According to
Luke, her father paid the poll tax of all the men who worked for him,

"and then automatically deducted the money from their wages when poll tax time was due." Mrs. Goins was herself ordained in 1936, and, she said, "It came naturally to me to take up and work with him because he was one of the first ministers that started this Ninth Ward Civic and Improvement League"—an organization Mrs. Goins led from 1955 through the end of the 1970s. The League's "main purpose" was voter registration as a means to obtain better "streets, lights, police protection, and better schools" for Ninth Ward residents.

This was often a frustrating task. After Louisiana's poll tax had been eliminated, other voting obstructions remained. The Supreme Court decision *Smith vs. Allwright* eliminated the white primary in 1944, but it did not affect black voters in the state until it was seconded by *Elmore vs. Rice* in 1948. Between 1940 and 1950, the number of black voters in the city rose from 400 to 26,209. This increase was largely due to local groups like the People's Defense League and other voter organizations. Black voters were an integral part of the constituency of Earl Long, who began his third term as state governor in 1956. Earl Long was a rural populist in the tradition of his brother Huey Long, the flamboyant governor, then senator from Louisiana in the 1920s and 1930s. Long courted the black vote, and provided state benefits to blacks within the segregated system. After 1956, further increases in the city's black vote were stymied by Long's political enemies, who tried to destroy his constituency by scrubbing poor white and black voters from state rolls. Between 1956 and 1959, the percentage of eligible blacks who were registered to vote in the state fell from 31.7 percent to 27.5 percent. Despite repeated voter registration drives by the NAACP and other black organizations, and despite increases in the city's black population, the city's black voters increased by only 10,000 between 1950 and 1962—out of a potential strength of 125,000 eligible voters.[3] Orleans Parish used a very complicated voter registration form that included a "citizenship" test that few blacks were allowed to pass. While these restrictive practices were legal under state law, Luke trained voters and personally accompanied them to the registrar's office as part of her work with the League.[4]

As a light-skinned child in a family that had a variety of shades, Leontine Goins had often been selected to go with her fair-skinned grandmother on errands. The older woman would always take the grandchildren "who could sit with her" when she passed for white on streetcars or in stores. "Her children knew her," Luke explained, and so chose the lightest of the grandchildren for the errands. "The children had no choice. We were *selected* by our parents to go with Granny." But passing "was an accepted part of life" in the New Orleans of Luke's childhood and youth.[5]

The Political Part of Life

Mrs. Virginia Young Collins was born in 1915 in Plaquemine Parish, a spit of land surrounded by marsh and water below New Orleans. She was the eldest of fifteen children from a "real radical" family—her father was a porter-embalmer, then a rag man, and finally an insurance salesman. His real vocation and love was his ministry and church. The Reverend Young was an admirer of Marcus Garvey, leader of a black nationalist, back-to-Africa movement of the 1920s. Young campaigned against the poll tax: "He was interested in the theory that if black people came together, then they would be able to do for themselves." And the vote was clearly a path to collective power. But Young did not believe that blacks needed to return to Africa—he was part of a group within the Garveyite persuasion that believed that "Africa is wherever Africans are," said Collins.[6]

The Young family believed strongly in education, Collins remembered: "you get educated so you have some *sense*, you know how to *reason*, you know how to think. . . . You had to go to school, but you had to be part of the political part of life." Educated as a schoolteacher and a nurse, Collins became involved with the Southern Conference for Human Welfare (SCHW) in 1938. The SCHW was an interracial group of Southern New Dealers and leftists who hoped to economically transform the South and eliminate racial discrimination. In the late 1930s and early 1940s, SCHW members backed the Southern labor and anti-poll tax movements.[7] Its educational arm, the Southern Conference Educational Fund (SCEF), which was established in 1946, conducted an insistent attack on racial segregation through its tabloid, the *Southern Patriot*, and in educational forums held in Southern cities.[8] Collins became involved in the SCEF, belonged to the Women's International League for Peace and Freedom, and joined other women's organizations and community groups that promoted quality education for black children, political power through the vote, and equal access to public accommodations. She became a leader in black parent-teacher associations as her ten children successively came of school age.[9]

Virginia Collins began her activity in local organizations after attending the initial meeting of the SCHW in 1938. She was first introduced to the "socialistic platform" of many SCHW reformers, and "was very fascinated by that meeting—I had so many ideas." At the time, Collins and her husband lived "in the country," in Iberville Parish, where he taught adult education and she worked as a home demonstration agent for a New Deal project. Collins taught black and white women canning and food preservation in a county school building. The women interacted well, until local police broke up a class and ordered her to keep the races separate. She subsequently taught the black women in the school building, and the white women in their own homes. This last arrangement did not bother the authorities because, as she said, "you could have a black person working in your house. They couldn't stop that. So the white people learned just like the black people."[10]

Experiences with the rural poor exposed Collins to the rampant illiteracy among whites. It surprised her: "I thought all white people went to school, and that they *knew*." She found that white tenant farmers and sharecroppers often kept their sons at work on the farms after a rudimentary eighth grade education. Collins understood black illiteracy—a shortage of schools, haphazard state support, and historic legal bars to black education had long handicapped Southern blacks. "But I was just alarmed and really baffled that [a white] man would let his boy stay home, and let the girl go on and get educated. And the mama didn't know either, in most cases. I had to read and write their letters." In 1988, Collins regretted that she had "no political sense" during her five years in Iberville Parish:

My whole time, I worked with white people and black people—naturally with my own. But I'm saying, I had a good relationship with the white people. And if I had the sense I had in 1954, and 1960, I would have begin to educate white people politically in that line, where black people and white people can work together and stuff. But I didn't know nothing about Marx or nothing else then.[11]

Like Leontine Luke, Collins saw racial designation as an arbitrary matter. In her own family, her grandmother, "a slave girl," had been the child of a white person, raised by black people—but educated in France as a nurse by her master's family. The light-skinned members of Collins' family often passed for white.[12] As an adult, Collins came to believe that white elites used racial difference to separate and polarize blacks and whites. In her work with both the black PTAs and with SCEF, Collins hoped to "break down that stereotype or myth" that separated whites and blacks.

She thought that "going to school together would bring about basic changes" between the races, which would result in "better living for black people because white people would begin to understand *them*, and wouldn't have to create" racial myths.[13]

The most important black minister in New Orleans in the 1950s and 1960s was the Reverend Abraham Lincoln ("A. L." formally, but "Jack" to his family and friends) Davis, pastor of the New Zion Baptist Church. Davis was born in 1914 in Bayou Goula, Louisiana. His father was the preacher for a congregation of sixty people drawn from two adjoining plantations. A. L. and his older sister, Oralean, were taught basic reading and writing by their mother, who kept a school in the church building. The children were later sent to a public school in Iberville Parish. In 1922, at age 11, Oralean was sent to high school in New Orleans. A. L. remained in Bayou Goula to work while Oralean and another sister finished their education. In 1935, Oralean began teaching in the city's black schools. The following year A. L. came to New Orleans, where he attended the local Baptist seminary. He was made pastor of the New Zion Baptist Church at age 20. During summers, he studied at the Moody Bible Institute in Chicago; this made him an unusually well-educated black Baptist minister in New Orleans. Davis pastored the New Zion Church for forty-three years; its congregation grew from ninety to more than 800 members.

Davis became an important political leader among the city's black ministers. As a member of the Southern Christian Leadership Conference (SCLC), Davis led the local Interdenominational Ministerial Alliance (IMA), which could quickly mobilize money and political action among the city's blacks. Davis also served as president of the Orleans Parish Progressive Voters' League (OPPVL), an organization that regularly backed Democratic Party candidates. He became a transitional interracial leader in the 1950s and 1960s—a man holding strong ties to deLesseps S. ("Chep") Morrison, the city's Democratic mayor of the 1950s, and also mobilizing his black constituency to protest segregation and discrimination in numerous instances. Although Davis preferred negotiation to confrontation in his dealings with powerful whites, he gave assistance to the young militants in the Congress of Racial Equality (CORE) when a chapter was organized in 1960.[14]

Albert Dent was a different kind of black leader from Davis. As president of Dillard University for twenty-eight years, Dent was formal and austere.

He was born in Atlanta in 1905, the son of a live-in domestic for a wealthy white family. The light-skinned Dent never knew the identity of his father. Because his mother did not want to raise her son in her employer's household, Dent was informally adopted by the Thomases, a couple who were friends of his mother. In 1987, his son Tom recalled that much of his father's "iron will to present himself in a certain way had to do with having come from nothing, having come from a lot of vagueness. It was like he made a decision when he was very young that he was not going to let *that* stop him."[15]

In 1978, Albert Dent remembered vividly the deprivations of segregation—of being unable to join the Boy Scouts as a child, of segregated streetcars and theaters. He taught Sunday School while a student at Morehouse College in Atlanta, and later became involved with the Commission on Interracial Co-operation (CIC), a bi-racial organization founded in 1920. The CIC took an active part in the anti-lynching movement in the South, and sought to alleviate the difficulties faced by black servicemen returning from Europe. Dent became a vice president of the CIC, and also served as vice president of its successor, the Southern Regional Council (SRC). He met Will Alexander, his lifelong mentor and friend, in the CIC.[16] As Dillard University's acting president, Alexander brought Dent to New Orleans in 1932 to be superintendent of the Flint-Goodridge Hospital, a teaching hospital owned by Dillard. In 1935, Dent also became business manager of Dillard, and was appointed president in 1941.

Albert Dent developed into a very skillful racial negotiator, effective with philanthropists, white and black educators, and people of power in New Orleans and in the South. He spent much of his career working with powerful whites who did not believe in or would not endorse racial integration: people like philanthropist Edgar Stern, who gave generous sums to Dillard but who never received Dent socially. Many of Dent's interracial accomplishments were the results of secret meetings with white elites who were afraid to be known as having met with a black of even Dent's status. Such subterfuge must have galled him. In the late 1970s, he maintained that he

did not believe in, I would not accept racial segregation. . . . This was ingrained in me early. Martin Luther King, Jr.'s father was in college with me. He's older— we were in college at the same time. The boys at Morehouse decided that they would not sit in a segregated balcony to hear anything. They didn't go. We wouldn't sit in a segregated streetcar. As a boy I walked all over Atlanta. Wherever I had to go, I walked. So this was not new to me. This sort of thing was not something he [King] had an inspiration about. . . . I knew Martin Luther King's grandfather. He was a Baptist preacher in Atlanta.[17]

Like his colleague A. P. Tureaud, local counsel for the NAACP Legal Defense Fund (the "Inc. Fund"), Dent was a self-conscious member of the city's black elite. Never a protest leader, he identified with other prominent blacks and whites—with men like Inc. Fund counsel Thurgood Marshall—who achieved status as racial negotiators.[18]

Dent became a mentor to Revius O. Ortique, Jr., a young attorney involved in black protest and in the Urban League in the 1950s. Ortique was born in New Orleans in 1924, the second of four children. Neither of his parents finished high school "but they both had the burning desire for us to go to college," said Ortique in 1988. As salutatorian of his class, Ortique attended New Orleans' Xavier University, then Dillard University during Dent's presidency. Dent, he said, "just sort of adopted me, and wherever he could, he always pushed me." While at Dillard, a sociology teacher encouraged Ortique to do graduate work in criminology at Indiana University. Once there, he began taking courses in the law school. When his time on the GI bill had elapsed, Ortique returned to New Orleans, where he worked for the state Department of Labor while he finished his law degree at Southern University.[19]

As a young lawyer, Ortique was mentored by Inc. Fund counsel A. P. Tureaud, a dignified, very patient man who fought numerous school desegregation suits in the state. From "just being around" Tureaud, he "got the sense" that segregation and discrimination could be eliminated by the law and legal change:

A number of us, every Saturday, went over to Mr. Tureaud's office, and just talked about the practice of law. A. P. Tureaud's office was always available. He had the best law library amongst any of the black lawyers and we would go over there and pick up a sandwich and a soft drink and just *talk*. And this went on for several years. Just talk, and I got a sense of the civil rights movement then.[20]

Dr. Leonard Burns was another young black professional in the 1950s. He had been born in New Orleans in 1922. His mother came from a close Creole family, and his father, a purchasing agent for a steamship company, traveled frequently. As a child, Burns was raised within his mother's family, and was very close to his mother. The family placed great emphasis on education, and on financial independence. His grandfather, a cobbler, had a typically Creole attitude: "he had this thing about being independent, about being your own boss." The family felt that Burns should become a doctor, a musician, a schoolteacher, or a minister—some independent profession. And very early, his relatives encouraged him to become a doctor:

They always had family gatherings, and always talk about, "You see that young man? Watch him. He's always washing his hands. He's always clean. He's gonna become a doctor." Well, this is the seed they're planting. They plant that seed, and I'm hearing it, and, naturally, I hear it as, "I'm gonna become a doctor, I'm gonna become a doctor." And you hear that often enough, you know that goes into your mind, and you start thinking, "I *am* gonna become a doctor." And when the time is ripe, you become a doctor.[21]

Burns' mother and grandfather encouraged his development in a number of ways. His mother never punished him physically, but reasoned with him. And Burns' grandfather, a "fabricator" of stories, gave his grandson important advice about making his way in the world. "He would tell stories in the most humorous way, but they would always have a punch line," said Burns in 1988. "He would make you laugh, and remember. And incidentally, I found that with laughter you can get to remember a lot more than you can with badgering or pointing a finger at somebody and saying, 'You must learn *THIS*,' with a dictatorial attitude." This approach became part of Burns' own life and style. He became a racial negotiator who used charm, courtesy, and an old-fashioned gentlemanliness to achieve community goals.[22]

Burns attended Xavier Prep, and entered Xavier University. In 1942, fearful of the draft, he enlisted in the Marines. He chose the Marines because the organization had the reputation for being the toughest unit of the military. After the war, he returned to Xavier, graduated, and went to medical school at Temple University in Philadelphia. He married while in medical school. In 1951, he returned to New Orleans. Anxious to build a patient load, he asked *Louisiana Weekly* publisher C. C. DeJoie how to build his practice. DeJoie advised him to join community organizations. This proved to be Burns' introduction to both community activism and civil rights leadership.

Having served in the military, and having spent time in Philadelphia, Burns "couldn't stand" segregation in New Orleans. After his daughter was born in the early 1950s, Burns spoke with NAACP attorney A. P. Tureaud about the possibility of desegregating Catholic schools. Burns also hoped to generate activism among the city's small, but influential black middle class and black elite. After associating with many middle-class blacks in community organizations, Burns became convinced that "fear prevented people from doing what they should have done—fear of reprisals. The [black] intelligentsia, the wealthy people with means enough to fight any case or stand up and be counted were fearful of reprisals." Burns was impelled to act out of self-interest, concern for his children's future, and from a sense of obligation to the race. In 1979 and 1988, he recalled being powerfully impressed by a commencement speaker at Dillard University, who told his audience that "any black person with an education is duty-bound and obligated to help his unfortunate brother to get somewhere out of the muck and mire and oppression of denial and segregation. These things can be overcome with education, and if you are fortunate enough to have it, use it to help your unfortunate brother." This injunction, said Burns, influenced "every dad-blasted thing in my life."[23]

Leonard Burns became a member of the Urban League, the NAACP, and several other groups. In 1953, Burns and several colleagues organized the United Clubs, an organization composed of four social and pleasure clubs and the local musicians' union. The group's first goal was to desegregate the Municipal Auditorium.

Through the Urban League, Burns and Ortique came to know several of the city's race relations liberals of the 1950s—especially Rosa Freeman Keller, Helen Mervis, and Albert D'Orlando. Of these three, Rosa Keller had the most influence with the city's economic elite. She was the daughter of the local Coca-Cola magnate, A. B. Freeman. Her brother, Richard Freeman, sat on numerous boards in the city, and another relative, John Minor Wisdom, was to achieve distinction as a scholarly jurist and civil libertarian during his tenure on the Fifth Circuit Court of Appeals. Keller was also a close friend of Judge J. Skelly Wright, the federal district judge who ordered numerous local institutions to desegregate. Through various interracial concerns, she also came to know Dr. Joseph Fichter, a sociologist on the faculty of Loyola University who organized interracial projects, Rabbi Julian Feibleman, leader of a large Reform Jewish congregation, and John P. Nelson, Jr., a young Catholic lawyer who had been educated at Loyola.[24]

Although Keller was wealthier than other white integrationists of the 1950s, she shared with them a number of characteristics. As a group, the white activists were independent of segregationist economic control. Almost all of the men were professionals; women activists were often married to wealthy men. They were scholarly in temperament, and valued interracial friendships and relationships as ways of learning about the other world of the South—the black experience, which assumed the status of forbidden knowledge in the 1940s and 1950s. Most of these white liberals were religious, adherents of a social gospel doctrine that stressed activism, and a this-worldly concern with social problems. They had been profoundly affected by the Depression and World War II, and several dated their politicization to those years.[25] And except for Keller, most of the whites active in interracial efforts of the 1950s were in some ways outsiders to the South and to New Orleans—Mervis, D'Orlando, Fichter, Feibleman, and Dr. James Dombrowski of SCEF had been born outside New Orleans, and educated elsewhere. Keller herself had developed a critical perspective on segregation by confronting anti-Semitism through her Jewish husband's family, and by living in different parts of the country during Charles Keller's service in the U.S. Army. The city's white liberals, then, had a distance, and an outsider's perspective on segregation. These perspectives were often sharpened by their exposure to the social sciences of the mid-twentieth century—to the sort of sociological research that had been used in the *Brown* decision.

Race relations activism became a way to satisfy needs that the prevailing social and political system did not meet. White integrationists gained knowledge, and experiences with a different culture and different racial experience. They often shared experiences of social marginality, as their activism increasingly alienated them from segments of the white community. But white activists also gained a sense of accomplishment, a sense of having made an impact on history. These gains would not have occurred had they remained complacent.[26]

Rosa Freeman Keller was born in 1911, the daughter of Louisiana's Coca-Cola pioneer. The Freemans were Presbyterians, and stressed "personal honor"; the children were lectured to "do what's right—even if it hurts you."[27] Rosa Freeman was educated in New Orleans, and spent a rebellious year at Hollins College in Virginia. She married Charles Keller, Jr., in 1932, a match that provoked some consternation in her family, because Keller was Jewish and an army officer. After the usual moves produced by army tours, Rosa Keller returned to New Orleans with her children while her husband was sent to Europe during World War II. In 1978, she recalled that

It was World War II that woke a lot of us up. . . . I'd married a Jewish fellow, and learned a lot about prejudice then. . . . I thought I could see the seeds of what got Germany in such terrible trouble right here.[28]

Keller threw herself into volunteer work in an effort to diminish her anxiety about her husband. She joined the League of Women Voters (LWV), and, when her mother died, she accepted Mrs. Freeman's position on the board of the YWCA. It was there that she met middle-class, educated black women for the first time—and had what amounted to a conversion experience. "I met people like Jessie Dent and Daisy Young. . . . They were ladies, lovely people, beautifully educated," she explained in 1978. "I didn't know they existed, the town was so sealed up in compartments." In 1945, she joined the board of the fledgling Urban League, an organization devoted to expanding economic opportunities for blacks. With this began Keller's long-term commitment to racial equality. She also became active in municipal politics. When deLesseps S. Morrison, a war hero, ran as a reform candidate for mayor in 1946, Keller and many of her "good government" allies backed him. He served as mayor until 1961, and became a political ally of Keller, recognizing his debts to both the reform constituency within the city's upper class, and to his base of support within the black community. As a strategic ally of the black elite, Keller was able to use influence to promote improvements for blacks within New Orleans, and to assist in the desegregation of several institutions. She was also able to create a career for herself as a reformer; civil rights became her "cause" and her vocation. It also became her way of staking out an independence from the men of her family—people who "did not understand" her commitment to an interracial society, and who were frequently known as obstructionists to racial change.[29]

Keller's first major project began in 1947. At a dinner party at the home of philanthropist Edgar Stern, Keller heard that a servant of the Sterns had been burned out of her house, and was unable to find another. Due to population increases from the war years, and to municipal building projects, black housing was in short supply throughout the city. With great indignation, Keller learned that blacks were unable to borrow money from banks to buy homes, because they were regarded as bad credit risks. Determined to prove that assumption wrong, she, her husband, and the Sterns decided to build a housing development for middle-class blacks. This would ease part of the housing problem of blacks in the city, and it would prove to banks that blacks were a good credit risk.

Ponchartrain Park represented a significant financial risk for the Kellers: Rosa and Chuck Keller invested a great deal of the money that she had brought to their marriage. And acquiring the financing for the project took a great deal of time. The development was built in the Seabrook area of the Upper Ninth Ward, and opened in 1954. It was backed by the Urban League. A. J. Chapital of the NAACP initially opposed the development—because it was known to be a blacks-only neighborhood—but other black leaders, recognizing the housing shortage in New Orleans, and trusting Mrs. Keller, applauded the project.[30]

During the late 1940s and early 1950s, colleagues in the Urban League "educated" Keller about the restrictions that blacks faced in the South. This knowledge often shocked her. In 1988, she recalled a discussion on black voter registration in the city. She asked one black union leader why he was not registered.

He said, "Well, I just don't want to get *killed* yet." And then he started telling me stories about people who would *dare* to do this. And how they got hurt, or their families would get hurt. Nobody wanted black people to vote.[31]

Keller was often appalled by the ignorance and hostility of whites of her own social class. She recalled an instance in which her daughter had asked J. Westbrook MacPherson, the black Urban League executive director, to address her Presbyterian youth group, which was then studying comparative religions and cultures. MacPherson spoke to the group until a church deacon entered the room, demanded to know his name, and announced "If you niggers think you can marry our white girls, do things like that ..." The teenagers froze as the man continued his tirade. "I simply couldn't believe that you could be that *rude* to anybody," Keller explained in 1988. MacPherson was "speaking to this *huge* roomful of teenagers. What earthly harm could that do to anybody? But [the deacon] was *sure* that all black men wanted to marry white women."[32]

Within this environment, Keller achieved a reputation as a race-relations pioneer. As president of the Urban League, she often took black leaders into the offices of white businessmen throughout the city, attempting to persuade them to hire black employees. "I'm very acceptable socially, and every other way, and there were plenty of times when people just couldn't tell me not to come," she said. "I kinda used my advantages to do these things." Her wealth, and her social connections, made Rosa Keller a rarity in race-relations leadership in the 1950s. The city's blacks did not have any other allies from the city's elite, the "blue-blood, King of Carnival" hierarchy to which the Freemans belonged.[33]

Helen Mervis moved to New Orleans in 1939, shortly after her marriage. She was born in Pittsburgh in 1917, the middle child of immigrant parents. In 1988, Mervis remembered her childhood in grim terms: as a child of "the only Jewish family for miles around" who experienced anti-Semitism from her working-class Polish neighbors; of seeing hills across the Allegheny River where crosses were burned by the Ku Klux Klan. "Very early on, we learned that they were out to get Jews," she said. Helen Mervis' family owned a grocery store frequented by the whites and blacks of their neighborhood. She recalled that her father was as prejudiced against blacks as some of her neighbors were against Jews. As a child, Mervis had tried to protect blacks from her father's bitterness when they came into the store. Her father's racism created an early and deep division between them: Helen began having arguments with him about blacks. Later, as a student at the University of Pittsburgh in the 1930s, she and her friends became involved in leftist anti-military and anti-war activities. Though not a Communist Party member herself, some of Mervis' friends were—which was enough to incense her older brother, who charged her with participating in "communist activities." Her political beliefs crystallized then; she would always consider herself a "liberal," she said in 1988. Like Keller, Helen Mervis found in politics and in activism a way to differentiate herself from the more conservative men in her family.

After her marriage to Leo Mervis, she moved to New Orleans, only gradually becoming involved in community organizations as her children matured. She became active in the Council of Jewish Women, and organized a local chapter of the Brandeis National Women's Committee in the early 1950s. Mervis found the exposure to the university and its scholars invaluable—particularly in the fields of sociology, economics, and psychology. Brandeis and its faculty became a "powerful influence" in her life, confirming her "very liberal" political orientation. The ideas she absorbed through Brandeis "had a lot to do" with her own feeling that "one world was where it was at"—and that the isolationism of her student days was "very wrong."[34] In 1956, she was recruited to join the Urban League by her friend Betty Goldstein. The League experience was the "culmination" of her evolving commitment to racial equality. It allowed her to fulfill important desires:

I just had that need in me to fight for everybody else's rights and in the process, fighting for my own. The fact that I am Jewish has a great deal to do with this; the sense of being different.[35]

Mervis' sense of personal difference—her identity as an outsider—was to some extent shared by other white integrationists of the 1950s. The Reverend Albert D'Orlando, pastor of the First Unitarian Church from 1950 through the early 1980s, was born in 1915 in Revere, Massachusetts. He was the eighth of fourteen children of an Italian immigrant family, and grew up in the Baptist church. The family owned a candy business, and all of the children worked in the business for some period of time. When D'Orlando finished high school in 1932, he went to work in the business, but entered Tufts University at 1940, determined to find a career in social service. In 1988, he claimed that his "spiritual conversion" to a socially oriented theology came during the Depression—"on the streets of small New England towns" where he made candy deliveries. In these towns, he saw "dozens and dozens of men," without work, and loitering. He also gave rides to numerous young men employed by the Civilian Conservation Corps (CCC), a New Deal program that employed youth to work in conservation and forestry. He became aware of "how much tension the CCC alleviated in these communities," and was "tremendously moved by the terrible waste of human resources" that large-scale unemployment produced. At the same time, he became impatient with the strictures of the Baptist church, and was drawn to the greater freedom of the Unitarians. As a theological student at Tufts, he "became more political," and became more convinced that government could, and should be used to relieve unemployment and poverty. Living with other theological students, he had long discussions about world affairs and the coming war. At this time, he became a member of the American Student Union, an organization under Communist Party sponsorship. When he graduated in 1945, he dropped his leftist affiliations, and took the pastorate of two small congregations in New Hampshire.

Aware of racial segregation in college, D'Orlando had participated in marches for integrated schools. But in 1950, after coming to New Orleans, he discovered a problem in his small congregation—the church was dominated by a very old segregationist family, which objected to the presence of black families drawn to the church during the 1950s. These black Unitarians expected to be full members of the church; they wanted to join other members of the congregation for after-service coffees, and to participate in all church activities. D'Orlando backed the claims of his black parishioners, offending some of the older white families. As the congregation grew, more black families joined, eventually provoking a split in the church. The segregationists seceded, leaving a far more liberal congregation than D'Orlando had first encountered. In the late 1950s, students from Tulane, Dillard, and other local universities met in interracial groups at D'Orlando's church.[36]

D'Orlando's "mixed" congregation and his student past would make him a controversial pastor in New Orleans of the 1950s, but he was not nearly as controversial a figure as Dr. James Dombrowski, the executive director of SCEF. In the 1950s and 1960s, SCEF, as a leftist and integrationist organization, was regularly red-baited by Mississippi senator James O. Eastland, by the American Legion, and, locally, by the local Young Men's Business Club (YMBC). Additionally, the Louisiana Joint Legislative Committee on Un-American Activities (LUAC) attacked the organization and raided its local offices in 1963, when SCEF was involved in a voter registration campaign in Louisiana.[37]

James Dombrowski came to SCEF out of a religious concern for social justice. He was born in 1897, the son of a prosperous jeweler in Tampa, Florida. In 1979, he recalled, "I had a comfortable childhood, with lots of love. I was exposed to all the good things. And Southern society can be very good if you get the breaks." His sense of the pleasantness of life was ended by World War I; he served as an ambulance driver on the Western Front for more than a year. Convinced that his attitudes were inadequate to confront the religious and moral dilemmas facing the world, he began a long period of intellectual wandering, culminating in study under theologians Harry Ward and Reinhold Niebuhr at the Union Theological Seminary. He received a joint doctorate from Union and Columbia University in 1936, writing a thesis on "The Early Days of Christian Socialism in America." In 1979, he described himself as a Christian socialist—"and a radical, in the best sense of the word."[38]

Dombrowski's studies led him toward social action. In 1932, as part of a small group of progressive Southerners, he helped organize the Highlander Folk School, an interracial institution that would train labor organizers and community organizers during the coming decades. Highlander's ties to the Southern labor movement, and to black voting efforts, made it a frequent target of red-baiting and violence by Southern conservatives. In 1965, Dombrowski asserted that, as a Southerner, he had wanted to spend his life in the South teaching religion and philosophy. "But very early I became convinced that my efforts in this field would be confronted by a far more fundamental problem, segregation. I felt sure that the little contribution I would make toward achieving a better world should be centered on this important issue."[39] Dombrowski was staff director of Highlander until he became an administrator for the SCHW. He found at Highlander a model of a democratic and communitarian way of life. The staff of twelve only drew subsistence salaries, and

we lived at the same level as the community—Appalachia, the poorest community in the United States. But the people shared each other; people shared, shared alike. Everybody was poor, and there was a certain dignity to that. We could decide what we wanted to do about it. We made decisions in common—it was a very democratic kind of group. We *felt* that we were in control of our daily lives, and that lent a certain dignity to it.[40]

Dombrowski differed from most Southern integrationists: he was a radical. As director of SCEF, he was a "lightning rod" within the community—absorbing right-wing charges of communism, and official investigations that left him without many visible allies in New Orleans. And yet, in the Southern reaction that is commonly known as Massive Resistance, even the most moderate integrationists were affected, and frequently attacked for their actions. Like the McCarthy era, the era of Massive Resistance stifled dissent and civil liberties in the South, subjected black activists to terrorism, and destroyed Southern liberalism as a political force for nearly a decade. It was in the context of this regional convulsion that New Orleans' black community organized for school desegregation, equal access to public facilities, and voting rights in the 1950s.[41]

Brown *and Massive Resistance*

Leontine Luke was one of the organizers of the lawsuit that eventually desegregated New Orleans' public schools in 1960. In November of 1951, she and a colleague from the Ninth Ward Civic and Improvement League chaired a meeting to organize parents for a class-action suit against the Parish school board. The suit, *Bush vs. Orleans Parish School Board*, was decided by the *Brown* decision in 1954, but would shuttle between the federal courts and the Parish school board's attorneys for almost a decade before the city's public schools finally and cathartically desegregated. In 1952, however, the *Bush* suit appeared to be consistent with a line of

NAACP suits initiated by A. P. Tureaud. The presence of school desegregation suits, like earlier equalization suits filed by the NAACP, forced
the Parish school board to pour more money into the chronically under-
funded black schools. NAACP litigation had achieved a number of victories: salary equalization for black teachers, and the desegregation of the
law school, graduate school, and nursing school at Louisiana State University (LSU) in Baton Rouge.[42]

The Inc. Fund's work was facilitated by the presence of a sympathetic
federal judge sitting at the District Court of New Orleans. J. Skelly Wright
was a New Orleans native, Catholic, and the second of seven children
from a working-class neighborhood. A product of public schools, he had
taught high school English while attending Loyola University's law school
at night. He served in the U.S. Coast Guard in World War II, and became
increasingly aware of racial problems in the military. After the war, Wright
returned to New Orleans, serving as U.S. attorney until 1949, when President Harry S. Truman appointed him to a seat on the U.S. District Court.
By 1952, he had ordered the admission of blacks to LSU's law school, a
turning point in his judicial career. Years later, he wrote that "ordering
LSU Law School integrated was my first integration order. Until that time,
I was just another Southern 'boy.' After it, there was no turning back."[43]

Like his fellow lawyer John Minor Wisdom, Wright had a fundamental
commitment to the rule of law embodied in the constitution and in Supreme
Court decisions.[44] But he also found his own personal attitudes changed
by the cases he decided in the 1950s. He could hardly help comparing the
claims of the black plaintiffs with the privileges demanded by segregationists. He was moved, too, by the character of attorney A. P. Tureaud—
"a repudiation of everything racism stood for," compared to the segregationists who visibly demonstrated "the structure, the hate, the ultimate
arbitrariness of white supremacy."[45]

Skelly Wright and Fifth Circuit Court judge John Minor Wisdom—
and the trial attorneys who took civil rights cases—played an important
role in the black struggle. First, they performed a gate-opening function.
Through litigation and appeals, lawyers and federal judges provided open-
ings in the political structure of the South. Second, they helped to mobilize
a national consensus on civil rights that helped to legitimate black protest
within the legal and political system. These activities of lawyers, judges,
and racial negotiators like Dent and Revius Ortique created links between
national political structures and black activists. Protest, litigation, appeals,

and positive judicial decisions linked social movement organizations like the NAACP, SCLC, SCEF, and, later, CORE and the Student Non-Violent Coordinating Committee (SNCC), to the larger political system.[46]

The U.S. Supreme Court delivered the decision later known as *Brown I* on May 17, 1954. Though the Court delayed its ruling on implementation for another year, black leaders saw the event as a historic milestone. *Brown* gave the black movement the sanction of the federal government and the federal courts. Like other optimistic black leaders, Albert Dent believed that the discrepancy between expressed white opinion on race and the attitudes that educated Southerners revealed in anonymous polls indicated that white Southerners felt fearful of expressing their pro-integration feelings due to public pressure. Like a number of his peers, Dent thought that *Brown* would sanction more enlightened views on race. Thus, he announced in 1954 that he did not believe that "there would be any real resistance" to *Brown*.[47] During a program in which he was interviewed by Harry Ashmore, editor of the Arkansas *Gazette*, Dent asserted that "Abraham Lincoln freed the Negro slaves, but the Supreme Court freed the white man."[48]

Within days after *Brown* was announced, the state legislature created the Joint Committee to Maintain Segregation, chaired by Senator William M. "Willie" Rainach of Claiborne Parish. Rainach led the drive to pass a pupil placement law making parish school superintendents responsible for assigning individual students to proper (meaning segregated) schools. A "Police Power" statute mandated segregation in all schools below the college level. Parts of the bill were drafted into a constitutional amendment. The legislature voted to cut off funding from any schools that integrated; admission into the state university system was closed to graduates of integrated schools.[49]

Thus began Louisiana's Massive Resistance. Between 1954 and 1960, the state legislature, often joined by other elected bodies, used a variety of methods to obstruct the desegregation of public institutions in the state. Much of the opposition to *Brown* revolved around New Orleans' public schools. Long threatened by the *Bush* suit, the city's schools appeared to be the most vulnerable link in the state's public system. Racial tensions heightened as the New Orleans' schools became a political combat zone between the legislature and the federal courts—with the legislature passing drafts of segregation statutes, and the courts declaring them unconstitutional.[50]

Between 1954 and 1960, the legislature "interposed" itself between the state's institutions and the federal government in an attempt to circumvent federal court rulings that voided new segregation statutes. In 1956, the legislature resurrected a Ku Klux Klan control law of 1924 to drive the NAACP underground by requiring the Association to file membership lists. The legislature also devised new technical strategies to scrub increasing numbers of black voters from registration lists and to keep new black voters from registering.[51] A law adopted in 1959 provided that those applying to register to vote must possess "good character," "understand the duties and obligations of citizenship," and be able to read and to interpret any clause of the state or federal constitution. This effectively discouraged poorly educated, uneducated, and black voters from attempting to register in the state.[52]

In 1954, white Citizens' Councils appeared for the first time in northern Louisiana; they were organized by the Joint Legislative Committee to Maintain Segregation, which was also known as the Rainach Committee. By the fall of 1955, segregationists had organized the Citizens' Council of Greater New Orleans—a group that claimed 50,000 members by 1960.[53] New Orleans' Council, like those elsewhere, was elite-led, with a largely working-class following. Known as the "Uptown Klan" by white liberals, the Councils claimed disdain for the terrorism practiced by the Klan, but participated in quasi-terroristic activities—harassing phone calls, death threats, economic reprisals against black activists. Councils also waged the "legalistic" battle against integration by passing state segregation statutes and other laws aimed at gutting federal court orders. By sanctioning disobedience to the federal law, the councils, and the elites who led them, covertly sanctioned the lawlessness that white extremists traditionally used to enforce segregation. For black activists and their few white allies, the results were frighteningly familiar—harassment, terrorism, and a pervasive atmosphere of fear that accompanied any assertion of black rights.[54]

The Citizens' Councils were a product of Massive Resistance, and claimed to pursue their political goals by legal, rather than extralegal means. From the Dixiecrat rebellion of 1948—in which the segregationist wing of the Democratic Party split to run a "State's Rights" ticket upholding segregation—to the defeat of the Citizens' Councils' legislative stratagems in the early 1960s, the agrarian Southern Right launched varied attacks on organizations and individuals supporting integration or black rights. In attacks on groups as disparate as the NAACP, the Urban League, and SCEF, the Southern Right placed tremendous pressures on civil rights advocates and activists. Council leaders frequently assailed black and white activists as communists intent on subversion, since the Southern Right equated racial integration with treason. Over the decade of the 1950s, the rhetoric and repression associated with this reaction increased.[55]

Within this growing frenzy of segregationist activity, New Orleans' black community achieved several important victories. The United Clubs opened the municipal auditorium for use by blacks in 1953 and 1954. The pretext was the annual ball to benefit the United Negro College Fund, but the object was to allow black citizens to use the segregated public facility.[56] In 1954 and 1955, the black community boycotted the annual McDonogh Day ceremonies of the city's public schools. In 1957 and 1960, the United Clubs called a Carnival Boycott to protest the segregation statutes passed by the legislature, and donated the proceeds to the NAACP's campaign against the "hate bills."[57] By late 1955, the city's libraries had desegregated, and by 1958, the city's buses and streetcars were desegregated.

The pattern of these victories suggests the limited and cautious options open to the black community, the multiple layers of cooperation within that community, and the monolithic nature of the institution of segregation. The desegregation of the city's buses and libraries also attests to the important role played by strategically placed white allies—people like Rosa Keller, Skelly Wright, and James Dombrowski.[58] Throughout the 1950s, segregationist pressures made New Orleans' black leaders cautious in their strategies, and inclined to use the influence of strategically placed whites to their advantage.

According to Leonard Burns, the United Clubs hoped to mobilize New Orleans' black middle class around a "cause" in the 1950s. Early in 1953, the group decided to try to use the municipal auditorium for a social event, but one that would draw wide support. They decided on an annual benefit ball for the United Negro College Fund. Through delicate negotiations, they obtained permission to use the facility, and through subtle, trickster stratagems, the group's leadership made a smooth preparation for the event. Burns only told the building's management that the event was a "university" function, and the club paid the rental fees well in advance. The event was a success, marred only by the intrusion of the city police, who were determined to break up the event because of the obviously "mixed" couples who were dancing and enjoying each other's company. Burns recalled that the police sergeant accosted him and said

"All these Negroes and whites are dancin together. They're not supposed to be— " And I said, "Where?" and he said, "Right there!" I says, "Oh, this couple here?" I says. This was Gerald Thomas and his wife. She was fair. And he was olive, a little darker than I am, Indian type. And I says, "Pardon me, Mr. Thomas, who is this lady?" And he says, "This is my wife! Don't you know my wife, Burns?" And I said, "Oh, pardon me, sorry." Officer say, "That man's wife?" I say, "yes, yes," I say, "come over here." Dr. Floyd and his wife. And Floyd looks like an Indian. Indian. Coal black hair, high cheekbones, brown. And his wife was very fair. Red hair. And I said, "Pardon, me, Dr., could you introduce this man?" "What do you mean?" I says, "Uhh, where's your wife?" "This is my wife! Don't you know my wife?" I say, "Now you see officer, we have all these people with their wives." I said, "this is no mixed affair." I said, "These people are university people, all educated people." He said, "All these people in here?" I said, "We're here for a cause. We're here to raise money for the university." I say, "Now you don't have any intentions of *arresting* anybody, do you?"

Now here's a sergeant, who may not have but a high school education, and dealing with all of these people from a university level—doctors this, doctors that, and he says, "No." Then one of the rednecks comes up and says, "Sarge, we gonna have to do something. We gonna have to stop this." And I says, "On what cause? If you stop this, I'm gonna sue you." And he looked at me as if to say, "Who is this guy?" He says, "Oh, this is a doctor. Don't be fooling with him. C'mon, c'mon, let's go."[59]

The dancers had a "rollicking good time," and raised more than $3,200 for the United Negro College Fund. The United Clubs held a second UNCF benefit ball at the Municipal Auditorium in 1954.[60] Burns and his colleagues had successfully mobilized the black middle class for the cause of black education, and had desegregated the Municipal Auditorium in the process. Burns had also outwitted the city's police by using the ambiguity of color and race in the city to confound racial stereotypes. In reality, Burns admitted, some of the dancing couples *had* been racially mixed.[61] In this action, Burns and his colleagues had used their class positions and social status to promote activism through the traditional social pursuits of the black middle class and elite. In their dealings with authorities and with the police, they had relied upon their class positions to defuse white protest and possible repression. The lesson of the event was not lost on Burns.

In January 1954, representatives of black parent-teacher associations and other community groups confronted the Orleans Parish School Board (OSPB) with objections to the arrangements for the annual McDonogh

Day ceremonies. The early May events were held to honor John Mc-
Donogh, an eccentric nineteenth-century philanthropist who had left much
of his considerable fortune to the public schools of Baltimore and New
Orleans. Children throughout the city attended schools named for
McDonogh. On each McDonogh Day, public school children were bused
to Lafayette Square, a park that fronted the old City Hall. School bands
played, the children placed flowers at the John McDonogh statue, and the
mayor awarded keys to each school's delegation. The event was segregated:
the white children passed the monument first, their bands played first, and
the whites met the mayor first. Black children stood in the hot morning
sun until every white delegation completed its ritual.[62]

In early 1954, the black teachers' associations protested the discriminatory practices of the event. They asserted that the segregation of the
event was a "humiliating experience" for the black children involved.[63]
The OSPB ignored the petitioners. By April, a number of black leaders
had decided to organize a boycott of the event. One was A. J. Chapital,
the NAACP president and a postal employee. He asked Revius Ortique to
make radio broadcasts urging black parents and students to boycott the
events. Ortique was then vice president at large of the Louisiana Council
of Labor, and worked for the state Department of Labor. His daily broadcasts to the black community, and his leadership role in the McDonogh
Day Boycott began his civil rights activism.[64]

The school board remained obdurate as the black community organized.
A. P. Tureaud, A. L. Davis, and other political and labor leaders backed
the boycott. Black organizations sent thousands of letters to the parents
of black schoolchildren, asking them to contact school principals and request that the children not be allowed to attend the event. On the May
morning of the ceremony, only thirty-four of the city's 32,000 black public
school children attended. Of the numerous black educators expected, only
one principal appeared to "unofficially observe" McDonogh Day. "We
were very, very angry with her," said Leontine Luke, a boycott organizer
in the Lower Ninth Ward. The woman never regained her status as a
leader in the black community for having violated this "first great boycott."[65] Ortique remembered that the event was "totally effective"—and a
silent sign that the black community could, and would, organize to assert
its rights. From his office above Lafayette Square, Ortique watched the
ceremonies:

As soon as the last white group had gone, you expected to hear the bands of the black schools . . . and there was total silence. You can imagine Mayor Morrison's chagrin when he stood on the steps of City Hall waiting with thirty-two keys in his hands.[66]

DeLesseps S. Morrison had built his career on an image of "progress" and municipal reform. One of the bases of this reform administration had been a durable and loyal black vote—regularly delivered by leaders like the Reverend A. L. Davis and others who saw Morrison as an improvement over previous administrations. Morrison was not an integrationist, but a man who dispensed patronage and services within the segregated system. As mayor, he had made—and supported—improvements for the black community, but these were carefully done, and segregated. He had built Shakespeare Park for his black constituency, and had backed the construction of Ponchartrain Park, a housing development for middle-class blacks. But Morrison, always ambitious for the governorship, would go no farther than reforms within the segregated system. For many of his black supporters, this was not enough. And for many of the segregationists who were on the offensive in the middle and late 1950s, Morrison's racial liberalism was too radical, and, even worse, too cosmopolitan. The McDonogh Day Boycott could have been read as the first sign that Morrison's fragile coalition—like those of other Southern liberals—was about to disintegrate.[67]

In March of 1954, two months before the McDonogh Day Boycott, and two and a half months before the U.S. Supreme Court handed down the *Brown* decision, Mississippi senator James O. Eastland brought members of the Senate Internal Security Subcommittee (SISS) to New Orleans to hold hearings on SCEF. In January, Senator William Jenner of Indiana had charged SCEF with "communist activities." The subcommittee subpoenaed Aubrey Williams, a former New Deal administrator and SCEF president, SCEF director James Dombrowski, and former SCEF board member Virginia Durr.[68]

Intense local publicity accompanied the Eastland hearings. Professional informers testified that SCEF was a "vehicle to promote communism." Dombrowski, a member of the Socialist Party as a young man, was asked repeatedly if he had ever been a member of the Communist Party. He repeatedly replied, "No." The committee subpoenaed SCEF's financial records, including a list of the organization's 3,000 financial contributors. Dombrowski refused to turn over the materials, citing rights to freedom of speech based on the First Amendment.[69]

The proceedings were volatile. Virginia Durr, a patrician Alabama liberal, refused to answer the committee's questions, but occasionally powdered her nose as a gesture of contempt for Eastland and his colleagues. Her husband Clifford Durr, an attorney who had defended loyalty oath cases during the Truman administration, grew overwrought during the proceedings, and collapsed.[70] James Dombrowski remembered that even "people with very little exposure to the civil rights movement" were

astonished or horrified at what took place—ignoring elemental civil rights, constitutional rights. It reminded one of what took place in Germany with the storm troopers. The hearings were held in the federal court rooms, with a number of these huge—they *looked* like storm troopers—standing around with brown belts and guns. They threw Myles Horton [the head of Highlander] out, and Cliff Durr, who had a heart attack, and could have died. So it was horrifying in many ways.[71]

Although SCEF attracted a number of liberal supporters due to their revulsion at the committee's tactics, the organization was effectively smeared as communist within the larger black and white communities of New Orleans. More moderate civil rights groups tended to avoid SCEF and its activities because they, too, fought the "communist" label. Segregationists adamantly insisted that racial integration was a communist-inspired program aimed at destroying American civilization. Such charges had repercussions. In 1956, the editor of the Chamber of Commerce newsletter was fired for his membership in SCEF; in 1957, the music critic of the *Times-Picayune* was fired after signing a SCEF petition.[72] In the red-baiting of SCEF, Dombrowski saw an "insidious" process:

If you can isolate a person or group from the rest of the community, and make people afraid to associate with them, you're a long ways toward a police state. People are afraid to say what they think. And that's been true in this struggle right on. There was a member of the legislature of Louisiana who said once on the floor of the house, "Integration is the Southern expression of communism." He put it very bluntly—and that's what most people thought.[73]

SCEF, like the SNCC, which it supported after 1960, had an "open door" policy, and did not prohibit communists from its membership. But, said Dombrowski, "actually, there were so few communists, you'd have a hard time finding any in the South." He thought that the segregationists who railed most against communism often had "the hardest time defining what they meant. Usually, it just meant someone who espoused the Negro cause—that's what they meant by communist in those days."[74]

The desegregation of the city's libraries illustrated the delicate use of negotiation and tactical discretion by the black community. In February of 1954, the New Orleans League of Classroom Teachers presented a petition to the city's library board urging the desegregation of the Latter Library, an elegant facility located in a fashionable uptown neighborhood. In March of the same year, three clergymen appeared before the board. They were led by the superintendent of schools for the Catholic Archdiocese, who urged New Orleans to follow the pattern set by Dallas and Fort Worth, Texas, both of which had recently integrated their library systems.[75]

The clergymen had appeared at the instigation of Albert Dent, who had been visited by James Dombrowski earlier in the year. Dombrowski had wanted Dent's cooperation in his efforts to integrate the city's libraries. Specifically, he wanted to present to the library board letters from other recently desegregated urban systems, which would document the success of integration. Albert Dent refused to assist Dombrowski, saying, "Jim, you're very unpopular here. I won't work *with* you, but if you'll let *me* do it, I will."[76]

Dent contacted the integrated library systems in Texas, and called "a Catholic, a Jew, and a Protestant." He asked the three religious leaders to take the evidence to the library board and urge them to integrate the city's libraries. He reminded them that blacks could not use the main library at Lee Circle, or any of the branch libraries. He refused to be a part of this delegation: "I told them, 'There were no Negroes around when you white people messed up this thing. Now, you white folks straighten this out.' "[77]

Rosa Keller had been agitating for library desegregation before the delegations appeared before the board. In 1953, deLesseps Morrison had appointed her to the board as a gesture of gratitude to his women supporters in the Independent Women's Organization (IWO), and the League of Women Voters (LWV), two of Keller's political affiliations. Keller recalled that she was informed by several board members that "it was all right to have a woman on the board, but that [I] was not expected to say or *do* anything."

She remained quiet and dutiful for months, but felt uncomfortable with the segregated library system. When a new branch was proposed for the Broadmoor section, she suggested that the board "admit all comers," since the neighborhood was racially mixed. The other board members were "horrified. I had succeeded in only making the board nervous."[78]

The board's discomfort was increased by the successive petitioning groups. Meetings became acrimonious and unpleasant. The board's decisions were traditionally unanimous, but with Keller urging desegregation, the board refused to vote. Several board members predicted the ruin of the library system if blacks were admitted. Keller left meetings disgusted and nauseated. Unhappy with the controversy, she decided to resign from the board. She made an obligatory call on Morrison to explain her position. At the conclusion of her story, Morrison stunned Keller by insisting that she not resign because her position was correct. Not long after their talk, Morrison called Keller to announce that the board would soon desegregate.[79]

The board had tried to avoid making the decision to desegregate. In March, it referred the matter to the mayor and to the city's Commission Council. At its April meeting, Morrison stated that he had met with Commission Council members and had decided to "advise the Library Board to allow" black patrons to use Latter Library. The board then requested from city government a formal policy statement on racial segregation in libraries. On May 21, the city attorney answered the board. In light of the *Brown* decision of May 17, he advised that "no attempt be made to enforce segregation in any of the libraries."[80]

By late 1955, NAACP president A. J. Chapital reported to the Association that "all branch Public Libraries" were open to blacks. The NAACP hoped to see Latter and other libraries integrated in 1955. Library branches were among the few public institutions in New Orleans that were opened to blacks without a lawsuit and sustained protests. Within the buildings, bathrooms and drinking fountains remained segregated.[81]

The actual desegregation of the branches was handled with discretion to avoid a hostile white response. When informed of the library board's decision, Rosa Keller called Urban League associates to make arrangements in the black community. Albert Dent, she learned, had already "made a deal," with influential friends in the white and black communities: if the board voted to desegregate, no publicity must follow. Instead, he told them,

I would call the presidents of the Negro colleges and the principals of the Negro high schools and tell them, 'Did you know the library is open to Negroes now? If you have some students who want to go to the library, tell them to go to Latter ...' Nothing was ever published in the newspapers.[82]

Like other smoothly achieved victories of the 1950s, the integration of libraries was facilitated by elite collusion—by the guarantee of little or no publicity, and by pressures applied by a strategically placed white elite.

But the library board was clearly pressured by *Brown* itself. Its members must have recognized, as did the city attorney, that integration was inevitable. With the desegregation of the city's buses in 1958, and of Tulane University in 1963, this pattern was altered only slightly. Both institutions were desegregated by lawsuits, and both were initially decided by J. Skelly Wright, who issued integration orders. The administrations of the city and the university were keenly aware of the inevitability of eventual desegregation—and of the costs of a protracted defense of segregation. The actual integration of the buses and the university was orchestrated by black community organizations, and done without publicity, in order to avoid a segregationist backlash.

When even cautious attempts to promote racial integration received publicity, black activists were routinely threatened, and white activists were ostracized and red-baited. An early instance of this occurred on September 15, 1955, when Rosa Keller and the Rabbi Julian Feibleman, an SCEF board member, led a delegation to the Orleans Parish School Board. Keller and her colleagues protested the board's intransigence on integration—the board had just hired two segregationist attorneys to fight the *Bush* case. Keller and Feibleman presented the OSPB with a petition circulated by James Dombrowski, and signed by 180 citizens, including Urban League board members Helen Mervis and Albert D'Orlando. Feibleman addressed the board, urging them to "face the issue of segregation in a realistic sense." The petitioners asked the school board to develop a plan for desegregating the city's schools.[83]

Keller didn't anticipate the school board's response. "They practically threw us out of the place, and such howling and screaming you never heard. . . . This is *very* unsettling when grown people behave like that. It was very frightening." The group's petition made the front pages of the next day's newspapers. Keller and Feibleman were "just pariahs for awhile after that." They "got sniped at with guns later on and it was *very* ugly." Keller began to doubt her own convictions:

somewhere along the way you'd get to thinking, maybe they *are* right, maybe I *am* the one that's wrong. . . . But people would come up—the ones who still spoke to you—and say, "You're all *wrong*. Those black people don't want to go to school with our kids. They *don't*. I've talked to my cook and she says, 'No.'" And they would convince *themselves*. They just couldn't encompass this kind of *change*. Change is hard on people. . . . You'd walk down the street, and you'd see other people walk across the street to avoid you. . . . And these were people I'd grown up with and gone to school with, danced with 'em at parties. And I give everybody the perfect right to disagree with me, 'cause this was *pretty sticky stuff*, but they don't have to not know your name anymore, just 'cause you're not working the same side of the street.[84]

Keller was president of the Urban League through 1956. Helen Mervis became president of the embattled organization in 1957. Revius Ortique joined the League in 1956; he was being groomed for the League presidency, which he would hold for five years in the late 1950s and early 1960s. Throughout 1956, the legislature continued to pass segregation statutes. Most were aimed at public schools, but several banned interracial sports, dancing, social functions, and athletic training. By the year's end, the Rainach Committee announced plans to eliminate "illegally" registered black voters from the state's registration rolls.[85] In May 1956, the NAACP was forced to suspend official operations in the state, and Leander Perez began an intensive mobilization against the desegregation of Catholic schools. This campaign would force the church to delay the integration of its schools until 1962, a year after the public schools had been desegregated. At a large public meeting in 1956, Perez attacked the New Orleans Urban League as a communist organization, and charged the League with promoting integration. At the same meeting, he read aloud a list of the board members' names. He urged Council members and sympathizers to boycott the businesses of all Urban League board members.[86] In 1957, the Community Chest, responding to Citizens' Council pressures, severed its relationship with the Urban League. Without funds of its own, the League was forced to raise its own budget. Helen Mervis, president in 1957, began "nickel and dime" fund-raising operations locally.[87]

In early 1957, Leonard Burns and his friends drew the United Clubs "into civil rights circles." The Clubs organized a black Carnival Blackout to protest the "hate bills" that had been passed by the state legislature. Mindful of the Montgomery Bus Boycott, which was occurring simultaneously, the Clubs urged black New Orleanians to boycott the Mardi Gras balls and festivities, and to donate the proceeds to the NAACP's legal campaign. The Clubs published ads in the *Louisiana Weekly* that urged, "Don't Dance," and "New Orleans Negroes Will Not Dance While Montgomery Negroes Walk." The blackout received support from 75 percent of the organizations the Clubs contacted, and raised an estimated $60,000 for national civil rights efforts.[88]

The blackout politicized the supposedly apolitical Mardi Gras festivities, making black carnival participation an act of complacency, at best.

Within the black and white communities, the blackout was controversial, according to Leonard Burns. "The caterer, the taxi driver, the man who was making the costumes, the man who was selling material for the costumes, even some of the stores on Canal Street that had black mailmen coming there, they were encouraging them to encourage me to lay low, to cool it," he recalled. Even the chief of police and the mayor became involved, according to Burns. The United Clubs had succeeded in getting the Zulu Club to cancel its parade. The Zulus were famous for the "African" costumes they wore in the Mardi Gras parades. Morrison and Police Chief Joseph Giarusso, said Burns, "paid [the Zulus] to go on with their parade." Some local blacks retaliated by threatening the Zulus. A woman scheduled to reign as Zulu queen was threatened, and refused to participate. Another queen took her place on the float, but, as Burns recalled,

because of some of the threats that people were making on the club, the queen that they did finally select arrived with four guard dogs on each side of her. A squad car sat behind the float, and everybody was shaky. And they said it was the fastest parade that they ever had. I mean, zoom, zoom, zoom, and it was over.

Burns remembered staying at home, listening to reports of the Mardi Gras festivities on the radio, television, and from phone calls.[89] This Carnival Blackout, like the Montgomery Bus Boycott and the Tallahassee Bus Boycott, was a signal that Southern blacks could mobilize money and people to protest segregation. But New Orleans' blackout was also significant in its leaders' use of indigenous festivities and class activities to protest segregation. In boycotting Mardi Gras festivities, they politicized a traditionally apolitical event, and withheld their money and participation from a local symbol of racial harmony and seasonal revelry.

In this atmosphere, the city's buses were desegregated after a "friendly" lawsuit. Davis and the Interdenominational Ministerial Alliance led the public campaign against bus and streetcar segregation in conjunction with boycotts led by black ministers in Montgomery and Tallahassee. Though the ministers threatened a boycott, they preferred litigation and negotiation. As it turned out, mobilization was not necessary. Skelly Wright deliberately gave his desegregation order at midnight on Friday, May 30, 1958—after the morning papers had been put to bed. Davis had been alerted that the order would be given, and had prepared his constituents. The Baptist minister sent telegrams to the NAACP and community leaders throughout the city. They met the buses in their neighborhoods, removed the "race screens" from the backs of the seats, and returned home. The city's bus desegregation proceeded smoothly, largely because of the discipline of the blacks who integrated the carriers.[90]

The presence of Skelly Wright on the federal bench aided the black leaders in their dealings with city officials and politicians. "When the integration of the buses came down, we had a strong decision from Judge Wright," Revius Ortique recalled. "We said to the leaders of the white community, 'Look, you guys, *this* judge will put people in jail if they don't obey.' And *that* changed overnight. One day the screens were on, the next day the screens were off. We had very little problem." When a city employee persistently "made trouble" on the buses, Ortique and his associates informed the man's supervisor:

in no uncertain terms that we could not afford to have public employees who were going to cause problems for the city of New Orleans. . . . We knew that we were saying "It doesn't take but *one spark* to ignite this and we just will *not* have that type of thing happen."[91]

The desegregation of buses and of libraries were certainly victories for the black community, but continued repression from the state legislature and the Citizens' Councils intimidated increasing numbers of once-sympathetic or even moderate whites. In 1958, Albert D'Orlando was thrown off of the Urban League board after being summoned to Washington to testify before the House Un-American Activities Committee (HUAC) about his activities in the American Student Union, and about his knowledge of Communist Party members in New Hampshire during the first years of his ministry. The First Unitarian church backed D'Orlando unanimously during this investigation. The board of the Urban League, however, felt pressured by a new state law that required organizations to certify that board members were free of communist connections. Revius Ortique, then president of the board, felt that failure to comply with the law would make the League "subject to conviction." The board split on a motion to drop D'Orlando from the board—but he was not notified of any meetings thereafter. In an interview of 1959, a researcher noted that D'Orlando was "sure of himself, but not at all sure of his place in the community."[92] The League's behavior hurt D'Orlando, who felt that he had "jeopardized the welfare of my family," and "put my life on the line" in New Orleans. He continued to preach against segregation, and against the McCarthy era from the pulpit. As a member of SCEF, he participated in the organization's integrated educational forums, and developed close ties to James Dombrowski and Virginia Collins.[93]

The ferocity of the segregationists, and the cowardice of liberal whites infuriated black leaders. In 1978, Albert Dent remembered this period with a mixture of irony and anger. He recalled a time when a white ministerial alliance invited him to speak, and he "shocked" them:

I told them that no man did I pity more than a protestant minister, because he couldn't stand in the pulpit and preach the truth—couldn't preach what he thought. I said, "You don't believe in racial segregation and deprivation such as we have— a dual system in the public schools, with Negro teachers being paid less than white teachers . . . you just can't possibly believe in that and be a Christian minister."[94]

Several of the ministers in that audience were men with whom Dent served on a committee on race relations. "Nobody *ever* came to me and said, "we think you are right. Let's do something about it." Dent recounted important dealings and negotiations, and secret conversations with the mayor, the chief of police, and various other white elites—men who would not let it be known that they conferred with blacks.[95] Such white cowardice galled him, even as it allowed him to achieve considerable stature as an interracial leader.[96]

By 1958, New Orleans' black leadership had achieved several victories in the face of rising regional and local repression. In 1959, several developments pushed the black community into active protest. A race-baiting gubernatorial campaign pitted deLesseps S. Morrison against segregationists Willie Rainach and Jimmie Davis. The black community, under the auspices of the Consumers' League, launched a boycott of white Dryades Street merchants. This successful boycott inspired several black students to organize a chapter of the Congress of Racial Equality in 1960. And in 1960, Judge J. Skelly Wright ordered New Orleans' schools to desegregate. Segregationist rhetoric and tactics achieved an almost hallucinatory quality between 1959 and 1961, and eventually forced New Orleans' business progressives to form a coalition of governance with the city's black leadership and their white liberal allies.

THREE

Desegregating New Orleans' Schools: The Political Generation, 1960–1961

*M*ANY of the men and women who emerged as activists between 1959 and 1961 became involved in one of two community crises. Several black lawyers and community leaders became advisers, counsels, and strategists for the protests launched by the Consumers' League, the Interdenominational Ministerial Alliance, and by the young people in the NAACP Youth Council and the Congress of Racial Equality (CORE). Additionally, a number of white liberals were drawn into the explosive school crisis of 1960–1961, when the legislature attempted to close the city's public schools rather than allow token desegregation, and sought to "interpose" itself between the federal courts and New Orleans' schools.

The crisis over public schools and escalating black protest made 1960 to 1961 a critical year for New Orleans, one that would result in a dramatic realignment of political forces. Faced with a choice between the federal courts and black petitioners on one side, and Massive Resistance on the other, the city's liberal and moderate whites chose to form a political alliance with the black leadership. This began a major process of change in the city's politics. By the late 1960s, the organized black vote would be

49

the most important constituency in city elections, and black political leaders—many of them active in the civil rights movement—would become members of the city's political elite.[1]

Motives for activism differed. Black leaders viewed the protest movement as a necessary step to racial liberation: all had angrily endured the indignities and restrictions of segregation since childhood. As adults, they were often the first in their families to acquire an education, and were certainly the first who could be openly involved in protest. Several had their aspirations broadened through service in the integrated U.S. Army, and through education in newly desegregated law schools. For these black leaders, the civil rights movement was a way to fight back, to destroy the system that had injured them, and to ensure opportunities for their children. It was also a way to claim the fruits of their labors—the economic, social, and political rewards that would accrue to lawyers and professionals. Often, the movement became a base from which to organize black voters, especially after the passage of the Voting Rights Act of 1965.

Many of the whites of this generation were involved with Save Our Schools (SOS), an organization that fought to keep New Orleans' public schools open and desegregated. SOS claimed between 800 and 1,500 members between 1960 and 1961. Many of its leaders regarded themselves as Southern liberals who had come to believe that segregation was morally wrong. The excesses of the legislature pulled them into active participation on behalf of school integration and racial justice. For a number of women, SOS was a galvanizing experience; it allowed them to "do something" meaningful to fight school closure and segregation. SOS and the school crisis also gave liberal whites opportunities to oppose the rabid segregationists whose excesses had been mounting since 1954.

White liberals resisted the Dixiecrats and Citizens' Councils from a mixture of moral and class motives; for many, the segregationists and their followers appeared to be a barbaric, race-baiting mob that symbolized the very worst that Southern political traditions had to offer. Like their black counterparts, many of the liberals were members of a relatively new class in Southern society, middle-class professionals whose numbers rose in Southern cities during the relative prosperity of the 1950s and 1960s.[2] They had neither economic nor class interests in maintaining segregation, and were often appalled by the back-country bosses and lower-class whites who violently resisted integration and black progress. Like the black middle class, they were excluded from participation in the segregationist-run political process, although for white liberals, this estrangement was sometimes a matter of choice. In rejecting the rhetoric and politics of racial segregation, liberal whites chose to ally themselves with the black protest elite, whom they came to know as fellow professionals who had interests and aspirations that were similar to their own. Brought into contact by the convergence of black protest and white violence, black and white professionals formed the working coalition that would guide New Orleans through its transition to an integrated city, and would create the bi-racial urban politics of the 1970s and beyond.

"The Most Radical Lawyers in New Orleans"

Robert Collins was born in New Orleans in 1931. His father was a printer, his mother a domestic, and, eventually, a masseuse who did private work for wealthy whites. Collins attributed his interest in the law to his mother: "she was from a good family, who themselves were not well-educated, but they were people who were ambitious." Many of her wealthy clients were lawyers, and "she thought that being a lawyer would be an important thing for me to do. She instilled in me at a very early age that this was something I should go for." He never wanted to pursue any other occupation. Collins' parents divorced when he was very young, and he counted his stepfather as a great influence on his development. Though not well educated, his step-father was well read and well travelled. He had served in France in World War I, and was keenly interested in world affairs and politics. Collins recalled that "it was always a mystery to me that a man who had his kind of intelligence had such a menial job—he worked at the washroom at the Roosevelt Hotel, which is now the Fairmont."

Collins attended high school at Gilbert Academy in New Orleans, a rigorous private school for blacks. His contemporaries at Gilbert included Lolis Elie, Andrew Young, and Tom Dent, the son of Albert Dent. Collins remembered Gilbert as an institution with high standards, where the best teachers instilled in students "a great sense of responsibility and seriousness in learning."[3] Black newspapers like the *Pittsburgh Courier* and the *Louisiana Weekly* were important in his education, because from them Collins learned of the progress that blacks were making in other parts of the country—in every place, it seemed, but the South. The papers gave him "an idea of what could be done, and what needed to be done," he said.

Collins attended Dillard University for his undergraduate degree, and was one of the first two blacks to attend law school at LSU in 1951. By this time, he "had a *reason* for wanting to be a lawyer—to do something" about segregation:

I wanted to use the law as a weapon to defeat the forces of discrimination and segregation. Because I guess the older I got, the more bitter I became at the system as it existed.[4]

Collins spent two years in the army after he graduated from law school, and entered briefly into a partnership with another black lawyer in New Orleans. He then taught for several years at the law school at black Southern University in Baton Rouge. While there, Collins decided to form a law practice with Lolis Elie and Nils Douglas, who had graduated from Loyola University's law school in 1959. Collins had known Elie at Gilbert, and Douglas at Dillard. All three were interested in taking civil rights cases.

While at Southern, Collins had come to know some of the young people on campus who were organizing for the Congress of Racial Equality (CORE), a national, pacifistic organization that sought to eliminate discrimination and segregation through non-violent direct action. Later, when students in New Orleans organized a CORE chapter, they asked Collins, Douglas, and Elie to represent them during the sit-in campaign they planned to wage in 1960. New Orleans' first sit-in case, *Lombard vs. Louisiana*, came to CD&E "because we were considered the most radical lawyers in the city of New Orleans," Collins said. As a young attorney, Collins was angered by the complicity of national authorities with the segregated institutions of the South:

The federal court house was located in the Wildlife and Fisheries Building in the French Quarter, and they had segregated toilets and segregated water fountains in the federal court. And in the civil district court. In all of the courts. There was segregation in the courtroom itself. Blacks were expected to sit in the back of the courtroom, or else blacks were expected to sit on one side of the aisle, whites on the other side. This was happening in the *very halls of justice*, to say nothing of public buildings. . . . It was kind of ironic that you'd go to the federal court to seek justice, and you were looking at segregated toilets, and segregated drinking fountains in that very courthouse that was supposed to be administering federal law.

Some of Collins' most vivid memories of the early 1960s included the times he went to the court to fight lawsuits to desegregate public accommodations. It angered him that "everyone" went along with the segregated system—the mayor, the district attorney, the judges, and others. "They were blinded to what they were doing. And these were supposed to be good, God-fearing people, you know, the pillars of society. It was a lot to take." Collins felt a sense of "outrage at what it all meant. It was a very bitter experience. I imagine that's how people in South Africa feel today. I felt then like they feel now about what's happening in South Africa."

Collins' partner, Lolis Elie, was born in New Orleans in 1930. His father was a truck driver and his mother worked part-time as a domestic during most of his childhood. His parents had four years of education between them; they were, Elie said, "not literate, but at no level were they ignorant." Elie was treated "special" as a little boy; his older sister Doris carried him around with her, pretending that Lolis was her own "cute little chocolate baby." He was always treated like a "prince" as a child. Elie's parents both provided him with examples of a very stubborn dignity and self-respect. They would not accept degrading treatment from white people, and told him stories that emphasized their own resistance to the common humiliations of segregation.[5]

Elie remembered the segregation of his childhood as a "series of petty meannesses that really did no one any good." At take-out places, blacks had to purchase food at special windows for "colored" patrons. They had to sit behind "race screens" on streetcars, which Elie later saw as "a calculated effort to deprive us of our dignity." Blacks needed a "special psychological make-up" to go downtown to Canal Street, he said, "because it was almost impossible to go on to Canal Street and not suffer some insult from some white person, either a policeman or some two-bit snippity white clerk." Blacks were not permitted to try on hats or clothing in downtown stores, none of which employed black sales personnel. While in high school, Elie regularly crossed Audubon Park on his way from his home to Gilbert Academy. "Each time I would walk across that park, or get a drink of water from a common fountain, there was inevitably some evil, racist white policeman who told us to keep on moving."[6]

Elie was a haphazard student for much of his schooling. He went to work early, selling papers, shining shoes, delivering groceries. When he neared high school age, his sister Doris paid the tuition that allowed him to attend Gilbert Academy. There, for the first time, Elie became interested in school, although he could not see any relationship between obtaining an education and receiving a good job. The best jobs in the black community were held by teachers and postal workers, and Elie's favorite teacher at Gilbert also worked part-time as a porter at a local country club.[7]

When he graduated from Gilbert, Elie took a job as a merchant seaman. While docked in New York City, he saw another world. A shipmate's relative took Elie on a sightseeing trip: "I saw Broadway, and I got myself a frankfurter and some orangeade, in a *highly integrated* situation, and I *knew* I was never gonna live in the South again," he recalled. Between 1947 and early 1951, Elie worked at a variety of jobs in New York: as a bootblack, a delivery man, and, finally, as an engraver. Though not a happy period, these were years of "real, real growth." He heard bebop greats play at clubs like Bop City and Birdland, and went to Harlem's famous Apollo Theater once or twice a week. In early 1951, he was drafted, and returned to New Orleans because he hoped to be sent north for his term of service. In March of that year, he began work as a "porter, bootblack, waiter, you name it," at the Audubon Park Golf Club. He earned $25 a week, plus tips, which gave him more cash than any of the young men in his neighborhood. He and his friends spent many evenings in the clubs, "cause there was a *lot* of music in New Orleans. I heard just about anybody anybody could name." He got inducted into the army in July 1951. "I said to my mother, 'They waited until I got a *good* job, and *then* they inducted me.'"[8]

"I got drafted, and here my life begins to change," he recalled. Elie's experiences in the army heightened his aspirations, and drew him into a world of reading and books. He served in an all-white unit in California. Among his friends were white college graduates who discussed politics and philosophy. Intrigued by their conversations, Elie began to frequent the post library, and to "really read" for the first time. One white friend, a lawyer, encouraged Elie to become an attorney when his service was finished. Elie decided to do just that. These experiences changed him: "I started really thinking of myself as really being smart," he said. "I started changing my speech patterns."

When his term of service was over, Elie returned to New York to live with his brother and work; he wanted to avoid going back to New Orleans and getting involved with his old group of friends. He worked briefly in New York before a telegram notified him of his acceptance by Howard University. "I have never felt any better since I have been on this earth. No experience that I had up to this point made me feel any better. . . . So here I go down to Howard," he laughed, "with my 126th Street Harlem wardrobe, big old hat and everything." Howard was tremendously exciting. It was 1953, and "*Brown vs. Board*, all the lawyers, everything is going on at Howard!" He studied hard and made good grades. That year at Howard, he "turned a corner. I am a very different person. I'm feeling smart and I'm feeling like I'm gonna be a lawyer." When he heard in 1953 or 1954 that Loyola University's law school had desegregated, he transferred to Dillard. Though the university was much less demanding than Howard, Elie found his mind opened by the philosophy courses he took. And he had changed from the person who had been afraid of the seductions of his neighborhood crowd: "I am now Mr. Black Ivy League. I've gotten a different walk, a different talk, a briefcase." He did well at Dillard, and was voted "Mr. Brains" during one of his years there. He took the minimum number of credits to qualify for law school admission, and entered law school at Loyola.

At Loyola, the gregarious Elie was popular, and became friends with Tommy Nelson, a white student whose older brother, Jack, worked as a lawyer in the district attorney's office. The two students often met at Jack Nelson's house for study sessions—an unusual practice in the New Orleans of the 1950s. Jack Nelson and Elie began a long, warm friendship; both would be allies and colleagues as civil rights lawyers.

In 1959, Elie finished law school with one other black student, Nils Douglas. No one recruited them in the last months of the spring term. Elie even considered filling out an application to work at the post office— he knew of three black lawyers who worked at New Orleans' office, and the federal post office in Washington had been "crawling with black lawyers" during World War II. But he did not send it in. He and Nils Douglas formed a law firm with Robert Collins, and became the principal attorneys in Louisiana for the Congress of Racial Equality (CORE) after 1960. "When I got my law degree, I would have been plenty satisfied to earn myself a living, and get myself a decent house, have two kids, and take a vacation every year," said Elie.[9]

In 1960, Robert Collins, Nils Douglas, and Lolis Elie opened a practice at Jackson and Dryades Streets, across from the Negro YMCA. Besides the civil rights cases, which brought little money to the three, the firm handled a mixed assortment of criminal and civil cases. This was a "ghetto practice," according to Collins. "We didn't have any clients of means. The irony of it is that most middle-class black people and the blacks who were in business, they gave all their business to whites—the very people who were discriminating against them." Collins found this very frustrating: "we had to scratch to make a living; we just eked out a very bare living in those days."[10] According to Elie, the firm's secretary made more than any of the attorneys.

Many white liberals came to oppose segregation through a long process of education, religious experiences, and individual relationships with blacks. John P. Nelson, Jr., was born in 1921 in Gulfport, Mississippi, the son of a bookkeeper, and the college-educated daughter of a wealthy Louisiana Cajun family. Nelson was strongly influenced by his mother, and by spending years on Valentine, her family's sugar cane plantation, during the Depression. He remembered a "kind of mutual respect for each others' customs" between the blacks and whites on the plantation, and a "strange affection" between the races. He also remembered that the young white boys like himself "got a lot of information from the older black men about life." From these men, Nelson learned why mosquitoes flourished at different times of the year, why crops grew or failed to grow. "It seemed to me that the black men, especially the older ones that worked around that plantation, had a lot deeper kind of communication with the young white boys than their fathers did," said Nelson. The black men taught Nelson and his friends how to fish, hunt, and farm, and how to interpret nature.

Nelson's life was changed by his service in World War II. He served in the infantry in the Pacific, received a Bronze Star and Silver Star for bravery, and was wounded badly. When he left the army after the war, he entered undergraduate school at Loyola, and entered law school in 1947. There, he came under the influence of Father Louis Twomey, a Jesuit who was active in race relations and labor education. "When I got out of the army, I really was hungry for education," said Nelson. Listening to Twomey in a class in jurisprudence, "I realized that that was where I should be. He sort of put into perspective questions that I had about that war, why we were in it, what were the consequences, and what were our responsibilities." Nelson had "some tough times" with the Japanese in the Pacific, and was trying to resolve his own feelings about them. Twomey's lectures put Nelson's own feelings about race into a different perspective:

His premise was simple. He said that man is created in God's image, and that therefore man has a sacredness about him. Because he has this sacredness, a quality he can do very little about, he is obligated to live a life in accordance with that sacred nature. And therefore he has a right to all economic, political, social, and cultural things that will enable him to live a life in accordance with this created dignity. And if he has a right to all of this, everyone else has a responsibility to see to it that he can exercise the right to live a life in accordance with that sacredness.[11]

It followed that any "sifting system," that separated a man from any of these rights, was contrary to Catholic and Judeo-Christian principles. "This was very revolutionary talk in 1947," said Nelson. After listening to Twomey, and thinking about the war, and about race, Nelson "began to understand" why World War II had been fought, and to resolve his own negative feelings toward the Japanese. For Nelson, the issues were religious:

If what Twomey says is true, then you start from a proposition of faith. And do I believe that there was a God and that God created man, or don't I? And if I did, then everything else, it seemed to me, would fall into place. And I was given the grace, I think, to believe. And once I came to grips with that, things were not too difficult.

Nelson began to attend integrated weekly meetings at Twomey's labor institute in 1948, and graduated from Loyola in 1950. He then worked for a firm that specialized in labor law, where he met intelligent, educated black labor leaders—people that middle-class whites rarely met, and did not know. His years until 1954 were quiescent, and from 1954 to 1958, Nelson worked in the district attorney's office. During this period, he became committed to racial equality and desegregation. In part, his commitment came from his perception of the segregationists. They were "so nasty and so uncouth in their defense of the system that I felt that I was *right*."

They were so bitter and vulgar about the position, that I felt, I do not want to be identified with these people—I don't care what their position is—because they *could* not be right. And my embracing a cause was not just because I felt intelligently that this was the best around, it was, "Man, this must be right, because these people are so"—

In these years, Nelson himself began to be red-baited for his opposition to segregation. After an Interracial Day held at Loyola in the mid-1950s, Nelson's name appeared in a newspaper article that identified him as a civil rights lawyer. In the district attorney's office, some lawyers stopped speaking to him. Nelson found it difficult to understand the whites' bitterness. On the basis of Twomey's lectures, and his own analysis of World War II and racism, he had become convinced that "segregation was wrong."

But after the article on Interracial Day appeared, he also realized that his dreams of 1950 were finished. He had wanted to become a prosperous attorney, a community leader, possibly a judge. But to be referred to as a "civil rights lawyer" was a

kiss of death. But I accepted it. It was about in that time, sometime between 1955 and 1957, that I said to myself, "I will accept this. I don't quite understand what it's gonna mean, but whatever it means, I will accept it."

He began to be invited to speak at black churches, and continued to attend Twomey's interracial group. And he established a reputation as a "hotshot prosecutor." In 1958, several Jesuits asked Nelson to run for the Orleans Parish School Board (OSPB), against Emile Wagner, a staunch segregationist who admitted that he would close public schools rather than see them desegregate. Nelson ran on a platform of keeping public schools open and obeying Skelly Wright's order to desegregate the public schools. In public meetings, however, the issues quickly devolved into "integration equals communism." Wagner always arranged to speak first:

He would always end his talks with communists. That this was a conspiracy man-ufactured in Russia, and then he would zero right in on me. . . . By the time I would start talking, these people were in a rage. . . . I really felt that a lot of people thought that this was a conspiracy to undermine the white race, and the communists were behind it.[12]

Nelson was hardly a leftist. Like most Cold War liberals, he opposed communism and totalitarianism. He had what he called a "scholastic phi-losopher's" attitude toward communism: "in those days, dialectical ma-terialism was anti-Christ, anti-God, anti-everything." He avoided leftists in the community like Ben Smith, an attorney who worked with the Na-tional Lawyers' Guild in the 1960s. He recalled that he thought the Guild's reputation would harm the civil rights movement: "We were trying to capture the minds and change the attitudes of people down here, and I thought that it had to be done, and it didn't include *them*. They had made their reputation representing people before McCarthy."[13]

Nelson lost the school board election in 1958, but felt that the issues of desegregation versus school closure had been aired. And many white mod-erates had been exposed to the vitriol of the other side, to the rhetoric of people like Citizens' Council leader and political boss Leander Perez and school board member Emile Wagner. Nelson became involved in Save Our Schools between 1959 and 1961, but would find his real entrance into civil rights with the *Lombard* case in 1960, a case begun when four students allied with the CORE decided to sit in at the lunch counter at McCrory's on Canal Street.

Like Nelson, Maurice "Moon" Landrieu was a product of Loyola University's law school. Born in New Orleans in 1930, he grew up in a racially mixed working-class uptown neighborhood. His father worked in a power plant, and his mother ran a corner grocery out of the front room of the family's shotgun house on Adams Street. Landrieu's parents taught their sons "fairness" and courtesy; Landrieu remembered feeling affection for the black women who came to do the wash and to cook: "but there was always that barrier," he said in 1988. "It's enough to confuse a child." His family maintained a complex relationship with blacks who were their neighbors, maids, and customers:

I can remember the women bringing their children in to be weighed on our scale. . . . You had small neighborhood grocery stores. The door was there, and we had a counter here, and the goods lined up, and a little icebox, and people came in and got milk and bread and cookies, and a bag of rice, bag of beans, and some kerosene that you pumped outta this machine. So people'd come in and buy things on credit, and you just put it on the nail, you know—"pay me when you get paid." This was Depression years. But the black parents in the neighborhood brought their babies in, not telling you they brought 'em in ten at a time, or every day, but it was a common occurrence so they could see whether the baby was gaining weight, and put 'em on the scale, on the grocery store scale. . . . I remember my mother huggin' those babies, as any woman would, kissing the babies. Big difference between that, though, and treating that person as a social equal.

Landrieu spent much of his childhood playing baseball, "puttin on my short pants and heading out to the park." Pushed and prodded by his mother, Landrieu went to Loyola University on a baseball scholarship. He spent most of his undergraduate years pitching for the team, studying, and courting Verna—the woman he would one day marry. She was a political activist who attended student government and city council meetings. Landrieu himself became active in student politics while in Loyola's law school, where he met two of Loyola's first black law students, Ben Johnson and Norman Francis. The two became members of the St. Thomas More Law Club, and also became Landrieu's close friends. These relationships influenced Landrieu's evolving attitudes toward race: coming out of a Catholic school, he "could never equate segregation with Christianity. It didn't follow. It was all contradictory."

Experiences as student body president of the law school also influenced

Landrieu's attitudes on race. In the early 1950s, he traveled to regional and national meetings of the National Conference of Catholic College Students. His colleagues from the Southern schools included several black students from Xavier University. This was "the first time that I was having contact with a black, on an equal level, but I didn't even realize that we couldn't stop to eat where we wanted to eat, or go to the bathroom. And all of that made a great impression on me; it angered me." He remembered that his black colleagues "instructed" him on their experiences, and on the problems they faced in the north and the south.[14]

Landrieu's relationships with Ben Johnson and Norman Francis, and his experiences as student body president, effectively changed his attitudes toward racial segregation. When the *Brown* decision was announced in 1954, he met one of his black friends on the campus, and said, "Thank God, it's over! You know, thank God, it's over!" He remembered being "terribly relieved that the decision was rendered"; he believed that the South had begun a new era in race relations.

In 1957, after two years' army service, Landrieu opened a practice in a relatively poor neighborhood on Broad and Washington Streets in New Orleans. Roughly half of his clients were black. He had begun to formulate "some very strong views" about race, and was appalled by the segregationist crusade of Massive Resistance. Landrieu was also making plans to run for the state legislature in 1959, when he would enter the Democratic primary in order to run in the election in 1960. As a "national Democrat" in orientation, Landrieu would run on a Democratic ticket with deLesseps "Chep" Morrison, New Orleans' moderate mayor. This election was to be a bitter, brutal, and dirty one—especially on the issues of race and schools.

During the 1960 school crisis, Moon Landrieu became acquainted with many of the women and men in Save Our Schools, a group organized in 1959 by uptown liberals. Ann Dlugos was an early recruit. She was an uptown Baptist matron from an old and respected family that combined "strong interests" in religion and politics, and equally strong traditions of dissent. Dlugos was born in 1927. Throughout her childhood, she heard family stories that emphasized the populist and progressive politics of her grandfathers, and family traditions of community service. Dlugos remembered growing up in an atmosphere of "complete freedom, acceptance, and tolerance." Her parents loved Franklin Roosevelt, and Dlugos' activist mother—"the steel hand in the velvet glove"—served as president of the local YWCA in the 1940s. Through her work on the YWCA board, Ann's mother met Rosa Keller.[15]

Dlugos did not remember any discussions of segregation until she attended college at Sophie Newcomb, the women's division of Tulane University. There, in the early 1940s, she took sociology courses from an East European refugee. These courses, and the sermons at her Baptist church, convinced her that segregation was "morally wrong. The social gospel was preached in that church," Dlugos said in 1988. "We had wonderful Sunday School teachers" who stressed "human dignity, the brotherhood of man, and the fatherhood of God."

Dlugos was most strongly influenced by one of her teachers at Newcomb, Mary Allen, who taught European history and labor history from a socialist perspective. Allen taught "social change, human betterment, and revolutionary movements—all the things that I think a Christian should be involved in," said Dlugos. Allen was involved in interracial groups in the New Orleans of the 1940s; Dlugos felt that she embodied the Christian beliefs that she had been taught since childhood. Dlugos' parents agreed: "my mother *loved* Mary Allen."

Dlugos finished college in 1944, and worked in New York for several years before returning to New Orleans after her marriage. In the 1950s, she worked part-time, and became very active in the League of Women Voters, which became the "great love" of her life. During the McCarthy era, Dlugos worked on a League program to counteract the attacks on the right to dissent. In meetings throughout the city, the League held discussions and workshops on civil liberties and dissent. Dlugos felt "awful" about the "smearing of innocent people," and the attempts of segregationists and conservatives to "smother dissent."

By 1959, the issue of school integration was becoming the central political issue in the Democratic primaries for the governor's race. The legislature had repeatedly passed school segregation statutes, and the NAACP was exasperated by the lengthy appeals that followed Federal District Judge J. Skelly Wright's order to desegregate the city's schools in 1956. In 1959, NAACP attorneys asked Wright to order the school board to prepare a formal plan to desegregate the city's schools.[16] Although liberals like Dlugos hoped that school desegregation might proceed quietly in the city, leaders like Rosa Keller and Gladys Cahn feared otherwise. In 1959, Cahn asked Dlugos to call together a group of people to form an organization dedicated to keeping the city's public schools open and desegregated. This organization, Save Our Schools, worked between 1959 and 1961 to change white public opinion on school integration, and to keep the public schools open. Dlugos saw her participation in SOS as an extension of her own liberalism, and of her LWV efforts. As secretary of SOS, Dlugos felt "alive" in this struggle: "You're not just letting *them* do it *to* you," she said.[17]

School desegregation was an explosive issue in the South of the 1950s. In 1957, Little Rock, Arkansas, experienced near-riots as black students attempted to enter Central High School over the opposition of Governor Orvall Faubus and mobs of whites. President Dwight D. Eisenhower broke the impasse by federalizing the National Guard and sending troops to Little Rock. In the polarized political climate of the Southern states, racial moderates increasingly came under attack by segregationist radicals. By the end of 1958, most Southern states had passed laws that mandated closing schools when threatened by racial integration. Louisiana was no exception.[18]

Some states carried out these mandates. On September 18, 1958, Faubus closed Little Rock's Central High School. In Virginia, the governor closed a rural high school rather than allow court-ordered desegregation, and subsequently closed the schools of Charlottesville and Norfolk.[19]

School closure alarmed middle-class whites and moderate businessmen. At the very least, it threatened to reverse the economic gains and "progress" that Southern cities enjoyed since World War II. In communities like Little Rock and Norfolk, groups of white moderates and professionals formed organizations to support public schools and to reject the proponents of Massive Resistance. The business community of each city, though slow to act, was eventually persuaded by the economic losses that followed school closure. Industries refused to move to areas without viable public schools. In these communities, as in New Orleans in 1961, segregationist pressures produced social turmoil and economic losses, and forced the formation of a coalition of moderate white and black voters that favored open and integrated public schools, and obedience to federal laws.[20]

Public school integration became an explosive issue in New Orleans because it forced into conflict both racial and class interests. The city was roughly 40 percent Catholic in 1950, and in 1962, some 39,000, or 47 percent of the city's white students attended Catholic schools. The city had well-established private, Catholic, and public schools; all three systems were segregated. Although the quality of public schools varied throughout the city, depending upon the affluence of the neighborhood involved, black public schools were acknowledged to be inferior to white public schools. Black children often attended schools on half-day "platoon" shifts in buildings that were dilapidated and in need of basic supplies. Black PTAs had protested these conditions throughout the 1950s, and the NAACP leadership hoped that school integration would equalize opportunities for the city's black children. But the public schools were the most vulnerable educational institutions in the city. Affluent whites preferred to send their children to elite private or Catholic schools, and ambitious black parents tried to educate their children in either private institutions like Gilbert Academy, or in the black Catholic system. It was not surprising that working-class segregationists interpreted school integration as class exploitation and victimization in the late 1950s and early 1960s. Many went to drastic measures to avoid the loss of status that racial integration signified. In the fall of 1960, their collective actions included demonstrations, picketing, acts of terrorism, and boycotting of integrated schools.[21]

In 1956, Judge J. Skelly Wright rendered a decision on the *Bush* case. He ordered the OPSB to cease requiring segregation in the city's public schools, but also granted the board a period "as may be necessary" for planning. He ordered the board to arrange desegregation of the public schools "with all deliberate speed."[22] A lengthy series of appeals followed, while the school board and the state legislature sought to stall school integration. Between 1956 and 1962, Wright threw out more than 100 segregation statutes passed almost unanimously by the state legislature.[23] On July 15, 1959, Wright ordered the OPSB to produce a desegregation schedule by March 1, 1960.[24]

Wright's decree appeared at a time of increasing political polarization. In Alabama, the racially moderate governor Jim Folsom signed successive interposition statutes drafted to nullify *Brown*. As governor of Louisiana, the populist Earl Long signed segregationist legislation that infuriated his black constituents. Throughout the South, racial moderates and liberals were smeared by race-baiting demagogues like Rainach and Perez.[25]

DeLesseps S. Morrison had run unsuccessfully for governor in 1956, despite the warnings of his wealthy political backers. He again ran for governor in 1959 and 1960, without the support of many of his prominent New Orleans supporters. In the first Democratic primary, Morrison's closest political rival was Jimmie Davis, a former governor and popular country-western singer. Davis campaigned on a theme of "Peace and Harmony," but the tone of this race, and the subsequent runoff, was set by Willie Rainach, who ran for governor as a states-rights segregationist. Rainach finished third in the fall primary. Morrison and Davis squared off for the final race. Each man knew that he had to win Rainach's segregationist constituency.[26]

The runoff campaign was a disaster for Morrison. Municipal stagnation had cost him support among his influential patrons in New Orleans. Convinced that the mayor could not win—and that they could control Davis—some of Morrison's strongest backers cynically invested in Jimmie Davis' campaign.[27] Morrison's attempts to appeal to the segregationist whites failed. His Catholicism and record of racial moderation hurt him in rural Protestant parishes, and his opponents smeared the mayor with charges of urbanity, liberalism, and Negro support. Davis won the governorship.[28]

Moon Landrieu ran on Morrison's ticket in both 1959 and 1960. The ugliness of the election forced him to think more deeply and broadly about the issue of race. "I had a lot of doors slammed in my face, and a lot of people called me 'nigger lover,' and [said] 'I wouldn't vote for you if you associate with Chep Morrison if you were the last man on earth,' " said Landrieu. A self-described "team player," who valued loyalty, Landrieu was offended by the racist attacks on Morrison. The opposition passed out photographs that showed the mayor jumping into a swimming pool with blacks. Landrieu continued to hand out Morrison's literature when he campaigned. He told more than one segregationist, "Spare me the indignity of having you vote for me. If I have to get elected on your vote, I don't want it." Landrieu won his election, having developed a "rather serious dislike" for Willie Rainach and Jimmie Davis. "My guy had lost," he said. "And I was kinda damn mad about it, and we'd lost on a purely racial basis."[29]

Landrieu early established himself as an opponent of Massive Resistance in the legislature. On his first day in the legislature, he opposed the reconstitution of the State Sovereignty Commission. When Landrieu returned to his hotel at the end of the day, segregationist leaders Willie Rainach and Leander Perez confronted him at the side door. Rainach "put his finger in my face and said, 'We know your kind and we're gonna get you.' " He then repeated the threat. Landrieu

looked at him and said, "take your best shot." You know, the kind of bravado that a 29-year-old kid would tell this to Leander Perez and Willie Rainach, these two giants. . . . So I guess from that point forward, I was kinda marked.

Landrieu had attended some early meetings of SOS and knew that the school issue was becoming critical for New Orleans. In legislative sessions held in the late summer and fall of 1960, the legislature passed a raft of new segregation statutes, all of which were thrown out by the federal judiciary. Landrieu remembered reading the stack of bills on his desk on the first Sunday night of the session. The next morning, he and legislator Sammy Anzelmo stopped by a Catholic church on the way to the legislature. He meditated, thinking about the "terrible decisions" that he would make on the segregation onslaught, and the fact that Davis—who was pushing the package—would surely win. Coming out of the church, he told Anzelmo, "Sam, they can't eat me. You know, the hell with 'em. I aint gonna do it." Having made the decision, Landrieu felt tremendously relieved. Political advisers warned him,

"If you don't go along with this stuff, you'll never get elected." I figured, "What the hell? I'll go back and practice law. If I ain't gonna be president, I'm not gonna be president. So what?" I'm not sure I would have taken that attitude at the age I am now, but I'm only 29 years old, think I'm the hottest thing going. I wish I could say that resolve carried me without fear throughout, but it didn't. Typically, you begin to worry about yourself, and the bills got tougher.[30]

The fall's bills and initiatives seemed relentless. "They kept putting these bills up. As fast as they threw them up, the court knocked them down, and it got to be a game. They were broadcasting this stuff live on the radio," said Landrieu. In various special sessions, the legislature voted to interpose the state of Louisiana between the federal courts and New Orleans' schools, voted to close schools that desegregated, cut funding from schools that operated "contrary to the laws of the state," and abolished compulsory attendance laws.[31] Segregationists defended the offensive in speeches and in newspapers. Some of Landrieu's constituents wrote letters, or phoned, asking, "How can you turn your back on the white race?" Almost alone, he voted against almost every segregation statute in that session.[32]

In April of 1960, deLesseps S. Morrison was a lame-duck mayor. The city's reform charter did not permit him three consecutive terms. His one hope of retaining a local power base rested on changing the charter to allow him a third term. After the race-baiting gubernatorial campaign,

Morrison was convinced that his best strategy on school desegregation was avoidance. He adopted a position of neutrality, and refused to take sides in the growing controversy.

In the fall of 1959, Rosa Keller and Gladys Cahn began to organize a group of uptown residents to support open and desegregated public schools. The women were alarmed by the events in Virginia and Arkansas, and hoped to rally white parents to support school integration. They decided that an all-white group could best mobilize support within the white community; black leaders Albert Dent and the Reverend A. L. Davis agreed. The group was sub-rosa until the spring of 1960, due to the leadership's fear of the segregationist attacks that had damaged the Urban League. SOS was led by Keller, Cahn, Helen Mervis, John Nelson, Mary Sand, and Ann Dlugos. Peggy Murison and Betty Wisdom also took important roles in the organization.

Though affluent, many of the SOS leaders were products of public schools, and educated their children in public schools in their uptown neighborhoods. Keller, Mervis, and Murison had children in public schools during the crisis, as did several other women. All believed that public schools were critical to a functioning democracy. "We thought that if we could show we had enough white people who wanted their schools to stay open, come hell or high water, then we could get [integration] done," said Keller. "But it didn't work. The political people behaved *outrageously*."[33]

Anxious to avoid the "communist" tag attached to integrationists, the SOS leadership stressed the economic and social importance of free public education. They publicized the negative consequences of strategies designed to circumvent federal court rulings. By 1960, states and districts had experimented with school closures, tuition grant subsidies to private institutions, and state funding of private, segregated schools. SOS directed its programs and publications to the white community. In particular, SOS hoped to reach the white parents who had responded to a school board poll in the spring of 1960 with an overwhelming vote to close public schools rather than allow "token integration."[34]

SOS leaders tried to recruit members and officers without obvious ties to the "cause" of racial integration—even though Keller, Mervis, Nelson, and Cahn were by this time "known integrationists." Ann Dlugos, as the group's secretary, tried to recruit eminent citizens and clergy for the group's board. She did not approach liberals or integrationists like Albert

D'Orlando or James Dombrowski who had been smeared as communists because

I just didn't think we needed it. Communists—that was what we didn't want to be called. We didn't care if they called us nigger-lovers. And we didn't care if they called us integrationists. But we really weren't out of the McCarthy era.[35]

While the school controversy simmered between the legislature and courts, the black community began to mobilize. In early 1960, the Reverend Avery Alexander, Dr. Raymond Floyd, and Dr. Henry Mitchell organized a boycott of Dryades Street merchants under the auspices of the Consumers' League, an all-black organization that fought job discrimination. The Consumers' League Boycott occurred simultaneously with the growing sit-in movement in Southern cities. The League's older leaders welcomed the participation of students from the black colleges in New Orleans, and the boycott and picketing became the seedbed for New Orleans' CORE chapter. The protests initiated by the Consumers' League spurred other protests by the black community, and led to the formation of the Citizens' Committee, a federation of black organizations that used a variety of tactics to pressure the city's white elite to desegregate downtown stores, businesses, and employment between 1961 and 1964. The League's successful show of unity also inspired the formation of the Coordinating Council of Greater New Orleans (CCGNO) a federation of black organizations that organized dramatic voter registration drives in the city between 1961 and 1965, and drew federal attention to voting-rights violations in the city.

In 1959, Dr. Henry Mitchell had a practice on Dryades Street, a large black shopping district. "I used to walk down Dryades every Friday and Saturday, and I would see just thousands of people shopping, just on Dryades Street. At that time, Dryades Street was the second largest shopping center in the city, next to Canal Street." Mitchell contended that the shoppers on Dryades Street were 95 percent black, but that he never saw any blacks working in the stores as clerks and managers. He called the director of the Urban League about the situation, and was told that the League had been trying to get jobs for blacks above a menial level, but had serious problems with the Dryades Street merchants. The men decided that they needed an organization to press the matter, so they met with the Reverend A. L. Davis, Dr. Raymond Floyd, and the Reverend Avery Alexander, and formed the Consumers' League. Attorneys Lolis Elie and Ernest

"Dutch" Morial provided free legal counsel for the group. After fruitless negotiations with the Dryades Street merchants, the group threatened to demonstrate. The merchants' answer, Mitchell recalled, was, "Go on ahead. Demonstrate, and march all you please. You're not gonna keep the black folks off Dryades Street." The Consumers' League challenged the merchants, and "we organized the first march that I can remember in the city of New Orleans for civil rights." Mitchell remembered that

We marched in Dryades Street. And it was a very, very emotional type thing. We had many, many people who joined us, people who immediately got the nerve to come out, pick up a picket sign, and march with us. And we gave [the merchants] a deadline. We told them that unless they started hiring blacks above the menial level, that we were going to boycott Dryades Street, and that we were gonna keep people out of the stores. And about two-three weeks before Easter, we set our plans, we hit them. And the Friday before Easter, Dryades Street was *dead*.[36]

By the end of April, a number of merchants had hired blacks in sales positions, and by mid-May, the Consumers' League could claim responsibility for thirty new jobs for blacks on Dryades Street.[37] The group next "attacked the Claiborne [Avenue] area, and that's when they started throwin' us in jail."[38]

Students Rudy Lombard, Jerome Smith, and Oretha Castle met on picket lines during the Consumers' League's boycott. Smith had known Castle in high school. Several white students also joined the pickets.[39] By summer, the group had organized themselves into the New Orleans chapter of CORE. They planned to conduct a direct-action campaign against racial segregation and discrimination in the city, starting with sit-ins at local dime stores. Rudy Lombard approached Collins, Douglas, and Elie to represent them in their efforts. At first, the three said no. Recently out of law school, they were concerned with earning a living. After the local president of the American Civil Liberties Union (ACLU) refused to represent the students, Elie and his partners agreed. They realized that their work would be controversial and risky. Whereas NAACP litigation was conducted primarily in federal courts, the public accommodations cases, and the picketing and protest defenses that CD&E would undertake "spoke directly to the state system," said Elie, a system with segregated courtrooms, all-white juries, and judges who often affirmed the racial beliefs of their segregationist constituents.

The Consumers' League protest, Elie remembered, was "in many ways a spiritual movement." Centered in the black community, led by ministers and doctors, the Dryades Street actions focused tangibly on dignity and solidarity. The sit-ins downtown were different. "To talk about hiring some black clerks in stores in a black neighborhood was one thing, but to start talking about social change, social life, going to the same restaurants, was considered to be *really* radical."[40] But after the first case, Elie's own fears "vanished." CORE members Julia Humbles, Castle, and Lombard encouraged blacks to hire Collins, Douglas, and Elie for their legal work. "We got a kind of protection from these young people," said Elie. "I got courage from them."[41]

The CORE chapter in 1960 was racially mixed; blacks from the Southern University of New Orleans (SUNO), and a few from Dillard and Xavier worked with whites from Tulane University and LSU-New Orleans. On September 9, seven CORE members held a sit-in at F. W. Woolworth's on Canal Street. They were charged with "criminal mischief," held briefly in jail, and released after black congregations and the ACLU raised bail. The next day, The NAACP Youth Council picketed Woolworth's to express sympathy with CORE.[42]

On Monday, September 12, Mayor Chep Morrison banned all picketing and sit-ins, stating that "the community interests, public safety, and the economic welfare of this city require that such demonstrations cease and henceforth . . . be prohibited by the police department." CORE representatives tried to negotiate a settlement with Morrison, hoping to arrange a meeting with variety store managers to open all of the city's lunch counters to blacks. A meeting with the mayor "accomplished nothing," according to field secretary Jim McCain. The CORE chapter voted to picket dime stores and conduct a boycott of discriminatory businesses. They also decided to test the legality of the mayor's order with another sit-in.[43]

On Friday, McCain and five members of the Consumers' League picketed a shopping center, and were arrested. The CORE field secretary and two other men were held in jail until Sunday evening.[44] Then on Saturday, September 17, 1960, CORE chairman Rudy Lombard, Tulane student Sydney "Lanny" Goldfinch, Oretha Castle, and Dillard student Cecil Carter sat down at the lunch counter at McCrory's and refused to leave until served. They were arrested, charged with "criminal mischief," and eventually released on $250 bail. But the district attorney also charged Goldfinch with "criminal anarchy," which carried a bond of $2,500, and a maximum prison sentence of ten years.[45]

Because Collins, Douglas, and Elie were inexperienced in criminal cases, and because they felt that Goldfinch, especially, needed a white lawyer, they asked John P. Nelson for assistance with the sit-in arrests of September 17. "I was called by Elie after the sit-in at McCrory's," said Nelson. " I was asked to come to municipal court to assist in a case. I agreed. I had no idea what kind of case it was." Nelson drove to the night court, found the four young people, and identified himself as their lawyer. "Once I'd done that, I was hooked. I knew this was something I wanted to do." Nelson had never considered himself a social reformer, but *Lombard vs. Louisiana* made him a civil rights lawyer. Although he later came to feel that *Lombard* was not the case that ruined him politically, he knew in the fall of 1960 that "I was committing political suicide, but it was not an act of despair."[46]

Collins, Douglas, Elie and Nelson hoped to prove that Morrison's ban on picketing and protest constituted state action, and was enacted "to implement and further the state's policy and custom of forced segregation for the races in public places."[47] Nelson argued the *Lombard* case before the U.S. Supreme Court in 1963, as one of the seven "sit-in" cases. In that decision, the Supreme Court affirmed the CORE lawyers' contention—that, in light of Morrison's ban on demonstrations, the actions of Mc-Crory's manager and the police constituted state action.[48]

In 1960, however, Morrison's ban on protests was strangely enforced. In December, CORE members were arrested for "leafleting without a license," while segregationist mobs harassed white and black schoolchildren without restraint. McCain, Alexander, and Mitchell had been jailed on September 17 under a new state statute that prohibited "blocking public sidewalks by picketing," but which excluded labor union demonstrations. On September 22, 1960, James Pfister, chairman of a new Legislative Committee on Un-American Activities (known as LUAC), charged that CORE was a "subversive" organization—a statement that CORE's national representatives protested.[49]

Within this racially tense atmosphere, the public schools were being desegregated. Judge Wright had ordered that school integration begin on November 14. On that day, four black first-grade girls entered two schools in a white working-class neighborhood in the Lower Ninth Ward. Immediately, white mothers rushed to the schools to withdraw their children from William Frantz School and McDonogh 19. Members of the Citizens' Councils and neighborhood whites harassed, threatened, and verbally abused the black children and the few white children who remained in the schools. On November 15, Citizens' Council leaders Willie Rainach and Leander Perez urged 5,000 supporters to boycott Frantz and McDonogh 19. Perez told the whites to "do something" before "burr-heads are forced into your schools." The next day, several thousand whites mobbed the school board's offices and city hall.[50]

Daily, through November and December, mobs of women met the children at Frantz and McDonogh 19 with screams, threats and racial epithets as they walked into the schools. They also made death threats to NAACP leaders, to the parents of all the children, and to the white activists in Save Our Schools, who drove the white children to the schools for the first four weeks of the crisis. The school crisis became the "Shame of New Orleans," covered by national news media and splashed in headlines across the country.[51]

As an NAACP leader, Leontine Luke had worked with the families of the black students during the months of October and November. She visited the families' homes, she said, "to encourage the people, and to assure them that they would not be harmed in going to school. However, that was only my great belief—because I did not know whether or not they would be." She brought food and clothing to several of the families, because "some of the children weren't from the best provided-for homes." The father of one girl, Ruby Bridges, was fired from his job when his daughter began to attend the formerly all-white Frantz school. Luke explained that

there were other people who, because they left their children in school where Ruby was, lost their jobs. I'm speaking of people of the white race, who left their children in school. They lost their jobs. People let them go. You know, I figured it was *mean* because they had no control over it. The law had passed. The courts had passed the law. And firing these men who had jobs so that their families would be in need, I don't think, you know, was the proper thing.[52]

Luke was appalled by the crowds. Whites threw rocks and eggs at the children and their escorts daily. The NAACP took care of the black children in the two Ninth Ward schools, but Morrison refused to involve the police in the fate of the white families who left their children in New Orleans' first integrated schools, and would not order the police to control the crowds at the schools. Throughout November and December, mob harassment of the children and their families continued.

The Citizens' Councils enforced a boycott of the two integrated schools. Local whites were either so hostile or intimidated that no white children were attending McDonogh 19 by the end of the first week of classes. Leona Tate, Tessie Prevost, and Gail Etienne were the school's only students. At Frantz, three families sent their children to school with Ruby Bridges. The Councils encouraged white parents to transfer their children to public schools in the adjacent St. Bernard Parish. Leander Perez and his associates backed the construction of a private "Frantz-McDonogh co-operative" to handle the overflow.[53]

The SOS leadership believed that the segregationists hoped that a total white boycott would close both Frantz and McDonogh 19. Whites could thus defy the federal courts by non-compliance. SOS assisted the families of the whites who remained in the schools, and tried to encourage other white families to return their children to Frantz and McDonogh. They were only minimally successful in both efforts. At the end of the school year, only forty-nine white children who had been enrolled in the two schools remained in the city's public schools; 684 attended schools in St. Bernard Parish, and 286 received no education at all.[54]

Leontine Luke knew some of the families who kept their children home rather than send them to an integrated school. " I told them, 'that's the worst thing in the world you can do—is keep your child home,' " she said. "But they kept their children home and they grew up, I say, almost infidels because there were no school habits, or church habits. It was just terrible— just the hatred that was in their mother and father. Race hatred."[55]

For the first few weeks of the crisis, SOS volunteers drove the white children to school, and escorted them inside the buildings. Liberals like Betty Wisdom, Ann Dlugos, and Peggy Murison were horrified by the violence of the crowds. Murison, a doctor's wife, drove a white child to school for several days. One day, a crowd stoned her car:

They came at us with great big *rocks* and *eggs* and threw themselves at the car. . . . One time they broke a side window, and in my stupid way, I thought, "*Wow!* That'll startle them so they'll *stop instantly!* They'll be shocked!" The hell it did! They were not people I was accustomed to dealing with. . . . And the things they said— I never heard some of those things. And I'd heard all sorts of things.

I was scared to death, naturally. And that poor little girl sitting next to me, she said, "I'll never volunteer for anything again."[56]

Liberals involved in the crisis were threatened and harassed. Betty Wisdom, who walked a white child into a school during the first weeks of the crisis, became the object of venomous invective and threatening phone calls. SOS president Mary Sand received anonymous phone calls in which her daughter's life was threatened. Judge Skelly Wright was hung in effigy, had crosses burned on his lawn, and had to be guarded constantly. His son was taunted by his schoolmates, and the little boy's life was threatened by hostile whites. John Nelson was smeared as a communist.[57]

These experiences affirmed white liberals' belief in the legitimacy of the black effort to desegregate the schools. The white crowds' violence horrified them. Betty Wisdom's experiences heightened her hostility toward segregationists, and made her welcome friendships with A. P. Tureaud and with Dutch and Sybil Morial.[58] John Nelson found his attitudes "hardened" by the school crisis.[59] Moon Landrieu emerged from the 1960–1961 sessions more adamantly opposed to the segregationists and their leaders. Throughout his difficult months in the legislature, his only supporters had been black voters, and the liberals in SOS, the National Council of Jewish Women, and some of the Catholic integrationists from Loyola.[60]

The school crisis was a product of numerous acts of malevolence and foolishness. The legislature's antics convinced working-class segregationists that the federal courts had no legitimate authority in school integration. Through its policy of Massive Resistance, the legislature and local segregationist leaders sanctioned white terrorism. The school board was also guilty of poor judgment. Hoping to appease the middle-class whites of the city, they sought to minimize desegregation, and stay within the boundaries of the law as it was defined by the legislature. When compliance was finally forced upon the board, its moderates chose to implement integration in accordance with Louisiana's Pupil Placement Act, a law designed to prevent integration. The Act mandated extensive testing and screening of applicants for transfer into white schools. The board chose to transfer only those black students whose test scores were equal to or higher than those of the white students with whom they would attend classes. The board also selected schools without regard to "political" considerations—which meant that uptown schools in more prosperous and more racially mixed areas were not chosen, and that the advice and cooperation of groups like SOS and the NAACP were neither sought nor accepted.[61]

The passivity of the city's political and elites compounded the school board's blunders. In the face of aggressive behavior by segregationists in the legislature and local Citizens' Councils, the mayor refused to become involved in the crisis, and refused to provide police protection for the children attending the two embattled schools, for their parents and teachers, and for the liberals in SOS. Additionally, the city's economic elite remained silent until it was clear that downtown businesses had suffered economic losses due to the crisis. In the winter of 1960–1961, several major retailers reported a 40–50 percent drop in sales. Hotel and restaurant trade had fallen off 20 percent.[62]

On January 30, 1961, elite support for the embattled board finally materialized. A group of business leaders organized a testimonial dinner for the Orleans Parish School Board. A crowd of 1,200 packed the Roosevelt Hotel's dining rooms for the event, and heard corporate lawyer Harry B. Kelleher praise the "gallant efforts" of the school board. Kelleher told the crowd that the basic issues of the crisis were public education and the rule of law. On both counts, he said, "this country and the South cannot go backward." With this speech, Kelleher became publicly identified as a Southern moderate—a pragmatic community leader who considered racial change preferable to the social and economic costs of Massive Resistance.[63]

The testimonial dinner was a turning point in the public resolution of the school crisis. The crisis was a watershed in New Orleans' politics: it effectively ended deLesseps S. Morrison's political career in the city. His unwillingness to take sides in the school crisis eroded his support among blacks and white liberals, and his attempt to change the city's charter and to allow himself to run for a third term failed. In June 1961, President John F. Kennedy appointed Morrison ambassador to the Organization of American States. Councilman Victor Hugo Schiro was appointed as interim mayor.[64]

The school crisis also marked a new departure for the business elite. Sensitive to the economic disruption caused by the crisis, they effectively pressured Schiro to post police guards at Frantz and McDonogh 19 to prevent further white terrorism during the year-long Citizens' Council boycott of the schools. Additionally, several members of the Chamber of Commerce, the heads of banking houses, and other local economic leaders formed a coalition, according to Kelleher. In late 1961, the group asked Kelleher to "take a hand" in negotiating a settlement to the protests at Canal Street's dime stores and lunch counters.[65]

According to Kelleher, the merchants' actions were triggered by the difficulties of Birmingham, Alabama. They were doubtless nervous about the continuing demonstrations and picketings conducted by CORE and the Consumers' League.[66] In order to avoid the kinds of disruption that Birmingham experienced, some fifteen business leaders and "twelve to fifteen black leaders" formed an "informal conference" to negotiate the desegregation of the downtown. Kelleher and attorney Harry McCall were spokesmen and negotiators for the white group. Lolis Elie and Revius Ortique represented the black federation, known as the Citizens' Committee. In negotiations that lasted for more than two years, these black and white leaders hammered out the largely peaceful desegregation of the city.[67]

The legislature and the federal courts sparred for another weary year and a half. Federal judges continued to declare unconstitutional the segregation statutes passed between 1960 and 1961. During 1961–1962, the city's public schools were only minimally integrated; black parents claimed that the board's testing procedures prevented all but the most exceptional black children from attending integrated schools. In April 1962, Skelly Wright ordered the first six grades of all public schools to be integrated in the fall of that year, sending shock waves through white New Orleans.[68]

Wright had recently been appointed to fill a vacancy on the Court of Appeals for the District of Columbia as a reward for his "unflinching support of *Brown*" in the *Bush* suit. Segregationists felt that Wright's order was vindictive, and placed great hopes on his successor, Frank B. Ellis. Ellis granted some relief, ordering only the first grades to desegregate in the fall of 1962. Ellis had in mind grade-a-year desegregation.[69] The *Bush* plaintiffs returned to court to reinstate Wright's decision. In August 1962, a three-judge panel ruled the state's pupil placement law unconstitutional, and allowed second and third graders to transfer schools in the fall of 1962. Only sixty-six black children had been transferred to all-white schools in the previous year.[70]

In 1962, negotiations desegregated New Orleans' parochial schools, which served almost half of the city's white students. Desegregation proceeded peacefully, without the boycotts threatened by segregationist Catholics.[71]

By 1961, the *Bush* suit had required nine years of litigation, five Circuit Court appeals, and seven proceedings before the Supreme Court, at a total cost of $96,000.[72] Between 1962 and 1965, the NAACP and black PTA repeatedly and angrily protested the pace and scale of school desegregation. The NAACP also fought a legislative device aimed at preventing school integration—state tuition grants that allowed parents to exercise "freedom of choice" in educating their children. By October 1962, such grants paid partial or total tuition costs for more than 5,000 children in Louisiana. In

New Orleans, tuition grants allowed 1,171 children to attend the Ninth Ward cooperative school organized by the Citizens' Councils, and subsidized attendance of others in private and Catholic schools. In 1967, these grants were declared unconstitutional, but they had already done considerable damage in undermining the city's public education system.

The desegregation crisis coincided with another development that thwarted real integration of the public schools. By the early 1960s, new suburban developments were built on recently drained marshlands surrounding the city. Throughout the 1960s, middle-class whites and some middle-class blacks moved into these suburbs. In 1960, blacks represented 37.4 percent of the city's population of 627,525. By 1970, blacks constituted 45 percent of the city's population of 593,467. In 1980, blacks represented 55.27 percent of a population of 557,515. New Orleans had become a city with a black majority in population, and an overwhelmingly black majority in its public schools. By 1971, the school system was 71 percent black. By the mid-1970s, New Orleans was becoming a far more segregated city than it had been in the 1950s.[73]

The cumulative impact of the school crisis and the upsurge in black protest was to unify the black community. Enraged by the legislative assaults, and by official complacence in the face of white mobs, black organizations throughout the city backed two related efforts between 1961 and 1965: the removal of segregation from all public accommodations and increased employment of blacks in New Orleans' businesses, and electoral power through an expanded black vote. In both of these efforts, the black community used an array of tactics, ranging from protests to lawsuits to negotiation. In the end, it was the threat of disruption brought by protest, the economic losses on Canal Street, and the assurance of federal intervention, that enabled the black community to win a largely bloodless battle for equal rights. In the process, the political leadership of the city was dramatically changed.

Four

"Would New Orleans Burn?" The Political Generation, 1961–1964

*B*ETWEEN 1962 and 1966, New Orleans became a desegregated city. Lunch counters in downtown stores opened to blacks, segregation signs were removed from public buildings, Tulane University integrated its classes, and employers began to hire black personnel in businesses throughout the city. For the black leadership, the process was sluggish, and, at times, frustrating, but it was largely peaceful. By the selective use of protests, litigation, and negotiations, the black community pressured the city's white elites, and through them, New Orleans' elected officials, to change racial policy.

The school crisis, and the behavior of the state legislature, united and galvanized New Orleans' historically divided black community. Under the auspices of the Citizens' Committee, the leadership of the Interdenominational Ministerial Alliance, the Urban League, the NAACP, the Consumers' League, and CORE applied a variety of tactics to gain basic civil rights. At the same time, black political organizations organized massive voter registration drives under the auspices of the Coordinating Council of Greater New Orleans (CCGNO). Through the CCGNO, the black leadership generated pressure and publicity about the parish registrar's practice of limiting the political influence of the black community by denying blacks access to the ballot box. In these two efforts—municipal desegregation and voting rights—three generations of civil rights leaders cooperated: first-generation leaders like Revius Ortique, Virginia Collins, the Reverends Avery Alexander and A. L. Davis worked with Lolis Elie, Ernest "Dutch" Morial, and Llewellyn Soniat. In turn, these two generations worked in an often volatile coalition with the leaders of the third generation—New Orleans' black students who had come to politics through protest activities with the NAACP Youth Council and CORE.

For most of the first- and second-generation black leaders, the negotiations of the 1960s were the natural, if surprising result of their long-term efforts to gain basic political and social rights. Many of the most active leaders of the Citizens' Committee were lawyers: Lolis Elie, Revius Ortique, and Dutch Morial had prominent roles in this effort. Their colleagues on the Committee were individuals who had long experience in racial negotiations—ministers like A. L. Davis and the Avery Alexander. They were advised and assisted by other community leaders: Albert Dent and C. C. DeJoie, editor of the *Louisiana Weekly*, were prominently involved. Dr. Leonard Burns represented the United Clubs and the Urban League. Oretha Castle, the only woman on the committee, represented CORE.

The campaign for voting rights involved several of the same actors. Dr. Daniel Thompson, a sociologist at Dillard University, led the Coordinating Council, which orchestrated the activities of neighborhood voting organizations, and more established voters' leagues. His assistant director and "activator" was Virginia Collins, and the Council's foot soldiers included hundreds of black college and high school students, recruited from wards throughout the city. Like CORE and the NAACP Youth Council, the Coordinating Council staged protests and demonstrations to dramatize its opposition to the tactics used to limit the black vote. Such protests eventually brought intervention in the form of federal registrars, who came to New Orleans after the passage of the Voting Rights Act of 1965.

An interesting array of whites worked with New Orleans' black political leaders during this period. Rosa Keller largely financed the suit that desegregated Tulane, and participated in voter registration projects in 1964. Helen Mervis formed the Community Relations Council (CRC) in 1962, and led the organization until 1967. In this effort, she brought together black political leaders and white liberals and political elites to attack specific problems within the city. During the 1960s, the Council held forums on police brutality, racism, and other human relations concerns. Often, the Council served as a bridge between black and white community leaderships, and served as a place for black leaders to find out "who was who" in the white community—which actors were most influential on specific boards and commissions, and how such men might be approached. In the CRC, black leaders Revius Ortique and Leonard Burns worked with Mervis and her white colleagues. The same black leaders also participated in Citizens' Committee negotiations with the white business leaders.[1]

White lawyers also participated, though at different levels. Harry B. Kelleher and Harry McCall became the chief negotiators for the white counterpart of the black Citizens' Committee. Both helped to create the Metropolitan Area Committee (MAC) in 1966, a bi-racial, private planning and educational organization that aimed to ease the process of desegregation. Its members included representatives from the city's black and white elites. In representing the city's white businessmen, Kelleher and McCall acted in the interests of an economic leadership that had agreed to acquiesce to the inevitability of racial integration, but that wanted to retain control over the pace and scale of desegregation itself. It was in the self-interest of such elites see that moderation prevailed in New Orleans: neither the white nor the black leadership wanted the tumult that "outside agitators" threatened—the kind of agitation that had led to disruptions in Birmingham, Alabama, in Albany, Georgia, and in Jackson, Mississippi.[2]

Other lawyers were also involved in civil rights work. John P. Nelson, Jr., argued the case that resulted in the desegregation of Tulane University, as discussed later in this chapter. He also continued to do legal work for CORE, and to take other civil rights cases throughout this period. As a state legislator, then city councilman, Moon Landrieu continued to build a political career based on a bi-racial constituency. And Ben Smith, Jack Peebles, and Bruce Waltzer took civil rights cases in Mississippi during the summers of 1963 and 1964, under the auspices of the National Lawyers' Guild. For these efforts, their offices were raided by state agents in 1963, and they, along with James Dombrowski of SCEF, were charged with subversion.[3]

The motives for such participation varied. For blacks, political power represented the key to larger social opportunities, to full citizenship. Men like Dutch Morial and Robert Collins saw political leadership, and political power, as the logical fruit of the movement itself.[4] White politicians like Landrieu and several of his peers saw the future of Southern politics in such a bi-racial electorate, and began their careers by backing the claims of blacks.[5] Wealthy whites like Kelleher and McCall, who represented both the economic and social elite of the city, saw black civil rights and political power as an inevitable change. As lawyers, they were aware that the federal courts and the federal government showed no signs of reversing the trend of policy decisions begun by *Brown*. Additionally, they knew that racial disruption had cost the city money during the school crisis, and that disorder in cities like Birmingham was producing even more expensive losses. They hoped that New Orleans could avoid both. Thus, the economic elites agreed to do what the city's and state's political elites would not. They agreed to negotiate changes in racial policy and practice.[6] Finally, white liberals like John P. Nelson, Jr., and radicals like Ben Smith were motivated by a mixture of political and moral convictions. As members of the miniscule segment of the white Southern bar that took civil rights cases, these men hoped to change the social and political system of the South through legal change itself.

Ernest "Dutch" Morial was born into a Catholic Creole family in 1929. His mother was devout Roman Catholic; she was ambitious, self-improving, and worked as a tailor. Morial's father was a cigar-maker who had been involved in organizing the cigar workers in the city. Morial's father was the "disciplinarian" in the family: "he taught us respect, punctuality, not to be late, you know, be a gentleman, that kind of thing, sit up straight, don't wear hats in the house."[7] The family spoke French at home, and Morial attended Catholic schools until high school. His "best times" as a child included running errands for the nuns—"going to the market for 'em on Fridays, taking their books back to the library, which was segregated." He was a religious little boy, attending mass almost every morning: "One time, I wanted to go into the priesthood."

Morial lived in one of New Orleans' many racially and ethnically mixed neighborhoods. He did not experience a brutal racism in this environment: many of his educational and social relationships included blacks and whites. Black and white children often played together, but separated before going home, or when whites headed for their own schools, parks, and playgrounds. Morial had both black and white teachers in the schools he attended: Irish nuns of the Holy Ghost order in grade school, black teachers at the public McDonogh 35, and a black and white faculty at Xavier University, which he attended on a scholarship between 1948 and 1951. After Xavier, he entered law school at Louisiana State University at Baton Rouge; he and Robert Collins were the only black law students in the school.

LSU's law school had been desegregated by a court order in 1950, a case argued by A. P. Tureaud, Louisiana's Inc. Fund counsel. Tureaud often visited LSU while Morial was there; the attorney was then working on a suit to desegregate the university's undergraduate division. Through an uncle, Morial had met Tureaud earlier in his life. While at LSU, the Inc. Fund attorney befriended Morial, and became a major influence in his career. As the only black attorney regularly practicing in Louisiana from 1938 to 1947, Tureaud hoped "to get more black lawyers" practicing in the state, according to Morial, and so tried to find "young lawyers to mentor, and who could succeed him"—young men like Morial and Revius Ortique, Jr.[8]

After law school, Morial served two years in army intelligence before returning to New Orleans. He began to practice with Tureaud, and became more active with the NAACP while he planned his political career. While in Tureaud's office, Morial worked on some of the major civil rights legislation in New Orleans. In the late 1950s, Morial became aware of the importance of the black Protestant churches, and began to appreciate the ministers' role in mobilizing the community. As a politically ambitious young attorney, Morial began to speak to church congregations, explaining the NAACP's programs and objectives.[9] As the Inc. Fund counsel's junior partner, Morial assumed a prominent position among the city's black Creole elite. Like Tureaud, he was light-skinned, aware of his class position, and a political moderate.

Morial became president of the New Orleans branch of the NAACP in 1962, and was part of the decision-making black elite who led the Citizens' Committee. At this time, he saw law as "an instrument to bring about change and social reform," as well as political change. Morial knew that many blacks seethed with anger, but took pains not to express it. What was critical in this period he said, "was the manner in which we manifested [the anger]. Cause we couldn't win. In the society at that time, to vent your hostility against the system of apartheid, would cause to happen to you what has happened to Mandela and others [in South Africa]." Morial developed a reputation as an extremely ambitious, "rigidly honest, and non-militant" civil rights leader.[10] In 1965, he became Louisiana's first black U.S. attorney; he worked in the civil rights division.

As a black Catholic Creole, Morial was from a different cultural tradition than the Protestant blacks of New Orleans. In the twentieth century, black Creoles formed an aristocracy in New Orleans' black community. Educated in private or Catholic institutions, they assumed positions of social and political leadership in the city. The light-skinned A. P. Tureaud was part of this tradition, as were Morial and his colleagues Dr. Leonard Burns and Norman Francis. Catholic Creoles participated in New Orleans' NAACP in the 1950s and 1960s: they were political moderates who favored negotiation over confrontation, and who deeply believed in an individualistic ethic of social mobility.[11]

Between 1962 and 1966, Morial, Burns, Elie, and Ortique conducted important negotiations with Harry B. Kelleher, a socially prominent corporate attorney. Kelleher, and fellow attorneys Harry McCall and Darwin Fenner, represented the white business elite in negotiations that stretched between 1962 and 1965, and eased the process of municipal desegregation.

"A Sort of Archaic Paternalism"

Kelleher was born in 1910 in New Orleans, the grandson of Civil War veterans. "As a child, I'd grown up with black servants in my mother's household," he said in 1988. From these experiences, he felt that he "knew and understood" blacks. His family had taught him that "civilized people don't abuse servants." Kelleher remembered his railroad executive father as a "very benign, generous" man, and his childhood as comfortable. Graduating from Tulane's law school in 1931, Kelleher began to practice law during the Depression, working for several years without salary.[12]

Kelleher believed that New Orleans' historic "milieu" of racial tolerance greatly facilitated the peaceful desegregation of the city in the 1960s. In New Orleans, he said, citizens traditionally faced disasters together—hurricanes, floods, "the horrors and rigors of the Civil War, and the rigors of Reconstruction." These shared experiences created a "certain bond of empathy for one's fellow man":

Now, granted, it was by today's standards a sort of archaic paternalism. When I was a child growing up, we had servants, and they became responsibilities of your family. If they were ill, you saw to it they got medical care. If their children or grandchildren got in trouble, got in jail, or anything else, you got 'em out. If they needed surgery, you saw it was *provided*.

As a representative of the white Citizens' Committee, he felt that all of his white colleagues had "grown up in this atmosphere, in this milieu, and black people were never their enemies. They were their fellow citizens, their friends, sometimes their very devoted friends."[13] He asserted that "the sort of racism that you had all over the Deep South—redneck against black—was never a reigning element in New Orleans." The city had long nurtured an "ethic of tolerance," and prided itself on being a "civilized community."[14]

Like many observers of New Orleans' class structure, Kelleher understood the power of the men that he represented on the Citizens' Committee. The white business community, he asserted, was an "oligarchy" in the 1960s; effective political and economic power rested in the leadership of five banks, and in several major businesses. "We had the levers of power," he said, whereas the White Citizens' Councils were regarded as an "upstart lunatic fringe."[15] Prior to the school crisis, the men of the white Citizens' Committee had influenced local politics through an organization known as Morrison's Cold Water Committee—so named because they tried to throw cold water on Morrison's bid to run for the state's governorship in 1956. After 1966, the same men would lead MAC, but, during the early 1960s, the group functioned as the white leadership who backed the Citizens' Committee's negotiations.[16]

Kelleher's involvement in this process had begun with his speech at the 1961 testimonial dinner for the Orleans Parish School Board. He agreed to speak at the dinner, and then to negotiate with the black leaders because "I was persuaded then, as I am now, that the alternative to the rule of law was chaos and riot and civil disorder and commotion." Kelleher had been raised in the tradition of "separate but equal," and "believed very firmly in the rule of law—and that [separate but equal] *was* the law until *Brown vs. Topeka*." But *Brown*, he maintained,

marked a turning point, a milestone in history, and the realities of the situation were changing. Social and moral values, too, I suppose, dictated a change in the approach to public education. And reality needed to be faced up to and recognized and dealt with intelligently and responsibly. It's just that simple.[17]

Between 1961 and 1966, black protest and white violence hit communities throughout the South. In 1961, CORE launched its Freedom Rides to test

a Supreme Court decision that prohibited discrimination in interstate trans-
portation. Whites attacked and burned a bus in Anniston, Alabama, and
brutally beat riders as they left a bus in Birmingham. During the summer
of 1961, CORE and the Student Non-Violent Coordinating Committee
(SNCC) sponsored other rides through the South. By the end of the summer, 360 riders had been arrested, and some spent prison sentences in
Mississippi jails.[18] In 1961 and 1962, SNCC and the SCLC staged demonstrations in Albany, Georgia. These were met with controlled police
repression, but nevertheless disrupted business in the community for the
period in which the Albany Movement was most active.[19] In 1963, the
Reverend Martin Luther King, Jr., and the Southern Christian Leadership
Conference (SCLC) launched "Project C" to confront the white political
and economic structure of Birmingham, Alabama, and were met with massive, well-publicized repression at the hands of the local police forces and
the Ku Klux Klan. Also in 1963, SNCC and CORE, using funds from the
Voter Education Project (VEP), launched a massive voter-registration campaign throughout the Deep South. Both organizations escalated these operations in the summer of 1964, and were greeted by increasing levels of
white violence. In communities throughout Louisiana, Alabama, and Mississippi, whites responded to the presence of the CORE and SNCC field-
workers with police harassment, outright terrorism, and increased intimidation of blacks. In Louisiana, Klan violence escalated in communities
like Plaquemine, Bogalusa, and Jonesboro between 1963 and 1966.[20] CORE
launched aggressive organizing and voter registration campaigns.

Increasing black pressures were necessary to gain the attention, and to
provoke the action of federal officials. Not until 1964, after sustained violence in Birmingham, Alabama, did the federal government pass the Civil
Rights Act of 1964. Not until three civil rights workers were murdered in
Mississippi in the summer of 1964 did the Justice Department respond to
requests and demands that the federal government provide basic protection
to civil rights organizers and black voters. Only unremitting black pressures
and escalating well-publicized white violence forced the federal government to guarantee voting rights in 1965. Violence exploded in many Southern communities in these years.[21]

The business leaders of a number of cities, however, took lessons from
the crises of Little Rock, Birmingham, Oxford, and St. Augustine. In Atlanta and Augusta, Georgia, in Dallas, Texas, and in Columbia, South
Carolina, businessmen and moderate politicians agreed to accommodate

their institutions and governments to black demands and federal pressures. New Orleans' business leaders followed these precedents in 1961.[22]

New Orleans' black leaders increased organizing efforts in response to the school crisis and the assaults from the legislature. Dr. Daniel C. Thompson formed CCGNO to conduct a massive voter registration drive over the next several years. Dr. Leonard Burns, president of the United Clubs, called for another Mardi Gras boycott—similar to the one of 1957—to protest the "hate bills" in the legislature. The money was pledged to the NAACP and to the Urban League. Burns and the United Clubs publicized the boycott widely. As a result, blacks canceled every major ball scheduled for the Mardi Gras season.[23] And between 1961 and 1962, Lolis Elie organized the black Citizens' Committee, a federation of organizations dedicated to pressuring the white community into granting blacks their basic civil rights.

In the Citizens' Committee's negotiations, the black community repeated its tactics of the 1950s, but added a new force and pressure. The force came from two sources: from the restlessness and militancy of the students in CORE and the NAACP Youth Council—who were often difficult to control—and from the conviction that the federal government would eventually back the claims of the black community. The black leadership knew that the disciplined and non-violent actions of the students could provoke violent attacks from the segregationists, which, in turn, might provoke a black response that could not be controlled. Black leaders also knew that the merchants and lawyers feared the disorder and lawlessness that the Citizens' Councils threatened. As Kelleher said, "thoughtful people feared the segregationists far more than the blacks." The Citizens' Councils represented "mobocracy at its worst."[24] Thus, the black leadership would again use strategically placed white elites—and the threat of white violence—to facilitate the desegregation of public facilities.

The events of 1960–1961 had made the city's white economic elites extremely sensitive to the costs of racial disruption. The school crisis had tarnished the city's reputation as a place of racial harmony. Throughout 1961, the students in CORE, and their elders in the Consumers' League, had staged pickets and protests on Canal Street and at other major shopping areas. With these protests, they challenged newly enacted state laws that prohibited picketing, and protested Louisiana's use of tests to disqualify black voters.[25] CORE members also participated in the dangerous Freedom

Rides of 1961, and fed and housed waves of riders who came to New Orleans. When city police beat two white riders in the city, CORE members staged a sit-in at the office of the chief of police, and picketed City Hall. Members continued to sit in and picket McCrory's and Woolworth's. In December, 1,200 black college students marched to protest recent arrests at Baton Rouge; 292 were arrested. During demonstrations at dime stores, whites behaved dangerously. One assistant manager waved a gun at CORE members, and other whites poured scalding coffee and ammonia on the heads of the demonstrators.[26]

Responding to this potentially explosive situation, a representative of the Chamber of Commerce contacted Harry Kelleher to ask him to negotiate with the black leadership. In meetings over the next two to three years, Kelleher and McCall met separately and collectively with the black and white committees; they also met with Chief of Police Joseph Giarusso and Mayor Victor Schiro. Kelleher said that he and McCall "took the position that New Orleans had a choice between an orderly transition and the riots and commotion that had characterized Birmingham and other cities in the South. And we felt that it was much more responsible and intelligent to work out negotiated, harmonious, peaceful solutions than to take to the streets."[27]

With Kelleher and McCall, the black leadership worked out a plan to desegregate Canal Street's lunch counters. The blacks publicly demanded the desegregation of *all* public places: the cafeteria in City Hall, and the facilities in the U.S. Fisheries and Wildlife Building, as well as Audubon Park and City Park. They wanted to abolish segregated rest rooms, and demanded the removal of all racial designation signs from the downtown. They also demanded that blacks be employed as salespeople and managers in Canal Street's stores.[28]

After the negotiators had devised an agenda, Kelleher and McCall embarked on one of their "most dramatic efforts": a series of meetings with the downtown merchants. "We had the facts and we had the statistics that showed what had happened to the Birmingham market," Kelleher said in 1979. "We said, 'Now, this is the *reward* for letting mass picketing, rioting, and civil commotion take over in *your* community—*that's* what's happening in Birmingham ...' McCall and I could talk to them like Dutch Uncles, 'cause nobody was paying us a *sou*, you see."

Throughout the summer of 1962, the negotiators and their committees planned how Canal Street's lunch counters would be desegregated. They "worked it out" in advance that no television station or newspaper would report the news for a week. Kelleher and McCall talked with store managers. Kelleher recalled:

We said, "Look, you have pretty good insights of your personnel departments, what kind of people you have. You know who the racists are and who they're not. You know who the rednecks from Mississippi are—the unreconstructable segregationists. We want 'em *all* gotten out from behind the lunchcounters."

The negotiators told black community leaders that they would need desegregation teams. Kelleher said that he and his colleagues told the blacks that "we want your best representatives," people who were "immaculately groomed," with "equitable dispositions, good manners, and pleasing appearances," who would know what to leave as a "proper tip" for service.[29] By September 15, 1962, some fifteen stores had desegregated their lunch counters.[30]

The men Kelleher represented had the power to make such changes when they desired. Kelleher felt that "the collective power of that group" was such that "nobody but the rabid segregationists had the temerity to challenge it."[31] The white leaders could control the press, the police, and the mayor's office when they needed to do so. They delayed and muffled media coverage of the desegregation of Tulane and of lunch counters. As a result, the majority of New Orleans' citizens only learned of these changes *after* each had been accomplished. Clearly, the Citizens' Committee's negotiations educated black leaders to the prerogatives of power and class in the city.[32]

Black negotiators took differing views of this glimpse of power. In the early 1960s Revius Ortique was a general troubleshooter within the civil rights leadership. During these years, C. C. DeJoie, the publisher of the *Louisiana Weekly*, paid Ortique a generous retainer to allow him to move freely within the black and white communities. Ortique wrote many of the articles on the Citizens' Committee that appeared in the *Weekly*, with the express purpose of telling both the white and black readers about the plans and accomplishments of the black leadership and its white counterparts.

Ortique had been chosen as a co-negotiator by Lolis Elie, who had organized the Citizens' Committee. According to Ortique, Elie had realized that he needed a negotiator who could be trusted by both the white elite—men like Darwin Fenner, Harry Kelleher, and Harry McCall—and by the black community. While a leader with the stature of Albert Dent would have been successful with the white elites, he would not have been trusted by the black community because "he had been very close to the Sterns, and to [other whites] they considered their oppressors."[33]

Ortique found the negotiations "exhilarating." He recalled many midnight meetings with Kelleher, followed by meetings with other groups the next morning. "I felt like I never wanted to leave those sessions," he said. Part of Ortique's sense of excitement came from the high stakes of the struggle. He and his colleagues were concerned that "brutality would not occur" to the young militants in CORE and the NAACP, but were also aware of the power of protest to force concessions from the white elite:[34]

I don't think that any of us were convinced that New Orleans wouldn't burn. I don't think that, as blacks, we would have been shocked, dismayed if it had happened. We were willing to work to prevent it, but as I recall, our attitude was, "Well, if we don't get this, then, the hell with it . . . Let it burn." And I think that was always in the back of my mind, and always the ace I had to play.[35]

In this process, Ortique and Elie worked hand in hand. Elie, said Ortique, "didn't mind speaking" the militants' language—"he used the jargon of the streets." He would meet with the young "actionists" of CORE, and, knowing that he couldn't "take these folks downtown directly," would ask Ortique to meet with them. Ortique would then meet with the young people, find out their "bottom line," and both men would then approach the white negotiators. "We worked with everything that got desegregated, everything that eased off," said Ortique. "The police brutality situation, the integration situation, school problems."[36]

Ortique appreciated the power of his white counterparts. In 1978, he asserted that "we always knew that we could call upon the top people in the community. I'm talking about the presidents of banks, the heads of corporations, I always knew that I could pick up the phone and talk to them at any time and make strong suggestions," and that the white leadership would try to be helpful. "I knew that they could call certain people and say, 'Look, this is gonna happen. This is the way its going to be.' " Especially, Ortique respected the power of Harry Kelleher and Harry McCall, his white counterparts. Kelleher was head of a law firm that represented major corporate interests, and McCall was the member of a law firm that represented a number of the downtown merchants.[37]

In these negotiations, Ortique refused to "play the numbers game" with desegregation by limiting the number of blacks who might eat at a lunch counter or restaurant. He saw his own role as a facilitator, a pressure point, and as a protector, making sure that the young blacks in the picket lines and marches were not harmed, and making sure that the white elite understood that basic changes in racial patterns had to occur.[38] This necessitated walking a fine line between the black protestors and white elites:

[Rudy] Lombard of CORE was an individual that I believed was determined that he would be a hero in the whole business. If that meant he got killed, it didn't bother him at all at that time; this was the role he should play. I . . . and others thought strongly that we should do anything we could not to allow something untoward to happen.

It was a matter of being prepared to act in a certain fashion because we knew that [a demonstration] was going to take place. If we learned that a group was going to march on city hall, we'd contact the mayor and say, "Mr. Mayor, these people are determined to march. Now, it seems to me that you don't want the repercussions of national headlines, that sort of thing. Now what can we do to make certain we don't have that?"[39]

Both Ortique and Elie were aware of the potential for violence that existed in New Orleans, and that flared elsewhere. Both men were involved in legal work and in bi-racial negotiations in communities in Louisiana and Mississippi in the years between 1962 and 1966. And both had a sense that they were making changes in New Orleans that could not be accomplished without violence elsewhere. "I knew that we were doing things here that people were not willing to do or able to do in other parts of the state or other parts of the nation," said Ortique. He was proud to have been a part of the meetings, even though he and his colleagues ran the "risk of other people referring to us as Uncle Toms."[40]

For Lolis Elie, the negotiations were an education in power and in class relations. "Bear in mind, I'd only been out of law school a couple of years, and I'd never had any experience that suggested to me that I was gonna be part of this," he said.[41] He was initially "astounded to discover that the people with whom I was negotiating, people who could make changes, were people no one ever votes for."[42] The negotiations also opened his eyes to the divisions within the white community. During the Dryades Street protests, Elie discovered that the larger business community "didn't give a shit" about what happened to the Jewish merchants on Dryades Street. Later, when a B'nai B'rith representative approached Elie with a suggestion that some of the Jewish merchants would be willing to hire blacks, a Chamber of Commerce representative told Elie to " 'keep those Goddamn Jews out of it.' " "There was no role for any Jews around," said Elie. Until he was thirty, Elie had been unaware of prejudice against

Jews. During the Citizens' Committee's negotiations, he discovered a "vicious anti-Semitism" within the white community.[43]

Of all the leaders of the black committee, Elie considered the Reverend A. L. Davis to be the most important: Davis could, and did mobilize thousands of blacks through the Interdenominational Ministerial Alliance (IMA). "If there was to be a mass meeting, there was only one way to get it—through the IMA," said Elie. "I think he was the best leader we had." And Davis trusted Elie: both were very dark blacks, different in culture and orientation from the "Creole lawyers" like Tureaud and Morial, who had traditionally acted as leaders of the black community. Elie also had the trust of the young people in CORE—Rudy Lombard, Oretha Castle, and Jerome Smith. Thus, he and Ortique functioned as twin mediators between the Creole black elite and the more militant young people of CORE, most of whom shared working-class backgrounds.[44]

The black leadership continued to pressure New Orleans' political and economic institutions throughout 1963 and 1964, with mixed success. Only the threat of "mass demonstrations" seemed to move the city's white political leadership and businessmen. In February, the Citizens' Committee threatened a selective buying campaign against Canal Street's merchants. After several merchants responded with "commitments" to hire black personnel, the black leaders postponed their boycott. By mid-May, Ernest Morial, the Reverend Avery Alexander, and Oretha Castle of CORE issued a statement that "some progress" had been made in "hiring above the menial level."[45]

During these months of negotiations, lawsuits, and protests, the *Louisiana Weekly* leaked word of the Citizens' Committee's activities to its black and white readers. Ortique, who wrote many of these stories, asked if the city had a " 'secret' bi-racial council." At a meeting of the U.S. Conference of Mayors, Mayor Victor Schiro had asserted that New Orleans was "getting along very harmoniously and making great strides on a citizen basis, working through an interracial council." The *Weekly* stated that "close observers of the progress of the bi-racial council movement across the South recall that only a few weeks ago Mayor Schiro said he would not appoint such a committee in New Orleans." The pointed news article made clear the black leadership's dilemma: while they had some influence with the city's economic elites, the community's political elites, and the institutions they governed, could be only sluggishly forced to act. The black community was spared the violence of wildly segregationist local officials like Birmingham's Bull Connor, and the controls exerted by the black leadership and the white economic elite effectively muted the potential for mass violence from whites or from blacks. The fragile unity of the black Citizens' Committee was the result of a clear consensus on very basic civil rights issues and goals—public accommodations, school integration, black employment, and the vote.[46]

The black leadership's greatest threat and weapon became that of "mass demonstrations," with their potential for interracial violence and economic loss. In July of 1963, the *Weekly* and Rev. Davis' IMA warned that "racial strife" would break out if the city did not correct the "lack of opportunity" available to blacks in New Orleans. But the IMA also commended the progress made by "private citizens both Negro and whites who for the past 18 months have worked untiringly to reach a just solution to racial problems." These "private citizens" had managed the desegregation of "virtually all the downtown lunch counters" and chain stores in other parts of the city, and had obtained "some" non-menial employment for blacks. The *Weekly* insisted that "no mass demonstrations" had yet occurred because of "communication"; a group of "15 Negroes" met periodically with "white business representatives and civil leaders." This group had obtained employment for more than sixty blacks in "formerly whites-only jobs," and had done so "in spite of the mayor and the City Council." The *Weekly* demanded that the city appoint an official bi-racial council, as Birmingham had recently done.[47]

On August 12, 1963, the black leadership announced that an agreement had been reached with Mayor Schiro. The city would remove its racial designation signs, would "refrain from appealing" court orders that desegregated local institutions, and the city's civil service would hire applicants on the basis of "qualifications." Schiro also promised that his administration would "refrain from harassing businessmen who desire to desegregate hotels, motels, restaurants, and other facilities." He also promised to hire black firemen and sanitation workers. In late August, Schiro himself confirmed that "desegregation proposals" had been worked out in a "'special bi-racial' meeting" between black and white leaders.[48]

By late September of 1963, however, six local civil rights groups called for a massive demonstration to protest the failure of municipal authorities to produce what they had promised. Blacks would stage a Freedom March from Shakespeare Park to City Hall and present a list of grievances to the mayor and city council. On the evening of September 30, 1963, more than

10,000 blacks and 300 whites marched to City Hall. The Reverends A. L. Davis, Milton Upton, and Avery Alexander, and Ernest Morial and A. J. Chapital of the NAACP, and Oretha Castle of CORE led the March. Neither the mayor nor the city council members met the marchers at City Hall.[49]

Oretha Castle, addressing the crowd, noted that the mayor and city councilmen were absent, and that City Hall was closed. But, she asserted, the attitude of the mayor was not important. "What we say together is important. . . . As long as we are held in economic and political slavery, they [the whites] aren't free either." She ominously predicted that there would be no peace "as long as Negroes 'are forced to live as we are now.' "[50]

"We probably had the largest peaceful march outside of Washington in 1963," said Dutch Morial in 1987. The black negotiators had warned the white negotiators to control segregationists during the march:

We told those people, "Look, if you don't let us demonstrate peacefully, and see that we demonstrate and do what has to be done peacefully, you're gonna have a situation and we are not gonna be able to control it." . . .We were trying to have cool tempers prevail. We didn't want demonstrations—which we know would have been legitimate—and then reactionaries creating some situation which the demonstrators might not have been disciplined enough just to demonstrate. The opposition was not disciplined; they were mobs.[51]

Harry Kelleher recalled that the black Citizens' Committee had announced that they wanted to march on City Hall. "The White Citizens' Councils said that if [the blacks] marched, they'd appear and break up the march." The negotiators called Schiro to a meeting and worked out an agreement. The white negotiators got the permit for the march, and received assurances of police protection. "We let it be known that the first person guilty of misconduct was going to jail, " said Kelleher. "I forgot how we got this message to them, but somehow, we got the same message to the White Citizens' Council. We told both sides this."

For Kelleher, the march to City Hall was a cathartic gesture to alleviate the buildup of black frustration. "The town was in a state of seething discontent," he recalled. "It was a time of long, hot summers." The white negotiators wanted to defuse the situation, so that they could "go on with these orderly, phased programs we were working on. We knew a major riot would disrupt the whole thing." The march was, then, an "intelligent safety valve" to cool some of the accumulated "emotional heat."[52]

In the week following the march, the Reverend Davis delivered the

Citizens' Committee's petition to the city council. In this document, the black leaders demanded the repeal of all segregation ordinances in the city, elimination of all forms of police brutality, appointment of blacks to all city and state boards, the desegregation of Delgado Trades and Technical School, and full desegregation of the city's public schools by 1964. The petition also called for full access to all places of public accommodation, hospitals, and places of amusement, the opening up of trade and professional associations, and the elimination of segregated unions in the city. Schiro responded by referring the requests to specific city agencies. He denied that he had the authority to intervene in the affairs of the city council, the school board, or the board of managers of the Delgado Trades School, or the city's hospitals, labor unions, or the Chamber of Commerce. He denied that there had been any police brutality in the city.[53]

Picketing and demonstrations continued through 1965. CORE members demonstrated at local theaters and other businesses. Between 1963 and 1965, the maverick NAACP Youth Council staged continued picketing of downtown Canal Street, violating the agreement reached between Citizens' Committee negotiators and their white counterparts. Raphael Cassimere, president of the Youth Council, maintained that the Citizens' Committee did not represent the younger group, and that merchants on Canal Street had promised more jobs than they had delivered. Cassimere and the Council kept the picket lines going until 1965. This infuriated their elders on the Committee. The *Louisiana Weekly* rebuked the young people with stories and editorials, but failed to break the picket lines.[54]

The one aberrant break in the bi-racial control of municipal desegregation occurred on October 31, 1963, when CORE members and the Reverend Avery Alexander attempted to desegregate the cafeteria at City Hall. When the group requested service, police arrested them. Officers carried Doris Jean Castle and Sondra Nixon from the cafeteria in chairs. Alexander sat down and refused to move, so police dragged him out by his feet. Alexander's head was bumped on two flights of steps as he was dragged to the building's entrance. Television cameras captured the spectacle of the dignified minister being dragged by his heels from the public cafeteria.[55]

Harry Kelleher saw films of the arrests on the evening news, and was appalled. He said that the arrests of Alexander and the group occurred because of a lack of communication. "That was the only breach that occurred between the white leadership and the black leadership," he said. "We made profuse apologies. We were mortified."[56]

Lolis Elie learned about the realities of power from the negotiations. He contended that political power was always subordinate to economic power in the city. He recalled a meeting of 1963, when the Citizens' Committee got the city to agree to hire black garbagemen, and to change the requirements for a plumber's license, and to allow blacks to use the facilities at Audubon Park. After the negotiators had reached an agreement,

I remember Darwin Fenner got on the phone to Vic Schiro, and he goes, "Vic, this is Darwin. Come over here, I want to see you." And in five minutes, here comes Vic. This agreement is shoved in his face, he signs it, and leaves. That was the *only* time a politician was involved.[57]

During the negotiations, Elie himself was in a momentous process of personal and psychological growth, which he attributed to his association with the intellectuals and activists in CORE.[58] His feelings about the Citizens' Committee's negotiations differed from those of Ortique. Although respectful of the power of the white lawyers and merchants, he did not fully accept the entrée it gave him into the local system of political power. He had begun to question the utility of integration, and to doubt whether the masses of whites would ever acknowledge blacks as human beings.[59] He therefore viewed his white counterparts simply as lawyers, and was "fascinated" to see how power operated. But he was also extremely sensitive to the amount of change that he could expect from the powerful whites with whom he dealt. He remembered a day when a powerful white attorney forgot that he was talking with Elie during a phone conversation: "he went on and on for ten minutes about how he wanted the niggers to have their rights. That happened on a couple of occasions with other people." Elie had perceived that this attorney was the most powerful man among the white negotiators; "I could tell from the way Kelleher deferred to him."[60]

Dutch Morial thought that the white committee's motives in the negotiations were fundamentally economic. "It was just out of self-interest," he said. He didn't think that any of the white elites in the 1960s saw segregation as "morally wrong. I don't think many of them today see it as morally wrong," he said in 1988. He believed that the negotiators like Kelleher, Fenner, and McCall "were cordial because they were gentlemen," and because the black negotiators like Elie, Ortique, and himself were younger men. "We were not their contemporaries, you know. So I guess that made a difference, too."[61]

Harry Kelleher was deeply impressed by the black leaders. In 1979, he spoke warmly about relationships with Elie, Ortique, and with DeJoie of the *Louisiana Weekly*. He claimed that New Orleans' black leaders were an "extraordinarily talented group" who had "constituencies that were loyal to them, that proved to be loyal and dependable." Kelleher was pleased by the "development of a spirit and attitude of trust between the black and white leaders" during the negotiations.[62] Similarly, Harry McCall wrote that the most significant effect of the negotiations upon him was "the forming of friendships and the creation of mutual trust between various members of the black community and myself, particularly Messrs. Elie, Ortique, Morial, [Norman] Francis and Drs. Burns and Dent. I feel that the city owes a deep debt of gratitude to the black negotiators particularly, since there were so many members of their community who were far more extreme in their views."[63]

McCall's and Kelleher's statements were echoed by Rosa Keller, one of the few white liberals of "blue-blood, Carnival status"—a status shared by Kelleher, McCall, and Fenner. Keller believed that New Orleans' racial progress during the 1960s was facilitated by the status and quality of its black elite. Men like Ortique, Dent, Norman Francis, and Dutch Morial were "just as self-respecting as anyone out of the Boston Club," and "never" felt that they were "second class." Keller, whose husband became an organizer of MAC in 1966, contended that the white elite's resistance to desegregation declined after they met the city's black leadership, and had been forced to acknowledge them as equals:

Once they had met the Albert Dent and the Norman Francis and the Revius Ortique, they got comfortable. [You had to get] over the initial thing of, "This is a black man; I've never talked to a black man"—you had this uncomfortable feeling: "Well, I didn't *know* he had a Harvard degree"—you know. It was socially *very* uncomfortable, their first exposures to each other. And then it got comfortable."[64]

Within the world of the Citizens' Committee's negotiations, Elie functioned as a politician, but his political views were undergoing rapid and dramatic changes. He had grown tired of the "progress" made by bi-racial committees; he doubted that these changes would solve the basic economic problems of blacks; nor would they do much to change white racism. He had begun thinking about black nationalism, and had begun to admire Elijah Muhammad, the leader of the black Muslims in America. He felt that he was different from many of the leaders of the black Citizens' Committee: "I came from a different place; I was born and raised in Niggertown. I spent a year at Howard." Most of his colleagues, he said, were "an ac-

commodating class. God knows, they felt that Malcolm X was a madman."
Elie was being drawn more closely to the perspective of the young militants
of CORE and SNCC. By 1963 and 1964, many of these men and women
were becoming radicalized, and disillusioned with the political system. "I
always listened to the young people," he said, because he had come to
realize that, with the exception of a few black leaders, the "older people
had no program." But the young people, he said, "were willing to take
some risk. They were people who understood that there's never any gain
without risk—in anything, personal or political." Additionally, his class
identity gave him a sharp perspective on the costs and gains of desegregation. When the lunch counters were integrated, he said, it was the poor
white, the angry segregationist who was dismissed from his job for harassing blacks, who lost something.

The people who were really giving something up—whatever that something was—
was that woman and that man behind that counter. The one thing that they had
was the fact that they were white. [Integration] was lessenin' their way of life.
They really had no one of their class to articulate their case for them.[65]

While Elie had doubted the ability of racial negotiations to change the
basic nature of racism, he saw the Citizens' Committee as a brief instance
of unity in a black community traditionally divided by color, class, and
religion. And the Committee did produce tangible gains. In October 1964,
the *Weekly* asserted that the "Freedom Marchers" had gained three out of
five objectives. A. J. Chapital of the NAACP had reported that three goals
had been met, one would be resolved by implementation of the Civil Rights
Act of 1964, and another issue awaited action by city officials. Racial designation signs were gone from municipal buildings, an NAACP suit had
desegregated the Delgado Trade School, and any city ordinances requiring
segregation would be removed by the CRA 1964, which would also eliminate a dual system of classification in the civil service. A fifth objective,
the appointment of blacks to city boards and agencies, still awaited action
by city officials.[66] Elie remembered the Citizens' Committee's goals as
narrow and limited, but of fundamental importance:

There was something on the surface that was even more important, I think. It was
a real struggle for dignity, which is difficult to define. I consider that to be a major
accomplishment. I think that as a result of the work of that Committee, blacks
gained a kind of psychological advantage, if you will, a kind of self-esteem. I think
prior to that, any time a black person decided to come downtown, they had to not
only put on their physical clothes; they had to put on a special psychological *mask*.

Because it was bound to happen—anywhere from City Hall to the Public Service to the telephone company to all of those stores downtown, someone was going to *abuse* you. And if you argued about that abuse, there was a fair chance that the *cops* were gonna get onto you.[67]

In February 1963, eleven black students enrolled at Tulane University. When the eight graduate students and three undergraduates began classes, the university's 129-year status as a segregated institution ended. As a result of a lawsuit, Tulane's board of administrators "voluntarily" admitted black students.

The suit originated with three whites: Rosa Keller, Henry Mason, and John Furey. Mason taught political science at Tulane, and Furey was on the faculty at Dillard University. All three considered themselves to be friends of the university, and feared that Tulane would be harmed if it remained segregated.[68]

The three decided to file a suit against the university because its board of administrators claimed that the provisions of benefactor Paul Tulane's will, which had provided for the education of white males from the city of New Orleans, prohibited Tulane from admitting blacks. By 1961, however, the university clearly violated these provisions; women attended Sophie Newcomb College at Tulane, and Chinese, Indian, and other nationalities studied as foreign students.[69]

Tulane University also had financial reasons to integrate. The institution had gone deeply into debt by making expensive capital improvements in the 1950s. Large foundation grants seemed to be the best answer to the university's financial strain—particularly some $6 million in Ford monies that were offered as a matching grant in the early 1960s. But Ford, and other foundations, were beginning to withhold funds from segregated institutions.

Rosa Keller was aware of the atmosphere on campus: "they were really losing some top-flight people" because of segregation, she said in 1978. But the board of administrators "could not make this decision, could not face this decision." Keller knew the board: her father had been a member, and her brother Richard Freeman was a member on 1961. Keller was convinced that the board had to be forced to integrate:

Somebody had to *do* this. They weren't going to do it for themselves. That sounds so silly, but they were gonna put it off as long as they could, even if it damaged the university. And *that* is the mentality that I think is so hard to explain.[70]

Keller, Mason, and Furey decided to file a suit to desegregate Tulane.

Furey recruited two women students, both graduates of Dillard University. Barbara Marie Guillory applied for admission to the doctoral program in sociology, and Pearlie Elloie applied for the master's program in social work. Keller put up most of the money for the suit, although the Unitarian church donated $1,000 toward expenses. The three approached A. P. Tureaud to see if he would take the case, but the Inc. Fund attorney refused because it was not, he explained, a policy-making case. They then approached John P. Nelson, Jr., who agreed to take the case.

Keller then visited individual members of the board of administrators to tell them of her plans. She visited Joseph Jones, the chairman of the board:

I told him what I was going to do. I said, "I don't ever want you to question my motives about Tulane." He said, "Oh, I would never question your motives—" I said, "Well, I think you will, before we get through."

But he told me, interestingly enough, that this had to happen, and he *knew* that it had to happen. And that he had *tried* to persuade his board to go on and *do* it. "Go on and do it—just set aside the old will or grant or whatever." He was just trying to persuade them that it had to be done and that they should do it peaceably . . . and they wouldn't. So he patted me on the back, and thanked me for coming, and said that everything was going to be *lovely*.[71]

In April of 1961, the board announced its decision on Elloie's and Guillory's applications. The administrators voted that the university "would admit qualified students regardless of race or color if it were legally permissible." To Keller, attorney Nelson, and the plaintiffs, this decision seemed to invite a lawsuit. From the wording of the board's statement, it appeared that the suit might be "friendly."[72]

"I took the case and I still cannot give a good explanation of why I took it," said Nelson in 1979. "Frankly, I always thought of myself as eventually being a rich, competent, well-respected lawyer, community guy." Nelson's most difficult experiences came with the Tulane proceedings:

The people that graduate from Tulane do not eat at McCrory's. They don't use drinking fountains in public places. They don't go to the local theaters. So they could care less about *that*. . . . But you don't touch their school.

Nelson could pursue two strategies in arguing the case against Tulane. He chose the more difficult, more controversial, and, ultimately, more explosive strategy. He challenged Tulane's status as a private institution.[73] Nelson believed that Tulane's attorneys expected him to go into state court and invoke a *cy près* doctrine, requesting that a judge reinterpret Paul Tulane's donation in light of contemporary circumstances. But Nelson felt that this procedure might have taken "six or seven years." He wanted to avoid going into the state courts with this kind of case because

I just didn't want to get involved in the politics of Tulane graduates and Tulane lawyers influencing state judges. Frankly, that was the basis of my decision. I just felt that the state courts would have been very sympathetic to Tulane, the judges were just as prejudiced as the board was. I would have been in an alien environment.[74]

Nelson thought that the Federal District Court, presided over by J. Skelly Wright, and the Fifth Circuit Court of Appeals, would be far more sympathetic to his argument. Wright had ordered the desegration of LSU's law school and its undergraduate divisions, and had recently weathered the state legislature's attack on the federal courts and the Orleans Parish School Board. The Fifth Circuit Court of Appeals had begun to establish its innovative record in civil rights and civil liberties cases.[75] Nelson went into the district court with his argument that Tulane had sufficient state involvement to be considered a public institution. Wright "rendered an opinion accepting my position," said Nelson. "At Tulane, people went crazy."

The case generated considerable controversy. Rosa Keller and John P. Nelson had difficult experiences during the trial. Nelson framed all of his medals from World War II, and hung them in his office "because I was tired of being referred to as a communist, and undermining the educational system of this country." He received abusive phone calls, and lost clients. Several times, he "reached a point where I considered moving to Washington, D.C.," but never actually did so. Because he devoted so much time to the case, his law firm dissolved. He had to "start all over again" after the case was concluded.[76] Keller remembered a highly pressured atmosphere:

All these people, you know, that you went to school with, the *kindest* approach anybody would take was that they were *troubled* about you. And it ranged from that to thinking you were *crazy*. You couldn't go to a party, you couldn't go *any place* that someone didn't come up and bother you. And it just made you *miserable*, just *miserable*.[77]

On March 19, 1962, Wright ruled in favor of the plaintiffs and declared Tulane a public institution and ordered its board to admit the plaintiffs.[78]

Already unpopular for his orders that desegregated the city's schools, Wright received additional criticism for the *Tulane* decision. Neighbors and peers in white New Orleans ostracized the judge and his family. "It was very, very, very bad," said his friend Rosa Keller. The Wrights had "cross-burnings, and their little boy was threatened. And it almost *destroyed*" Helen Patton Wright, the jurist's wife. Skelly Wright, said Keller, was "tough," and was "going to do what he had to do, morally and legally." But his wife

didn't have any of that. . . . She'd go to church, and everybody would move across the aisle. She was unacceptable in those circles. It was breaking her heart, that's what it was doing.[79]

Days after Wright gave his restraining order to Tulane's board, he was appointed to the U.S. District Court of Appeals in Washington, D.C.—a promotion due to his unflinching support of *Brown*. He was replaced by Frank B. Ellis, a Kennedy appointee. Tulane's lawyers immediately filed a motion for a new trial with Ellis, alleging that Wright had ignored matters of fact in his decision. On April 19, 1962, Ellis stayed Wright's injunction.[80]

Ellis vacated Wright's decision on May 8, 1962. At the trial held on August 3, he ordered the attorneys to address the main issue—whether Tulane had sufficient involvement with the state to change its private status.[81]

Nelson introduced evidence to support his claim that Tulane had sufficient state involvement to be affected by the Fourteenth Amendment. Tulane's attorneys used the same evidence to argue that the university was a private corporation, and immune to state interference. For Tulane's attorneys, the proceedings represented the university's last chance to maintain the school's private status.[82] On December 5, 1962, Ellis announced his decision in favor of Tulane. He found state involvement in the university's operation not significant enough to be considered state action. Ellis ruled that Tulane's board was not restricted in its admissions policy, but was free to "act as it wishes." Having restored the university's private status, Ellis left it free to desegregate. On December 5, Nelson filed an appeal to the Fifth Circuit. On December 12, the Tulane board voted to admit black students to the university for the semester that began in February 1963.[83]

So Tulane became an integrated institution. The university quietly desegregated, simultaneously opening all of its facilities to black students. Rosa Keller had requested that the local press refrain from making any reports on the students' initial reception for several days. Friends at the *Times-Picayune* and at WDSU-TV agreed, and no publicity attended the integration of Tulane.[84]

"After it was settled for them, and taken out of their hands, they [the board] behaved like the bunch of gentlemen they always thought they were, and they accepted it with great grace," said Rosa Keller. "It turned out to be a nice story in the end ... I think a lot of people realized that Tulane would be irreparably damaged if they didn't go on and do what they all knew by that time they had to do." Once again, strategically placed white elites facilitated the opening of a major institution to black petitioners—for an array of reasons. Just as Keller, Wright, and Nelson were committed to racial integration, their colleagues and peers were committed to maintaining order and autonomy in local institutions. In the instances of Canal Street and Tulane, New Orleans' white elite demonstrated that they valued local autonomy over segregation. When confronted by the federal courts, by losses in revenue, and by local black pressures, New Orleans' most powerful whites acceded to black demands, in order to retain some control over the pace and scale of racial integration.

A longtime member of SCEF, Virginia Collins had gone to the organization's offices on Perdido Street on the morning of October 4, 1963. She regularly did "volunteer" work for SCEF, "filing, and stuff like that," until she went to her afternoon job as an "activator" for the Coordinating Council. That afternoon, she learned that police officers and prison trustees had raided the SCEF offices, the law offices of Ben Smith and Bruce Waltzer, and the homes of Smith, Walzer, and James Dombrowski, the executive director of SCEF. The officers confiscated the papers and files of Dombrowski, Smith, and Waltzer, arrested the men, and charged them with "violating the state Subversive Activities and Control Law and the Communist Propaganda Control Act." The officers packed SCEF's files and documents into a moving van and took them to Baton Rouge.[85]

"They raided the office, they took everything," said Collins. "They raided Jim's house, they took everything. All of the papers, all of Jim's library. Its a shame, what they did." Officers even confiscated Dombrowski's autographed photo of Eleanor Roosevelt.[86]

The Louisiana Joint Legislative Committee on Un-American Activities (LUAC) had authorized the raid. It charged Dombrowski and Ben Smith with operating a subversive organization—SCEF—and Walzer with belonging to a subversive organization, the National Lawyers' Guild (NLG). Significantly, Walzer and Smith had been arrested at an integrated NLG-sponsored meeting at the New Orleans Hilton. Smith was then SCEF treasurer, and involved in planning the NLG defense work for the Mississippi summer of 1964. The SCEF raid and arrests were a product of state officials' desire to halt the operations of an integrationist, white-led civil rights organization that was deeply involved in promoting the black vote. Mississippi's James O. Eastland was also involved in the raids: he had telephoned LUAC chairman, State Representative James Pfister, on the night of the raids to inform him that he was issuing a subpeona for SCEF's records. Eastland had attempted to obtain the organization's files—with its membership lists—in 1954, as part of his attack on integrationist sentiment and "communism." After LUAC's raid, when Waltzer, Smith, and Dombrowski attempted to regain their files, they were informed that the materials had been transported to Woodville, Mississippi, and part of them had been sent to Washington, D.C., for photocopying. Eastland was using his authority as chairman of the Senate Internal Security Subcommittee to attack SCEF and its members.

In the shambles of James Dombrowski's office, Virginia Collins searched for membership lists or any documents that would help to reconstitute the organization in the aftermath of the raids. Finally, she found an old galley in a closet, and she and her children went to work on putting together SCEF's mailing list. Her son Walter remembered that he spent much of his sophomore year in college "putting SCEF back together"—constructing a mailing list on three-by-five cards. Prior to the raids, Collins recalled, SCEF had been considered a "really very mysterious" organization that kept in the background of events. Most local board members and supporters were blacks and white professionals from local universities. "It was considered a communist organization," said Walter Collins. "After the raid, things changed." Pfister and his colleagues in LUAC made SCEF "a very popular organization in the black community."[87]

The attack on SCEF had more significance regionally than locally. It was clearly aimed at the organization's South-wide activities, particularly SCEF's cooperation with SNCC and other militant organizers in rural areas of Mississippi and Louisiana. These areas were still controlled by an old agrarian elite which enforced its opposition to black rights through quasi-"legal" repression.[88] Perhaps because such mainstream groups as the Young Men's Business Club (YMBC) and the American Legion sporadically attacked SCEF as "subversive," SCEF's leaders held no important positions within New Orleans' civil rights leadership. Rather, it was SCEF's symbolic status as a largely white, integrationist organization, and its ties to the National Lawyers' Guild activities in Mississippi, that prompted the raid and the indictments of Dombrowski, Waltzer, and Smith. The attack on SCEF was a final effort of repression by rural elites who had largely exhausted all other remedies.[89]

Through a series of suits and actions, Dombrowski and SCEF tried to restrain Eastland from using SCEF's documents, and charged Pfister and his committee with false arrest. At a committee hearing on November 8, Pfister labeled SCEF a "communist front." The legislative committee then resolved that SCEF was "in fact a Communist front organization and is also ... subversive ... because it is aiding and abetting the Communist conspiracy." A LUAC counsel described SCEF as a "big holding company" in the communist drive into civil rights organizations in Louisiana. He linked SCEF with demonstrations in numerous Louisiana cities and towns.

At an initial hearing in New Orleans, a local judge dismissed the case because LUAC presented "no evidence" to support their charges of subversion. WDSU-TV and radio roundly criticized LUAC for its "dangerous" techniques and its "shoddy performance." The Louisiana authorities moved to the state courts in their prosecutions. SCEF's lawyers William Kunstler and Arthur Kinoy, both NLG members, moved to the federal courts. On November 12, SCEF's lawyers filed a suit in the Federal District Court that challenged the "constitutionality of the state Subversive Activities and Communist Control law, and requested a three-judge court to issue a declaratory judgment that the state law violated the U.S. Constitution."[90]

In *Dombrowski vs. Pfister*, attorney Arthur Kinoy charged that Louisiana's subversion statutes violated the First Amendment by their breadth, which made them "susceptible of sweeping and improper application." Kinoy also asserted that the arrests were part of a program of harassment aimed at discouraging Smith and Dombrowski "from asserting and attempting to vindicate the constitutional rights of Negro citizens of Louisiana."[91]

Kinoy's and Kunstler's argument was rejected by a three-judge panel composed of E. Gordon West, Frank B. Ellis, and John Minor Wisdom. Wisdom, however, wrote an eloquent dissent of the majority opinion, that provided the basis for Arthur Kinoy's appeal to the U.S. Supreme Court. For Wisdom, the issue was central to the federal constitutional system:

whether the federal courts had a duty "to determine whether a state court proceeding is or is not a disguised effort to maintain the State's unyielding policy of segregation at the expense of the individual citizen's federally guaranteed rights and freedoms."[92]

On January 29, 1964, Dombrowski was indicted by the Orleans Parish Grand Jury on two counts of being a member and officer of SCEF. The grand jury indicted Smith on those two counts, as well as for his membership in the National Lawyers' Guild. Waltzer, Smith's partner, was indicted for his membership in the Guild. In June of 1964, the U.S. Supreme Court agreed to hear Kinoy's appeal in *Dombrowski vs. Pfister*. On April 26, 1965, the Court ruled in favor of the three men.[93]

The SCEF raids and arrests shook New Orleans' civil rights organizations. According to Virginia Collins, "Everybody was up in arms. Cause, we were doing things, too, that the police was on us, too. So the black community had no choice. It had to respond." The Coordinating Council called a meeting and protested the SCEF raid, as did many other black organizations. The Louisiana Civil Liberties Union, the Rabbinical Council of New Orleans, and the First Unitarian Church objected publicly to the state's action.[94]

While black and white liberal groups within the city protested the raids on SCEF, that organization's left-wing reputation was reinforced by the latest round of official red-baiting. SCEF remained an outsider to most civil rights groups within New Orleans, as it did to the national organizations of the NAACP and CORE. Local activists found the "communist" smear simply too controversial to contest. James Dombrowski was admired by a number of black leaders; he was considered "ahead of his time," by Albert Dent, who had not wanted to be associated with him publicly on the issue of library integration. Lolis Elie believed that Dombrowski represented the "very best of white people"—but also noted that "he was so far ahead of anybody else" that the "liberal white community—because of his Marxist views—didn't want to get near him."[95] For somewhat similar reasons, Elie, Jack Nelson, and Leonard Burns kept a respectful distance from SCEF treasurer and NLG lawyer Ben Smith. All concluded that the "communist" image was something that the local civil rights movement did not need. To Rosa Keller, even the ACLU, which was led by Ben Smith and Albert D'Orlando in the 1960s, was "a little shrill" for New Orleans. Thus, the SCEF raids confirmed the lingering power of McCarthyism in the changing South. They reinforced SCEF's outsider status by directing the state's police power and force to a small interracial or-ganization that combined militant integrationism and leftist politics. The object of the raids was not so much SCEF's operations in New Orleans, but in the larger struggle—particularly, in the organization's activities with the NLG and with the planned defense of SNCC's Freedom Summer participants.[96]

The national CORE responded to the legal assistance program of the NLG by launching a lawyers' organization of its own. In 1964, the Lawyers' Constitutional Defense Committee (LCDC) was organized by CORE counsel Carl Rachlin and representatives of the ACLU and the American Jewish Congress. The impetus for the LCDC had originally come from the offices of Collins, Douglas, and Elie—the three were simply swamped with the task of representing the numerous clients involved in civil rights actions throughout Louisiana and even in Mississippi. Very few black law-yers practiced in these states, and white Southern lawyers were notoriously unwilling to handle civil rights cases. Hence, the NLG program, first launched in 1962, filled a desperate need. But Rachlin and his colleagues in the ACLU and American Jewish Congress had another agenda: by re-cruiting lawyers to represent black plaintiffs, they would prevent the NLG from being the major legal organization to defend civil rights activists in the South. Rachlin's attitude reflected a long-standing suspicion of SCEF and the NLG as "communist" organizations within the civil rights move-ment.[97]

New Orleans' political leadership resorted to an almost passive resist-ance to black demands, a resistance characterized by foot-dragging recal-citrance rather than violence. Mayor Victor Hugo Schiro's responses to black protest in 1963 had reflected city officials' attitude toward a black voting constituency kept deliberately small by periodic voter purges. He had won his election of 1961 with mild race-baiting, but altered his stance dramatically by 1965, when he appealed to black leaders for their support. Schiro changed his official attitude because he recognized the increasing importance of the black vote within New Orleans, and of escalating black pressures to enlarge the size of the black electorate.

In 1963, black leaders asserted that 125,000 potential black voters lived in the city, but only 36,000 were registered to vote. Some 8,000 blacks were eliminated from the registration books in 1963 alone. In 1963 and 1964, the Coordinating Council of Greater New Orleans (CCGNO) staged mas-sive voter registration drives in the city. The results were frustrating in the short run, but provided ample evidence for federal intervention in the wake of the Voting Rights Act of 1965.[98]

According to Daniel Thompson, a sociologist at Dillard University who organized the Coordinating Council, the black leadership "tried to convince the population that you could have 80,000 to 100,000 black voters, and *nobody believed it*." Since successful registration depended upon filling out a complicated form that included a "citizenship" test, the Coordinating Council established voter education schools in offices donated by the longshoreman's union. After schooling the applicants in voting qualifications, the Council sent busloads of prospective voters to the parish registrar. "We knew that out of forty people, no more than *two* would ever be registered, and sometimes none," said Thompson. Blacks were variously rejected for insufficient identification, for "mistakes" in filling out the registration cards, and for numerous other reasons. "We were not getting anywhere."

The Coordinating Council was working closely with the Commission on Civil Rights in Washington, D.C., whose representatives watched the voter examinations "very closely," documenting the irregularities in the procedures. The Council sent matched pairs of voters to register, each prepared to give the same answers to the questions asked by the registrar. Invariably, the whites were able to register, the blacks were denied. "Then they had a hearing in New Orleans on voter discrimination. There were fifteen proven cases, and five came from our group."[99] In October 1963, the U.S. Justice Department filed suit against the state of Louisiana, requesting that a federal court forbid the state from using its voter registration forms as a "test to discriminate against Negroes." The suit charged that registrars throughout the state used the application form as a qualification test, with the aim of maintaining white supremacy by eliminating black registrants.

Virginia Collins was working as the "activator" and assistant director for the Coordinating Council in 1963 and 1964. In the summer of 1963, she helped organize the Council's "Youth Voter Crusader Corps" of 300 high school and college students to conduct door-to-door canvassing in wards throughout the city. As a result of the students' work, more than 1,000 blacks attempted to register to vote by October of 1963. Less than 350 people were able to register; black high school and college graduates were repeatedly rejected. In response to these tactics, the students and the leaders of the CCGNO picketed the Municipal Auditorium, the office of the registrar of voters, and City Hall. Collins was arrested several times in these protests.[100]

Collins then hoped the black vote would cure "some of the ills" of the black community, but "didn't have no illusions about class, that some people would have, and some people wouldn't."[101]

In December of 1963, Collins described the frustrations of the voter registration campaign. After months of canvassing by the student volunteers, 500 fewer blacks were registered in December than in March of 1963. "In that time we tried to register around 3,000 people, and succeeded in registering 1,000, mostly after five to eight tries—one schoolteacher had to go back eighteen times. But more than that were dropped from the books, mainly people who'd moved." Collins believed that a quota of black voters existed: "just enough are let in to replace people who've dropped." And the registrar had the discretion to permit or prohibit voters from taking the test, and then to decide whether the applicant had passed it. Collins admitted that she was sometimes discouraged by the seemingly endless efforts that resulted in minor changes, as she and other black activists waited for federal suits to strike down the procedures that allowed state officials to limit the size of the black vote.[102]

The numbers of black voters stayed frustratingly low until 1965. By August 29 of that year, 1,000 new black voters had been added to the rolls of Orleans Parish after the President Lyndon Johnson signed the Voting Rights Act into law. Simultaneously, the IMA and four other black organizations asked the Justice Department to send federal registrars into the Parish to stop the "foot-dragging" of the registrar of voters. The Consumers' League, the United Voters' League, and the New Orleans branch of the NAACP also requested federal registrars. The black organizations protested the continued "scrubbing" of black voters from the registration lists, and planned mass rallies to boost registration.[103]

The passage of the Voting Rights Act transformed electoral politics in New Orleans. By 1966, 66,000 black voters had registered, nearly doubling the black vote totals of 1961. By 1965, these voters had made their presence felt in municipal elections: Victor Schiro, a vaguely segregationist mayor in his first term, actively courted the black vote in 1965. Running against a conservative opponent backed by lower-middle-class whites who traditionally followed a segregationist political appeal, Schiro needed the black vote. His covert appeals to black leaders, including black ministers, netted him more than 30 percent of the black vote. He was re-elected by a very thin margin.[104]

In the wake of the Voting Rights Act, black civil rights leaders made active efforts to form new black political organizations, and to run candidates for office. Collins, Douglas, and Elie organized the Southern Organization for United Leadership (SOUL) in 1965, which soon became the dominant black political organization in New Orleans. SOUL was based on the black homeowners and middle-income and lower-middle class blacks of the Lower Ninth Ward. In 1969, Collins led a group of black professionals to organize the Community Organization for Urban Politics (COUP), based in the Seventh Ward, traditionally the home of Catholic Creoles. Both SOUL and COUP actively ran candidates in the middle- and late 1960s, and were instrumental in producing the black vote for the 1970 election of Moon Landrieu as the mayor of New Orleans.[105]

For Robert Collins, these victories were logical goals of the civil rights movement. "Its all about the same thing," he said. "Getting your just desserts. Justice could not just be obtained through demonstrations. It had to be obtained through the intelligent use of political power, obtaining power and using it wisely." Collins benefited from the changes he had helped inaugurate: between 1969 and 1972, he was appointed judge-ad-hoc of the Traffic Court of New Orleans to fill temporary vacancies. In 1972, he was appointed magistrate-judge of the Criminal District Court by Louisiana governor Edwin Edwards. While serving an eight-year term as magistrate-judge, Collins was nominated by President Jimmy Carter to the position of U.S. district judge of the Eastern District of Louisiana. In 1978, this nomination was confirmed by the Senate, making Collins the first black federal judge in the South.[106]

As a state legislator and city councilman, Moon Landrieu had cultivated black support. "Once that session of the legislature ended," he said, referring to the months of the school crisis, "there was nothing I could ever do. First of all, I was pleased with who I was, and the more angry that some whites became with me, and the more blacks showered me with appreciation, the harder I tried." Landrieu had attempted to simplify the state's voter registration form, and lobbied to desegregate Audubon Park. These actions marked him. In 1962, he was defeated in his first election attempt for a seat on New Orleans' city council, on what he thought was a "purely racial" vote. By his inauguration in 1970,

I got to be known as "Moon the Coon." That was a common reference term.

That's a badge of honor I wear with pride. People call you "nigger-lover," and I'd say, "You right, I am. I flat am, without any shame or apologies." But you don't get there overnight. Those kind of epithets in a Southern society will rock you the first time you hear them.[107]

During his two terms as mayor, Landrieu deliberately brought blacks into the political system. He increased the percentage of blacks serving in city government from 10 percent to 40 percent. Blacks and whites believed that he had rewarded blacks for their support by giving the control of the community action and model cities program of the War on Poverty to black political organizations. His success set the stage for the developments of the late 1970s and 1980s—the dominance of black political organizations and their candidates in city politics. Locally, this resulted in the election of Dutch Morial as mayor in 1978, the election of Revius O. Ortique to a judgeship in 1979, and Robert Collins' appointment to the federal judiciary in 1978.[108]

By 1966, New Orleans' black leadership had won the civil rights guaranteed by the Civil Rights Act of 1964 and the Voting Rights Act of 1965. They had conducted protests, litigations, and negotiations with the city's white elite, stressing the threat of protest to the city's tourist revenues and economic well-being. As in the 1950s, strategic white elites acted as allies of the black movement, and facilitated the transition to a desegregated community. These elites included white liberals like Rosa Keller and J. Skelly Wright, and business moderates like Harry B. Kelleher and Harry McCall. The reasons for their interracial activism varied widely, from economic pragmatism to a committed integrationist perspective. The black community was able to effectively use these elites to obtain its goals.

In the process of these negotiations, a new black leadership emerged. These men had political ambitions, and eventually acquired political influence and power. They were the young professionals of the black community in 1960—men like Robert Collins, Dutch Morial, Norman Francis, and Leonard Burns. In the 1970s and 1980s, they would join ministers like the Reverend A. L. Davis and Avery Alexander in acquiring political positions in the city, as New Orleans' population, and its voters, became increasingly black. But they had been pushed to positions of leadership, and, ultimately, to political power, by forces that they could only marginally control. They had become racial negotiators due to the explosive potential of racial protest—particularly, the protest ignited by young blacks who, in 1960, launched the black student movement throughout the South.

FIVE

"Terror and Solidarity":
The Protest Generation, 1960–1965

*T*HEY came of age in the shadow of *Brown* and the Montgomery Bus Boycott. By 1960, when they were in their late teens and early twenties, the members of New Orleans' protest generation were ready to act. Several had joined the Dryades Street protests, and were anxious to launch an assault on segregation throughout the city. These leaders—Jerome Smith, Rudy Lombard, and Oretha Castle—were the products of ambitious, highly supportive working-class black families, the first generation to attend college, and the first to engage in active protests. But these three, and their activist colleagues, also had stringent parental models of dignity and resistance who supported their attack on the segregated system.

The blacks who made up the nucleus of New Orleans' CORE chapter were young intellectuals. They were drawn to CORE's emphasis on direct action, and to its philosophy, which mixed pacifism with moral absolutism in the cause of social change. Their years in CORE tested the non-violence that all initially accepted as a tactic and goal, and also tested their own beliefs in democracy and in the political process.

Within New Orleans, CORE was a catalyst for change. Demonstrations and sit-ins disrupted business on Canal Street in 1960 and 1961. Continued demonstrations—and the threats of further direct action—propelled much of the Citizens' Committee's success between 1962 and 1964. After 1965, many CORE members worked in War on Poverty projects as community organizers and project staff members. Inspired by the cultural nationalism of the black protest movement in the mid-1960s, they focused increased energy on cultural affairs in the black community from the late 1960s through the 1980s.

But it is as leaders of the black movement in Mississippi and outstate Louisiana that New Orleans' CORE leaders found their most fruitful and painful political testing. The lessons that they learned in the dangerous small communities of the rural South awakened them to the conditions of oppression that existed in a continuum of black poverty and desperation in New Orleans, and beyond. These lessons—which mixed a respect for indigenous black culture with a profound skepticism about the possibilities of meaningful political change—made their returns to New Orleans bittersweet. In the 1970s and 1980s, the "CORE family" of the 1960s would be an ongoing cultural force in New Orleans, but one that largely renounced the political leadership in which they had been so intensely trained.

Jerome Smith was born in the late 1930s in New Orleans, the son of a merchant seaman who was "talented with his hands," a man who fought and defeated anyone who challenged him. His father taught Jerome to "protect the house" in his absences, and to demand courtesy for his mother from any whites who came to the door. Jerome Smith's mother was his "great strength": she read poetry to her children every night, and told her son about her hero, Paul Robeson, and about Mary McLeod Bethune. As a child, Jerome Smith was impressed by the Labor Day parades in New Orleans. His grandfather was a longshoreman, and

I can remember as a baby, at least at age 3 or 4, they had all these men with these huge hands. I would stand with my grandfather, I could see all these big hands, these strong men, all these hands run up and they would grab me. I always felt big when I left them.[1]

Smith was also inspired by the example of the Mardi Gras Indians, the black krewes that sewed elaborate costumes and "masked" and marched both at Mardi Gras and on St. Joseph's Day to honor the patron saint of labor. Smith felt that the traditional Mardi Gras of New Orleans was a poor shadow of the Indians' celebrations in the black neighborhoods: "I never saw Rex [the white elite krewe] on Mardi Gras," Smith said. "We always seen Rex as nuthin'. We always felt that, one, they wasn't equal to us, and, two, none of the costumes would be as pretty as what we could do." He learned this kind of pride from Toudy Montana, the king of a black krewe or tribe. Smith started sewing costumes as a young boy, and remembered that

Toudy Montana unconsciously made statements about black power . . . the whole thing about excellence, about uniqueness, about creativity, about protecting your creativity—I learned that in those houses [of the Indians].

Police would try to run the Indians off the street, but we had a thing. You don't bow, you don't run from 'em, not black or white or grizzly grey.[2]

Smith's rebellion against segregation started early. Imitating his father, he tossed a race screen from a street car at age 11. Around the age of 16, he decided that he would never enter the military. From talking to uncles who had served in the armed forces, he determined that the military was "just another form of slavery." Later, while a freshman at Southern University at Baton Rouge, he read about the struggles in Africa. When student demonstrations broke out at Southern in the spring of 1960, Jerome Smith joined them. He then dropped out of school in order to devote himself to the movement, and returned to New Orleans, where he worked as a longshoreman, and did "free-lance" work as an activist, picketing for the Consumers' League boycott of Dryades Street. While working on the waterfront, Smith dreamed of integrating the black and white longshoremen's unions, and making Local 1419 an autonomous and controlling force on the docks. "But I didn't stay there long enough to see that because I was bitten by this other bug, and I guess my generation had to move to that drummer," he said in 1988. "But it started at my Mama's. It was formalized at Southern University. I heard at Southern, that there were people meeting, talking about doing some things locally, and it just so happened that I went to one of those meetings on Dryades Street, and that was my initial involvement with CORE."[3] He met Rudy Lombard, the student body president at Xavier University, on a picket line. He knew Oretha Castle, a young woman who also picketed for the Consumers' League, from high school.

Oretha Castle was born in 1940, and her sister Doris Jean in 1942. They spent early years in Oakland, Tennessee, where their grandparents on both sides were farmers. One set of grandparents were independent landowners;

the others were sharecroppers. Doris Jean recalled that both grandmothers gave the Castle children pointed advice about dignity and self-worth. She remembered her sharecropper grandmother

saying things different things like, "Don't ever bow to anybody when you feel you're right, or you know you're right." Or she would say things like, "I would rather pick with the chickens than be beholden to somebody." Which I didn't understand then, was a great way of expressing what her dignity was all about to her. . . . Whatever pickin with the chickens meant, I come to realize, had to do with going hungry or doing without before you bow or beg or whatever to anybody.[4]

John and Virgie Castle, the girls' parents, moved to New Orleans in 1947. Both worked full-time, and raised their children to be close and "fiercely independent." Oretha and Doris Jean were expected to excell in school, and to be goal-directed. They saw their parents accomplish important goals like property and home ownership. Eventually, both grandmothers came to live with the Castles in their double-shotgun house at 917 North Tonti Street.

Oretha Castle was a student at Southern University of New Orleans in 1960, and worked at the Hotel Dieu Hospital. She was drawn to the Dryades Street boycotts and to direct action from her sense of what was happening in the rest of the country, and the growing consciousness and awareness of young people. Out of the Dryades Street actions, "several young people" came together in 1960. "We had some very definitive ideas about the kinds of activities we felt should be engaged in here in New Orleans—to attack, you know, the problems as we perceived and understood them at that time," she said in 1978.[5] Most of the students were NAACP members at this time, and they talked to the local branch about the possibilities of undertaking a direct-action campaign. "Of course, they felt this was real kind of militant and radical action—to be talking about sitting in and all that kind of stuff. And they really didn't want to have any of it." Independently, Oretha Castle, Jerome Smith, Cecil Carter, Joyce Taylor, and Rudy Lombard decided to organize themselves into a group. According to Castle, Lombard was "the leader—the person who was really instrumental in pulling us together."[6]

Doris Jean Castle was pulled into protest by "following my big sister, following Oretha." Following her graduation from high school, the Castles gave Doris Jean a trip to Chicago as a present. While in Chicago, Doris Jean learned from her mother that Oretha had gone to jail for carrying a picket sign. When she returned to New Orleans, she accompanied Oretha to a Consumers' League meeting, where she met James T. McCain and other members of the Congress of Racial Equality (CORE). "People were talking about—we were going to start a CORE chapter," said Doris Jean. "These people came in and out several times a week. It was really about organizing demonstrations. I wasn't really into it like Oretha was. I guess I developed a role myself, and I developed that role in relationship to her." She saw herself as an "enabler" for her commanding older sister.[7]

Rudy Lombard was born in 1939, in Algiers, a community across the river from New Orleans. His father worked as a hospital orderly, his mother as a domestic. He became aware of segregation early. When Lombard was very young, his mother took him with her to work at a fashionable uptown residence. "She worked in the main house, and I lived in the slave quarters, the servant quarters. And I was not allowed to go into the house. So, as far back as I can remember, one would *know* that," he recalled. Rudy Lombard believed that he modeled himself after his father, "a very defiant person, very aggressive. He thought it was important for us to see ourselves as good as anyone else, that we shouldn't tolerate abuse of any kind, and he was forever mocking the system of segregation." He watched his father fight a white man who had almost run into his mother with a car. As an old man, the elder Lombard "had a fist fight with a sheriff in Jefferson Parish who was notorious for having killed other blacks." Lombard's first demonstration occurred in elementary school: he tossed a ball into a whites-only playground, and invited his friends to join him there. After the recess was over, the neighbors "called the police, and there was a big hoobrah of sorts." When Lombard returned home, his father rewarded him with a case of Barq's Root Beer—"a very favored drink then."[8]

Lombard spent a year at the University of Michigan after high school, then returned to New Orleans to attend Xavier University. While at Xavier, he worked as a longshoreman, hoping to eventually make a career in union leadership. He wanted to use the union as a political base "to develop other resources in the community." But, he said, the movement came, and his own "ambitions got bigger. I wanted to turn the whole country upside down." When Lombard met Marvin Robinson and James McCain in 1960, he was immediately interested in organizing a group to attack segregation in the city. He felt that his frustration—and hopes—were shared by the other black students who had participated in the Dryades Street boycotts:

We thought people were well-intentioned and basically good willed, and if they

Illustrations

1. Doris Jean Castle, a member of CORE, is removed from City Hall in a 1963 demonstration after refusing to leave the council chamber. Courtesy *New Orleans Times-Picayune.*

AN ANGRY WOMAN was restrained by police after she shoved Mrs. James Gabrielle against this tree behind the school zone sign Wednesday afternoon as the latter was walking her daughter, Yolanda, home from the integrated Wil- liam Frantz Elementary school. A group of men and women followed Mrs. Gabrielle from the school to her home, al- though she was accompanied by police. —Photo by Vernon Guidry, Times-Picayune Staff Photographer.

2. An angry white woman is restrained by police after confronting Daisy Gabrielle, a white mother who was accompanying her child home from the integrated William Frantz Elementary School, and shoving her against a tree. Courtesy *New Orleans Times-Picayune.*

—Photo by The Times-Picayune.

THE TARGET of jeering remarks of these irate women at Frantz Elementary school Thursday is Sydney Goldfinch, a Tulane university student who recently led a group of Negro sit-ins at a New Orleans lunch counter. Goldfinch, who was kicked by one of the women before departing the scene at request of police, said, "I didn't think they'd recognize me."

3. Sydney Goldfinch, a Tulane University student, sit-in leader, and CORE member, is jeered by irate anti-integration demonstrators at Frantz Elementary School. Goldfinch, who was kicked by one of the women before departing the scene at the request of police, was quoted as saying, "I didn't think they'd recognize me." Courtesy *New Orleans Times-Picayune*.

4. Judge J. Skelly Wright is hanged in effigy during 1960–1961 school crisis. Courtesy *New Orleans Times-Picayune.*

5. Judge J. Skelly Wright, 1981. Courtesy *New Orleans Times-Picayune.*

6. Dutch Morial, celebrating his 1978 mayoral election victory. Courtesy
Amistad Research Center, Tulane University.

7. Albert W. Dent, president of Dillard University, 1941–1969, circa 1936. Courtesy Amistad Research Center, Tulane University.

8. CORE member and Freedom Rider Jerome Smith, 1961. Courtesy Amistad Research Center, Tulane University.

9. John P. Nelson, Jr., during the Tulane proceedings. Courtesy Tulane University Archives.

10. Matt Suarez during Mississippi Freedom Summer, 1964. Courtesy
Matt Suarez.

11. Rosa Freeman Keller, Urban League and Save Our Schools member, circa 1970. Courtesy Amistad Research Center, Tulane University.

12. Tom Dent, during his days at Morehouse, circa 1951. Courtesy Tulane University, Amistad Research Center, New Orleans.

13. Tom Dent, writer, playwright, poet, 1991. Courtesy *New Orleans Times-Picayune.*

14. The Reverend A. L. Davis, protest leader of the 1950s and 1960s, circa 1970s. Courtesy Amistad Research Center, Tulane University.

15. Moon Landrieu, mayor of New Orleans, 1970–1978, 1970s. Courtesy Amistad Research Center, Tulane University.

16. Richard Haley, field secretary for CORE, 1960s, circa 1970s. Courtesy Amistad Research Center, Tulane University.

17. Richard Haley, 1980s.

18. Leonard Burns, Urban League member and NAACP leader, 1970s.
Courtesy Amistad Research Center, Tulane University.

19. Judge Revius O. Ortique, Urban League and Citizens' Committee member, circa 1977. Courtesy Amistad Research Center, Tulane University.

20. Mrs. Leontine Goins Luke, NAACP and Ninth Ward Civic and Improvement League member, circa 1977. Courtesy Amistad Research Center, Tulane University.

21. Oretha Castle Haley, CORE leader, who was active in New Orleans from 1960 to 1964, 1980s.

22. Dr. Rudy Lombard, national vice president of CORE in 1963 and a regional CORE leader, in New Orleans, 1986. Courtesy Matt Suarez.

23. Lolis Elie, standing next to a statue of a Maroon, a fugitive Negro slave who refused to be enslaved by the French in the Caribbean, 1984. Courtesy *New Orleans Times-Picayune*.

were confronted under pressure, they would change—and not only under pressure; they had some righteous qualities about them. . . . We wanted to be sure that they were not misunderstanding our feelings about what was happening to us. We knew that there were some people who would rather *die* than change.

Underlying all of this was the feeling that we'd been abused, and didn't like it. And we wanted to change it right then and there—for all time.[9]

Yet Lombard knew that attacking segregation was dangerous. "You grow up knowing that whites did not value black peoples' lives," he said.

You know that blacks are killed for little or nothing, that the police might do it, or some mob might do it, and you would always hear about these things locally. Some blacks being abused or murdered or hanged, whatever. Locally. I remember when the first sit-ins started, I kept saying to myself, 'that's never gonna happen here. Because the police are too *mean*. They would kill somebody if they tried to. Or they would do them some kind of serious physical harm.' Well, you grow up with that, you know that the way the segregated system was perpetuated was that whites would not hesitate to do any act of ultimate violence to a black person. . . . You hear about Emmett Till, the Klan, and so forth—that happens to blacks everywhere. And that was the climate. And rather than this being the exception, you understood the *meanness* of the system, and the meanness of the spirit of the people who had an interest in keeping it the way it was. Or thought they did.[10]

By the summer of 1960, black students and several whites who had joined in the Consumers' League picket lines formed a CORE chapter in New Orleans. Most of the blacks attended Southern University of New Orleans, and came from working-class families. Very few black students from Dillard and Xavier Universities joined the protests. Oretha Castle believed that the black students' class backgrounds gave them "black concepts of values and class"—which made them very different from most of the white intellectuals from Tulane and LSU-New Orleans, who came to civil rights as part of an emerging leftist consciousness. Many of the black students in CORE were religious, and believed in CORE's philosophy of interracialism, non-violence, and redemptive love.[11]

Matt Suarez became involved with the CORE chapter in 1961, when he returned from his service in the U.S. Navy. Born in 1938, Suarez had grown up in the Seventh Ward, the child of a light-skinned Creole father and a dark-skinned mother. Many of his father's relatives passed for white, and found it "unforgivable" for a family member to marry a dark black. As a child, Suarez felt pulled in two directions by his family: he identified with his mother's family, but also felt the influence of the distinctive Creole value system:

The Creoles had a philosophy, which was that they were above all that. . . . It didn't matter what the white folks did, or it didn't matter what the black folks did; they had their own thing. And they were superior to all of 'em. But you had to treat 'em differently. With the whites, you had to outthink them and outslick 'em, and with the blacks, you could just order 'em around.

Suarez grew up in an integrated neighborhood, in the heavily Creole Seventh Ward. He had a classic first experience of racism and segregation. During a ball game played by both white and black boys in his neighborhood, "one of the little white guys got called in by his mother, and I asked why he couldn't finish the game, and he had to go to a birthday party that only the little white kids were invited to. Now, we all played every day, but none of the black kids were invited to the party. And that sticks in my mind very vividly. It was one of the things that really slapped it up in my face and made me know that there was definitely a difference and that we weren't quite as good as other folk, right?" His childhood rebellions against segregation took the form of sabotage: sitting with his friends in the balcony of the Orpheum Theater, letting juice from meatball sandwiches drip onto the whites below, or spraying Cokes above the white crowd.

These rebellions occurred, despite the options open to light-skinned Creoles like Suarez, who could pass for white if they chose. An uncle who worked as a furniture repairman for a department store routinely passed for white. When he married, he discovered that his wife had also been passing—neither had known that the other was black. When the Catholic schools began to conduct integrated sports competition in New Orleans, "they had my two first cousins playing against each other. One was white, one was black, right? And they were playing against each other."

Within his family, Suarez differed from his grandfather and father. His grandfather was a hunter and fisherman, a pharmacist who "spent every waking moment of his [spare] time in the woods." His father, who worked as a veterinarian's assistant, was a "sports fanatic" who played baseball and bowled several nights a week. Suarez, however, considered himself "a strict mind person, political animal." From his earliest memories, his chief interests were business and politics. "As a teenager, the fellows used to play baseball. Afterwards, you could always find me sitting—either sitting with a bunch of girls on the steps, or sitting with a bunch of old people who were telling me what was going on."

As a teenager, Suarez experienced the conflict between the two cultures when his light-skinned friends urged him to go with them, and pass for white as they went to French Quarter bars and clubs—places darker-skinned blacks couldn't enter. Suarez usually stayed with his darker friends, but felt the pressure of the Creole value system in other parts of his life. "Creoles believed in being self-employed, being in business for themselves, and making lots of money. They always figured to be boss. And they always chose their own paths." Accordingly, Suarez planned to make money, prosper, and succeed as this kind of independent, self-starting individual. He joined the U.S. Navy after high school, and his tour was stormy: Suarez was repeatedly busted for insubordination. He never believed in non-violence.[12]

Yet, he returned to New Orleans after his discharge from the service because he was curious about the Freedom Rides, and the emerging Southern student movement. "At first, I thought that they were assholes, a bunch of crazy niggers," he said. "But something about it aroused my curiosity. I came back to find out what this civil rights movement, what these freedom rides, was about." Initially, he was drawn to the CORE chapter by its "fine-lookin' women." But after he met Oretha Castle, and he became fascinated by her arguments for a more "humanitarian" approach to life and to political questions. The two argued for more than a year. During this time, Suarez began doing volunteer work for the CORE chapter—making picket signs, bringing food to the members at meetings—although he would not join in any direct action or demonstrations.

At one protest march, Suarez made a critical choice. CORE had planned to make a massive march downtown, where Suarez would meet the marchers, and distribute picket signs that he had made on the previous evening. After police arrested the marchers, Suarez and one white CORE member found themselves alone on Canal Street. Suarez knew that it was important to keep the picket line going—day after day, CORE members had maintained the line for eight months. Reluctantly, Suarez and the white student each took a side of Canal Street. Suarez warily began his task:

I was walkin' with that picket sign, and I said, "If one of these motherfuckers tells me somethin, I'm gonna wrap this sign around his fuckin' *head*." And really, that's how I got involved. I was walkin the line, and there were about five white boys standing up, and I looked at 'em, and they looked country, and *hard*, and ready to wear my ass out, right? And I'm walkin with this sign, and I'm walkin, and I'm saying, "If any one of these motherfuckers come tell me anything, just one of 'em, we gonna get it on out here, right?" And son of a guns comes over, they says, "Excuse me," and they got this heavy accent. They want to talk to me about the civil rights movement in this country. They were from Sweden. And they were supportive of what I was doing. And that made me feel better. Then this old white woman comes up—"I'll never shop in McCrory's again." After that, I just got heavily involved in everything with the CORE chapter.[13]

Although he was not a chronological member of New Orleans' protest generation, Richard Haley became a member of that political generation through his involvement in CORE. Haley was born around 1925 in Ohio, and educated there. His father was a barber and a staunch Republican Party member. In 1960, Haley was a music instructor at Florida A & M University (FAMU) in Tallahassee, and an unlikely candidate for activism. He was a deliberate, soft-spoken man, careful and precise in his diction.[14]

"I'm not really an activist," said Haley in 1979, referring to his temperament. "I'm one of those people I don't have a great deal of respect for. I think they are 'living room liberals'—people who sit and talk about human relations, who have opinions, and who feel strongly about their prescriptions, *but* they tend to limit their actions." As a member of a bi-racial group of academics and professionals in Tallahassee, Haley was familiar with such conversations. "Living room liberals are people who looked at the situation and said, 'There's really nothing I can do about it.' And that's the position I was in at FAMU." But in 1959, CORE field secretary James T. McCain appeared in Tallahassee at the behest of two FAMU students who had attended a CORE workshop in Miami during the previous summer. The students were anxious to conduct a direct action campaign to desegregate Tallahassee. An interracial CORE chapter was soon active, and mounting a campaign to erase segregation in public accommodations in the city.[15]

In 1979, Haley recalled that the students' philosophy clashed with the attitudes held by the members of the bi-racial committee. "It wasn't that the [adults] were trying to do something and not having success, but that what they were trying to *do* had next to no bearing on the problem. They were trying to, really, *talk* problems away." When the sit-ins came in 1960, many of Haley's colleagues on the committee felt that the students were pushing too hard, moving too fast, and that their confrontational tactics would make race relations worse—would provoke a violent white response. In this climate, the students in CORE asked Haley if they could use his office and classroom for a meeting. By February of 1960, CORE was "really established on campus," and organizing sit-ins and protests in downtown Tallahassee. These climaxed in March, with arrests at Woolworth's and

McCrory's dime stores, and a jail-in at the county jail. Haley's involvement with the students grew; he became one of four adults in the community whom they trusted. For this involvement, FAMU terminated Haley's teaching contract. By the fall of 1960, he was a field secretary for CORE.[16]

Haley decided to back the students, and to risk his job, for several reasons. "At the time, I was living alone," he said. "I had a little car that was paid for. I had no children. My wife was employed and self-supporting in Chicago. I was in an ideal position to risk—whatever—because of—whatever." Many of his colleagues were not in his position: they had children, homes, and roots in Tallahassee and in Florida. "But I had no roots there," he said.[17] Haley also believed in CORE's goals and its strategy. In a conversation with writer James Baldwin in 1960, he described the assumptions of CORE partisans:

"What we're trying to do," he tells me, "is to sting [the whites'] consciences a little. They don't want to think about it. Well, we must make them think about it.

"When they come home from work," Haley continues, "and turn on the TV sets and there *you* are—" he means *you* the Negro—"on the way to jail again, and they know, at the bottom of their hearts, that it's not because you've done anything wrong—something happens to them, something's got to happen to them. They're human beings, too, you know . . ."[18]

The euphoria of direct action, of changing hearts and minds through redemptive suffering, captured the imaginations of many of Haley's colleagues in CORE. "In the beginning, we snapped our fingers at social change through legality," he recalled. "For a time, we even decried the emphasis on voter registration." At the time of the sit-ins, CORE believed that it effectively attacked the conscience of the country through direct action demonstrations—and that moderate whites would find their beliefs and attitudes changed by witnessing the undeserved suffering of the young actionists. "We very willingly gave over the operation of the legal side to the NAACP."[19]

So Richard Haley began his involvement with CORE. He felt that his role was "more symbolic than anything else" within the organization. "I was not young, past 40," he recalled. "I was not a firebrand. In fact, I was a queer kind of bird, who appeared to be more conservative than progressive. I was the only one of this kind in CORE." He was, in fact, a mild-tempered and reflective man who remained "apolitical" within the factional disputes of the organization over the next five years.[20]

Another third-generation leader, Tom Dent, was born in 1932. The oldest son of Albert and Jessie Dent, he grew up in the shadow of his father's expectations. Albert Dent registered Tom for Morehouse at birth. Tom remembered his father as a powerful man who relished the deference that his position at Dillard brought, a man who expected a similar deference at home—although Jessie Dent defused her husband's pretensions with humor. According to Tom Dent, his mother's "very appropriate nickname" for his father, "which was given with a lot of affection, but also hit the target, was 'Big Shot.' . . .'Big Shot, go get my hat!' He loved it!" The family made little rituals of Dr. Dent's likes and dislikes—his cigarettes, his milk shakes—"having him play boss, having him sit at the head of the table," said Tom Dent in 1987.[21]

As a small child, Tom was largely raised by his father's mother, "Gran," while his mother finished her music degrees at Oberlin. Albert Dent had brought his mother from Atlanta to look after his first son, freeing her from her work as a live-in maid. Albert Dent had purchased a house in Atlanta for his mother when her friends, and his foster parents, the Thomases, had died, and Tom's Gran traveled back and forth between New Orleans and Atlanta during her grandson's childhood.

Tom Dent felt tremendous affection for and allegiance to his paternal grandmother. "Gran was poor, but intelligent, and could read, even though she never went to school. She read the paper every day. If you wanted to know what was in the paper, you didn't have to read, just ask her." When Tom was a student at Morehouse, he tried to correct his grandmother's grammar: " 'Gran, you don't say 'ain't'; you don't say 'doozent,'—you know? She'd say, 'Listen, child, Gran never went to school.' . . . Yet, I realized, as you can only know instinctively, that this was a very, very intelligent woman, and that my father's intelligence came from *her*. She was just *bright*, and alert, mentally, and perceptive. But that had been suppressed, and there was no way of seeing it developed." Throughout his life, he would feel "a tremendous emotional attraction to people who do not have an education, but who have sacrificed."

Living in his father's household, Tom Dent became a reading child, tracked toward the best schools and a distinguished career. But he developed between two sets of influences—the musical talents of his mother and public prominence of his father, and the black folk influence of his grandmother—poor, hardworking, sacrificial, in awe of her son's meteoric rise.[22]

Tom Dent attended Gilbert Academy, where he met Andrew Young, Lolis Elie, and Robert Collins. His memories of the city and the academy were polarized into the dichotomies of his early childhood. "Mrs. B," Gilbert's principal, warned her students of the dangers of the "underworld" of South Rampart Street—"the commercial center of the struggling black nation within the city we had all emerged from and were now, attitudinally, being trained to escape from." Gilbert Academy promoted hard work, upward mobility, self-conscious cultural striving—the kind of culture represented by Albert and Jessie Dent, not that of the black clubs, bars, jazz and pool halls. As Mrs. B. instructed her pupils, "Because of the deplorable condition of our race, there is no place for dreamers. Unless they are *purposeful* dreamers. You must work, work, work. Too much dreaming, too much thinking, too many questions, especially too many questions, do not, do not, I remind you, build personal or racial uplift."[23]

Tom Dent was a dreamer, a solitary boy who relished the long ride on the St. Charles streetcar that ran between Carrollton Avenue, past Gilbert Academy, and on to Canal Street. He found the famous streetcar "most favorable to fantasy—it traversed the center of a high-prestige boulevard of sprawling nineteenth-century mansions and spacious lawns, rocking from side to side as it crawled along the track, clanging its bell at intersections, stopping every two blocks for passengers." In the fall and spring, Dent would

throw the shutter-like shellacked brown windows up to enjoy the beauty of the warm air and the relaxed promenade of the avenue, where it seemed no persons of color resided or could ever hope to reside. St. Charles was the street where the mothers of many of my classmates worked: five dollars a day plus roundtrip carfare—14 cents. A magical ride through a forbidden city representing the grand "out thereness" that we might aspire to—the dream world of possibilities Mrs. B. and visiting speakers always aluded to, a world beyond the barriers of FOR COLORED ONLY, beyond Negroidness or Negroid reality.[24]

Tom Dent graduated from Gilbert Academy at 15, too young, his parents thought, to enter Morehouse. They sent him north for a final year at a Quaker school in Poughkeepsie, New York. "It was a severe *jolt* for me," said Dent in 1987. "Never having had any intimate contact with anybody who was not black *at all*, but living in this school that had only three black students and 150 white students, and being in the North. . . . It was a tremendously jarring experience. I literally spent four months before I said anything to anybody." When he had only begun to adjust, he had to leave to enter Morehouse College in Atlanta. That, too, was a shock: he disliked the Baptist culture of black Atlanta, the disdain for the frivolity, the gaiety, and the creativity he had remembered in New Orleans' culture. He felt that a "great fear" permeated black colleges like Morehouse—a fear of black creativity that was not connected with the church. "There was a fear that there would be *anger* if there was a student newspaper or literary journal—because everybody knew that anger was there!" Dent feels that Ralph Ellison's description of the fictionalized Tuskeegee captured the "suppressed" anger of black colleges during the late 1940s and early 1950s. In spite of his dislike for Atlanta, Dent did well in school, acquired mentors, edited the student newspaper, and began to write.

Dent then entered graduate school in international relations at Syracuse University, the logical direction for his degree in political science. His faculty adviser wanted to groom him for an ambassadorship to one of the newly emerging African nations. But he felt unhappy in his work. At the end of four years, he decided to leave. "That was the beginning of my taking control of my life," he said. "I was 24 years old. I had never made a decision like that. It was necessary for me to say, 'Hey, wait a minute, I'm gonna do what I think I should be doing, or at least put myself in the position where I can find out, instead of getting on these trains that other people put me on, and saying, 'Go that way,' you know, 'Just go. Something good'll happen to you.'" He went to New York, working briefly before he was drafted. In 1959, he returned to New York City from the army. He was determined to become a writer.

He worked at a number of jobs in New York: as a reporter for the New York *Age*, as a door-to-door cosmetics salesman, as a social investigator for the Welfare Department, and as public information director for the NAACP Legal Defense Fund between 1961 and 1963. He was consciously searching for other black writers and artists—people he had never known in his school life. He began to know Calvin Hernton and David Henderson, two young black poets, and then became active in poetry readings held at coffeehouses on Manhattan's Lower East Side. A group of black writers coalesced, and called themselves "Umbra"—"from one of Lloyd Addison's strange poems in which he was talking about the 'penumbra and umbra,' and we thought that it was very sophisticated, and very unusual way to say 'black.' So we did call ourselves 'Umbra.' 'The Umbra People' and 'The Umbra Poets' has become one of the legends of the black literary world which won't go away."[25] The Umbra poets became part of a revolt of young black writers who would explore the black experience in avant-garde, experimental styles.

The young people who gravitated toward New Orleans' CORE chapter and toward direct action were part of a worldwide generational youth revolt. The civil rights movement was the well-spring of both the New Left and the women's movement in the United States, and the model for student peace movements in Europe. Both CORE and SNCC had close ties with the black churches and black colleges, and both shared a commitment to non-violent direct action as a strategy to awaken the consciences of individual, and hence, collective white people. They were, as Rudy Lombard said, "young idealists" who believed that they could remake the Southern social system, and eliminate segregation, through the pressure that their moral witness would place on both public authorities and private citizens.[26]

CORE drew students like Lombard, Oretha Castle, and Jerome Smith because it was an "intellectually oriented organization, concerned as much with broad intellectual issues as with racial equality." CORE had been founded in 1942 in Chicago, by James Farmer and a number of students from the University of Chicago. An integrated, white-dominated organization in 1960, CORE was centered in northern cities, supported by middle-class intellectuals who were pacifists, or who had adopted pacifist principles. According to Aldon Morris, "The overriding goal of CORE members was to demonstrate that large social problems could be solved by non-violent means." According to James Farmer, CORE's national director after 1961, the means of non-violent direct action were "perhaps more important in the minds of many of the persons there than the ends being sought . . . it was means, finding some way to use nonviolence to show the world that nonviolence can solve racial problems."[27]

CORE entered the South in 1957, when James T. McCain, a former district school principal from South Carolina, became a CORE field secretary charged with organizing CORE chapters and leading the training of new members in the techniques of non-violent direct action. McCain generated a great deal of respect from the students in CORE: he was an older man, well-educated, and willing to take risks in the cause of social change. In 1979, Lombard recalled that "one of the more endearing" aspects of CORE was its mixture of mature adults and young people. The adults like Haley and McCain provided activists like Lolis Elie and Rudy Lombard with important role models that aided their own growth and transformation.[28]

Like their colleagues in SNCC, people drawn to CORE felt an intense sense of making history, of changing social relationships, of liberating black people. After 1960, New Orleans' CORE members felt themselves connected to an exciting student movement that offered them dramatic risks, visible political victories, and intense intellectual stimulation. In 1962, an estimated 39 percent of all black students in the South took part in the movement's activities; in 1964, the total had risen to 69 percent. According to Doug McAdam, these students were those who were "most integrated" into campus activities and politics—like Lombard, who was student body president at Xavier, and Jerome Smith, who had been a drum major in high school.[29]

New Orleans' student protest was sparked by the protests of early 1960, and by the success of the Consumers' League boycott. CORE members were inspired by the first sit-ins in February of 1960, when four students at North Carolina A & T University sat at a whites-only lunch counter and refused to move until they were served. In the spring of 1960, protests at Southern University in Baton Rouge also inspired New Orleans' activists: Smith was moved to quit school for the struggle, and Rudy Lombard was excited by the example of the Southern students' demonstrations. In April of 1960, SNCC was formed. Although Louisiana would remain a predominantly "CORE state" in the organizational geography of the black student movement, the leaders of New Orleans' CORE came to work closely with SNCC members in Alabama, Mississippi, and in other places.[30]

New Orleans' CORE picketed discriminatory merchants, and conducted direct action demonstrations in late 1960 and 1961. When the national CORE office launched its Freedom Rides to test a Supreme Court decision that banned discrimination in interstate transit in 1961, a number of the local activists—Jerome Smith, David Dennis, Julia Aaron, and Doris Jean Castle—took part in the dangerous journeys through Alabama and Mississippi. Jerome Smith and Doris Jean Castle spent time in Mississippi jails. Later, New Orleans' CORE tested towns in Mississippi and Louisiana with Freedom Rides—and encountered white hostility and violence in these tightly segregated communities.

When the Citizens' Committee's negotiations got under way in 1962, New Orleans' CORE was guided by the Committee's decisions—Oretha Castle, the long time chapter chair, was a leader of the black committee, and Lolis Elie, one of CORE's attorneys, was its chair. Both Castle and Elie were aware that the Committee made progress in New Orleans that proved almost impossible in other communities. Accordingly, the Committee's decisions moderated the the local chapter's activities.

But New Orleans' chapter also suffered from the larger movement's focus on voting rights in Mississippi, and of the statewide program launched by the Council of Federated Organizations (COFO) in 1963 and 1964. After 1962, Jerome Smith and Matt Suarez were on CORE's field staff in Mississippi; Rudy Lombard, though in graduate school at Syracuse, spent his summers working on CORE projects in Plaquemine, and West Feliciana Parish, Louisiana, in 1963, and in Philadelphia, Mississippi, in 1964. George Raymond, Jr., and David Dennis also worked full-time in the Mississippi campaign. Matt Suarez told an interviewer in 1969 that

everything that the civil rights movement had in the South, just about primarily everything came from either New Orleans or Nashville. All of the Nashville people that started the movement went to work for SNCC, all of the New Orleans people went to work for CORE. CORE drained New Orleans of all its current, SNCC drained Nashville, so there wasn't any people left here to keep a movement going.[31]

Richard Haley seconded Suarez in an interview of 1969. The Mississippi campaigns drained New Orleans of many of its ablest leaders. While Oretha Castle was a strong-willed and dynamic CORE chair in the early 1960s, most chapter members who remained after 1962 were primarily workers, rather than leaders. Haley felt that the New Orleans members who became part of CORE's staff in Mississippi "were just young, firey, and they were much more the SNCC-type than the CORE-type."[32] These young leaders—Suarez, Smith, Lombard, Raymond, and Dennis—would have the definitive movement experience of Mississippi. It was an experience that was both liberating and disillusioning.

It was liberating because the movement offered an intense experience of personal growth, strong personal relationships, and a political education. At their best, CORE and SNCC provided intellectual stimulation, a "beloved community," and a sense of personal and collective transformation. But this experience exposed its most dedicated leaders to intense political and personal frustration, as activists and the communities in which they worked continued to be the brunt of white terrorism from the early to mid-1960s. The terrorism, in fact, increased as the movement's successes grew, and as interracial tensions wracked SNCC and CORE. Out of this discordant mixture of experiences, New Orleans' CORE leaders, like some of their colleagues in SNCC, emerged at once transformed and disillusioned. Most lost whatever faith they had possessed in electoral politics as a means of racial change. Many also rejected integration as a solution to the problems of black people. By the mid-1960s, many worked for War on Poverty programs in New Orleans, and supported projects that promoted the distinctive contributions of black culture to the city.[33]

After the massive demonstrations in the spring of 1960, Marvin Robinson, the expelled student body president of Southern University, contacted Rudy Lombard in New Orleans. He talked with Lombard about organizing a CORE chapter. After this meeting, several of the black and white students who had taken part in the Consumers' League picket lines met at the Negro YMCA on Dryades Street. New Orleans' CORE chapter was formed.

By late summer, the group planned a direct action campaign against segregated public accommodations in the city. At this time, other students—Alice, Jean, and Shirley Thompson, and Doratha and Carleen Smith—were attracted to the group. Within the CORE chapter, they began to admire the people who emerged as local and national leaders—Rudy Lombard, Oretha Castle, and Jerome Smith. All were committed to CORE's non-violent ethos, and Jerome Smith led other members of the chapter in fasts, hoping to increase the group's discipline and morale.[34]

In the fall of 1960, the group started its sit-in campaign. On September 9, seven CORE members entered the F. W. Woolworth store at Canal and Rampart and refused to leave until served. Police arrested the five blacks and two whites, who were charged with "criminal mischief." Police held them in jail until nine that night. Black congregations raised bail money, and an ACLU attorney represented the group. The next day, the NAACP Youth Council picketed Woolworth's to express its sympathy with CORE.[35] On Monday, September 12, Mayor deLesseps S. Morrison banned all picketing and sit-ins. The CORE chapter decided to test the legality of the mayor's order with another sit-in.[36] Oretha Castle recalled the reservations that accompanied her decision to participate:

We knew it was going to result in going to jail, and that wasn't just a little easy thing, you know, back at that time to talk about doing. . . . I was working. And I knew I *had* to work. OK? I *knew* that if I was in that sit-in, where I was working, I would no longer be working. Which exactly did happen. I was working at the Hotel Dieu Hospital for the *good Catholic nuns* over there. And I mean, we were arrested. Of course, it was in the newspaper and all that sort of stuff. When I went to work they had my pay check ready for me. The good nuns said, take that pay check and don't ever come back any more.[37]

On Saturday, September 17, CORE chairman Rudy Lombard, Oretha Castle, Dillard student Cecil Carter, and Tulane student Sydney "Lanny" Goldfinch sat down at the lunch counter at the downtown McCrory's and refused to leave until served. They were arrested and charged with "criminal mischief," and eventually released on a $250 bail. But the district attorney charged Goldfinch, who was white, with "criminal anarchy," which carried a bond of $2,500 and a maximum prison sentence of ten years.[38] The group was represented by Collins, Douglas, and Elie, and by John P. Nelson, Jr. Nelson won a favorable decision from the U.S. Supreme Court in 1963; he argued *Lombard vs. Louisiana* as one of the seven sit-in cases.

Though a small contingent within New Orleans, CORE's morale was high, even though New Orleans' class-divided and culturally fragmented black community was difficult to organize. In statements to the press, CORE leaders expressed their sense of hope and possibility. After the sit-in of 1960, Rudy Lombard remained in jail for several days. From jail, he announced that "We, the members of CORE are willing to make any sacrifice [to gain] the support of the community. If we cannot secure your backing, then we must carry on this struggle alone."[39] At a mass meeting, he admonished the black community to "Be not discouraged by the threat of jail, or by the criticism of those who oppose equality. . . . Fight against the smugness of our community." He stated that "No man can imprison the desire to be free. I speak with confidence when I say, not even the threat of death shall silence the cry of the Negro for liberation from the imprisonment of segregation."[40] The CORE members were deeply immersed in Gandhian philosophy, and spent hours in discussion, concluding that they were willing to give their lives, if necessary, for the cause.[41]

Like Lombard, Doris Jean Castle felt tremendously hopeful in the early 1960s. Although not religious, she accepted Dr. Martin Luther King's ethos of redemptive suffering as a strategy. She thought that the movement would liberate and uplift blacks: "I truly, truly believed that the basic lives of black people in America was going to change." The assault on public accommodations was a first step: "I felt that we should have an opportunity to do, to seek, to find, to *be* without the indignities that was thrust upon you because you was black." Yet she did not see integration as the goal of the movement: "I never felt that we should want to be like white people." Her own motivation rested on the belief that "you took a stand, you stood for something. You wasn't just rolling with the punches, going with the flow." In this struggle, as in her later opposition to the Vietnam War, she saw the real contest—and real division—in class terms, between the "have and the have not."[42]

Doris Jean's and Oretha's parents supported their daughters' activism in generous ways. The family's house at 917 North Tonti became the headquarters of the local CORE, and a meeting place where Freedom Riders and other actionists planned strategy, slept, ate, and held long, involved discussions into the night. According to Doris Jean,

It was just like ... they were the parents. They expected us to go and do what we were doing, and we expected them to be available to do what was necessary to allow us to do that.... I mean, nobody ever asked them, was it all right for 375 people to parade through your house, you know, and would you feed them?[43]

Matt Suarez felt that "there will be no way of repaying [Oretha's] family for all that they did because that's a one, two, three ... five room house and one bath and there was times when sixty was sleeping in there and her mother cooked and fed all of them three meals a day, you know, without getting any money from anybody, or any food or anything like that, this was strictly out of her paycheck and her husband's paycheck that she kept them going."[44]

Oretha Castle felt that her parents were unusual in the New Orleans community. "My parents weren't themselves action-oriented," she said, adding that her father had "questions and reservations about some of the kinds of activities we used to engage in with the non-violent philosophy. He couldn't cope with that; he could not understand it. However, he never made an effort to dissuade us from participating in these activities." Other than her parents and her grandmothers, the surrounding family members "thought that we were crazy, and didn't know *why* our parents allowed us to get involved in this stuff. Generally, that was the kind of attitude that prevailed in those early years."[45]

Parental support was important for CORE members, because they were clearly a minority among New Orleans' black and white students. The city never had a "real student movement" like a number of other Southern cities. Administrators at the black Dillard and Xavier universities penalized student demonstrators, although the dean at Southern University at New Orleans did not. As a consequence, very few middle-class black students participated in direct action demonstrations. The working-class students who joined CORE often found themselves impatient with the goals and tactics of the moderate NAACP and Urban League leadership, and with the "apathy" of the black community. Within New Orleans, blacks often crossed CORE's picket lines to patronize discriminating merchants. Additionally, many older blacks were openly suspicious of the interracial organization, especially when the whites and blacks in CORE began to openly socialize and to date.[46]

Within this relative isolation, the black CORE leaders' allegiance to each other, and bonds with each other tightened. This sense of solidarity was strengthened by several events: by experiences in the dangerous Freedom Rides in 1961, by the expulsion of many whites from the chapter in 1962, and by experiences in community organizing in rural Mississippi and Louisiana in the summers of 1963 and 1964. These were the years of the greatest testing and public triumph of the movement, and its activists shared experiences of danger, personal growth and communal closeness, and often bitter disillusionment as the attitudes of the white Southern majority remained seemingly impervious to change.

CORE's national office organized the Freedom Rides in May of 1961 in an effort to test the Supreme Court's *Boynton* decision that banned discrimination on interstate carriers. Integrated groups of riders planned to journey from Washington, D.C., to New Orleans by Trailways and Greyhound buses, stopping at stations along the way, and integrating the facilities. After a group of riders was badly beaten in Birmingham, and a bus was burned near Anniston, Alabama, SNCC volunteers from Nashville confronted CORE executive director James Farmer, insisting that the Rides be continued. Farmer instructed his staff to recruit a group of volunteers from New Orleans' CORE to also continue the rides from Montgomery.[47]

Doris Jean Castle, Jean Thompson, Jerome Smith, and Julia Aaron were determined to go on the rides. The evening before they left, the group got Dave Dennis drunk enough to convince him to join them. Doris Jean Castle recalled the terror of the journey to Montgomery:

I know we were all afraid that night when we got on the train at Union Station and left here and went to Montgomery. I know I was, and I know Julia [Aaron], Jerome [Smith], Dave [Dennis], and Jean [Thompson] was. I can clearly remember that no one was in that particular section of the train but us and the FBI. They pretended they don't know who we are, and we pretending we don't know who they are. Us knowing that they were not there for any reason other than what they say they are—to investigate. Not to help, not to stop, not to prevent, not to do anything. And you approach Montgomery, and you see all these blue shirts with sticks in their hands, who are state troopers, and you don't know what their orders are, you know? But nevertheless, you don't waver one way or the other, you just do it. . . . We had to be out of our minds.[48]

The experience was one of fear and connection—connection with other activists, and terror of white violence. Jerome Smith remembered the greetings the riders received as the buses rolled across the Alabama line into Mississippi: "the people wavin' to us from the fields, you know, dropping their tools of work. These were the elders. And they would sneak these waves to us. That put it on my mind, put myself up." Such examples of courage and support from other blacks and fellow activists "postured" him up when he was frightened or apprehensive of violence.[49]

After their arrests in Jackson, Doris Jean and Julia Aaron decided to spend their full sentences in jail. They stayed in Parchman Penitentiary for sixty days.

To say that we were frightened was an understatement. But I don't think that any of us realized, except to reflect back on it later, just how frightened we were. I think that the warfare that was going on at that time was more psychological than anything else. . . . The effort was really to break the spirit of the people, and the things that were done to accomplish this, in retrospect, was really so cruel, I can't help but to say I don't know how we stood it. Except that we had enough armor of what we were all about, that our cause was right, you know, and God was on our side, that it overshadowed the fear that had to have been there all along.[50]

The CORE members who went on this Freedom Ride, and on other test rides during 1961, became a very cohesive group. The dangers of the rides, and the brutal beatings that Jerome Smith received in McComb, Mississippi, gave them stark experiences in terror and solidarity. But with their visible presence in New Orleans as pickets and demonstrators, and as the welcoming chapter for the hundreds of Freedom Riders who journeyed South to fill Mississippi's jails in the summer of 1961, the CORE chapter began to attract numerous new recruits. Many were white males from Tulane University and LSU-New Orleans. The chapter, which had been a cohesive group of perhaps twenty, swelled to between "350 to 400 people," according to Matt Suarez, who estimated that perhaps 60 percent of these members were white.[51] Very quickly, racial tensions simmered within the chapter, due to two developments—interracial dating, and the whites' attempts to dominate the decision-making processes of the group.

Within the exanded CORE chapter, interracial dating and partying became a point of concern for Oretha Castle and others. Castle felt that "the word was, the CORE chapter was the place where you could come into contact with black women without *any* problems." She felt that this was simply a replay of the white male's traditional exploitation of black women, and had nothing to do with her notions of what CORE was about, or what the struggle itself was about.[52]

But black chapter members were also angered by the presumption of authority by the white students. Castle saw the conflict in both class and racial terms:

you had all of the whites coming in with their tremendous amount of education and sophistication and then you had blacks who, we really felt, "boy is we some dumb compared to those white kids." They would come in meetings and they'd be talking about the philosophy of this political philosopher as opposed to that, and we never even heard of what they were talking about. And too it was that kind of intimidation on our part by what we thought was their smartness. . . . but, you know, like we always do, we'd be mumbling certain things: "Boy, they sure want to run everything and tell us what we have to do."[53]

When older people in the community became angered by some of the public partying of the CORE chapter, Oretha Castle convened the all-black membership committee. At a meeting in early 1962, "we decided that as far as we were concerned, that wasn't what the struggle was all about. So what it amounted to, we put every last one of the white people out. Every last one of them." Although the membership committee later readmitted some of the white males and their black partners, the racial breach never healed. According to Oretha Castle, "after it became clear that some white folks weren't going to be the leaders, most of them of that group who were involved in CORE at that time kind of dropped by the wayside."[54]

CORE's national office resisted this action, and dispatched field secretary Richard Haley to resolve the situation—the interracial organization did not want a "resegregated" affiliate. Haley was unable to mend the split, which prefigured subsequent ejections of white members from SNCC and CORE that accompanied the move toward a black power ideology in the mid-1960s. He saw it as an example of the conflict that plagued CORE "in varying degrees" between 1960 and 1965—the "tug of war" between blacks and whites. The white students were accustomed to leadership roles, and inevitably took charge of an organization.[55] "Maybe it was *right* most of the time, but it was not proper," said Haley. He felt that blacks needed to learn leadership through the process of leading, but, "more significantly, this *understood* relationship between blacks and whites, this traditional, habitual relationship between blacks and whites, *had* to be broken."[56]

While CORE members experienced police harassment in New Orleans, their elders' communication with white elites, and the restraint of the local police chief, prevented the brutality of a Birmingham or a Selma. They had very different experiences outside New Orleans, in the small towns of Louisiana and Mississippi, where CORE conducted voter-registration and community-organization drives. These events, and the arrests that accompanied them, frequently bound the CORE partisans and their attorneys in shared experiences of terror and solidarity. CORE members experienced the field as part of an intense intellectual and emotional ferment that had begun in New Orleans.

Rudy Lombard, who had left New Orleans to attend graduate school at Syracuse University, spent his summers working on CORE projects in North Carolina, Louisiana, and Mississippi. His experiences in Plaquemine, Louisiana, and Philadelphia, Mississippi, were especially frightening— and eventually disillusioning. While national vice-chairman of CORE, Lombard worked on a voter registration project in 1963 in the town of Plaquemine, a Klan stronghold. That August, police brutally dispersed marchers during several rallies and protests. On September 1, black ministers held a mass rally at Plymouth Rock Baptist Church. After the rally, marchers started toward the downtown, while surrounding whites urged police to "string them up now."[57] As the blacks marched on the central square, police attacked the crowd with electric cattle prods. The marchers fled back to the church, where CORE's national director James Farmer waited with the Reverend Jetson Davis, brother of New Orleans' A. L. Davis. As the crowd poured into the church, police turned firehoses into the building. Mounted police pursued the marchers. "They bombarded people with tear gas," said Lombard. "They were trampling people."[58] Police lobbed tear gas into the windows of the parsonage, and scoured the black community for James Farmer, who, with a number of other blacks, had found refuge in a black-owned funeral parlor.[59] Lolis Elie was among the blacks who packed the funeral home after running from the gas-filled church:

When I saw that door open I went in there and it was a wake. I was really almost hysterical. I remember thinking that that child in the casket was better off than anyone else. . . . I was looking out the window, and I could see troopers on horses—any black person they saw, they would jam [the] person back against the wall [with a] cattle prod and the other started beating them with billy clubs. . . . [Then] a trooper stormed up to that door and they said, "we want that nigga Farmer." I saw one of the most courageous acts I've seen in my life. It was a lady who owned the funeral home who said, "You have no right to come into my funeral home making that noise, causing a disturbance." He said, "there's a disturbance in here." She said, "there ain't no disturbance but the disturbance you are causing." I've never seen anyone more courageous than that. I think the troopers were going to kill Farmer.[60]

Farmer was smuggled to New Orleans in a hearse that trailed Collins, Douglas, and Elie: "we all met at my house and got drunk or tried to within ten minutes," recalled Elie.[61] Lombard, who had earlier tried to calm the black crowd when police violence began, fled from the church and the tear gas, and spent the night in a fig tree. Though genuinely afraid for his life, he said, "We would just not give up. Nobody expected us to come back out."[62] He and his colleagues felt that

if there was a situation that spoke to danger, that was probably where we wanted to be. We thought it was important to grab this thing by the throat. So if it was dangerous, that only meant that it had to be dealt with. And if you were serious, you weren't gonna be intimidated by anything.[63]

Richard Haley experienced a similar terror during his participation in the William Moore Memorial March in May 1963. Moore, a white postman, had decided to stage a solitary freedom march from Chattanooga, Tennessee, to Jackson, Mississippi, to protest segregation. He was murdered during the walk on April 24. Following his death, CORE's steering committee initiated a Freedom Walk along Moore's Route. On May 1, Richard Haley led a group of CORE and SNCC marchers from Chattanooga through Alabama.[64] Although Haley had initially opposed the William Moore Freedom March, he decided that once CORE was committed to the project, he would go. "I thought that I had as much responsibility, perhaps a little more, than anybody else. . . . because it was soooo comfortable to sit in a New York office and discuss, and make decisions about what some other people were gonna *do*." For Haley, the march became an experience of solidarity and fear. In Tennessee, he met Bob Zellner, a legendary white SNCC activist from Alabama. Among the marchers,

I found myself in a group where, because of our union on this particular project, the vast difference in backgrounds, points of view, among us never caused a moment of friction. It doesn't have anything to do with civil rights. I think it does have a whole lot to do with human relations, and the capability of people of putting aside differences which actually turn out to be superficial, but which in ordinary circumstances can cause you to be [uncomfortable].[65]

But the march also provoked a white violence that underscored the contradictions of racism. Haley remembered the moments when the group encountered hostile whites near the town of Little Fawn, near the Tennessee-Alabama border:

It was spring, and I remember how we were walking through the hills. . . . I was struck my the—I won't say dazzling beauty, because it was something that didn't *shine* bright, it sort of permeated your *insides*. You can sort of imagine the feeling an old farmer has when he goes out in the young spring and picks up a handful of dirt, and looks at it, and smells it. And you feel the same kind of way: fields, forests, little redwings, trees, flowers, the only discordant notes were people.

Crossing into Alabama through the town of Little Fawn, Haley thought, "such a beautiful name for a little town—and you get all these bucolic pictures of a little village nestled in a hillside, you get pictures of people who are at peace with each other and the rest of it—oh, you get *all* these pictures," he laughed. What met the marchers at the town was a line of hostile, howling whites:

One thing that really struck me was a boy of about ten, he was standing there. We were just walking by, and they were yelling and screaming, and somewhere over the hubub, I heard that little 10-year-old boy, "*black sons of bitches*—" The thought just crossed my mind: for a child so young to be already infected with that particular virus is as tragic as anything I'd seen.

The group was met by police at the state line, but also by a crowd of perhaps 500 hostile whites. Haley remembered that when the integrated group became visible, "there was a roar from that other side, and the only thing that I could connect it with in my mind was the roar of the Roman crowds when the lions came out." The marchers were "much more pleased than hurt" when the Alabama state police arrested them, and took them to a small prison at nearby Fort Payne. Later the group was transferred to Kilby State Prison, where they spent a month after refusing bail. Haley recalled that

when they carried us through the entrance, all the prisoners were *lined up* behind bars, but there was the same roar that came from the incident at the top of the Alabama hill. . . . And, somehow, it struck me as a little *odd*: here they are, all of them, back up these bars, for some transgression or other, but they're all in agreement with the system.[66]

Jerome Smith also had experiences that mixed terror with solidarity. Being smuggled out of communities by night, rolled into a blanket and hidden in the back of a station wagon, he would joke to driver Matt Suarez, nicknamed "Flukie," that he might prefer a Mississippi jail to the speeds of Suarez' driving. "Man, this friendship is gonna kill me," he recalled exclaiming during a particularly harrowing escape from police. Suarez, like most drivers who worked for COFO, refused to stop for pursuing white police because to do so invited brutal beatings or, in the case of Andrew Goodman, James Chaney, and Mickey Schwerner, death. Smith met activist-comedian Dick Gregory, Lena Horne, and James Baldwin in the movement; he also encountered Justice Department lawyer Burke Marshall, and Attorney General Robert F. Kennedy. He grew especially close to his CORE colleagues Dave Dennis, Rudy Lombard, and Ike Reynolds. In 1988, Smith's strongest memories were those of intense solidarity and collective empowerment:

My strongest memory is not ever being isolated, you know, never, never being isolated. Because of the collective involvement, I think the strength of dedication to a purpose that was bigger than each of us, and that no individual strength was enough to achieve that purpose. The absence of loneliness is my greatest memory of that time, the magic of every moment being wrapped in love—that kind of spiritual thing was, to this day, the greatest thing.[67]

Within the movement, Smith found five colleagues from New Orleans' CORE whose approach to activism mirrored his own. "We were like the direct actionists of reputation; we were looked upon as folks whose feet were constantly in the dust. We were always standing in the fire. And the kind of allegiance we had to each other was known throughout the country, wherever we went," he said in 1988. "We just had a great comfort in being with each other regardless of what the situation was."[68]

For Smith, the years in Mississippi amounted to a conversion experience for many ex-students like himself. He saw people who were "drenched in the sophistication of books, learning from people who could not spell their name, about books they read." The inspirational sources were the Mississippi blacks, particularly the older people and the children. The dangers of the field were frequently mixed with moments of spiritual transcendence. One memorable episode involved being "trapped in Smith County," and spirited out of a community by a black minister:

He said, "they're lookin' for you, and I'll bring you back." So this old minister walked me through the woods. I don't know how many miles we had walked, we got to an opening. He said, "I'm gonna leave you here, and say a prayer for you before I leave." I said, "you know, I feel bad, you have to go back by yourself." He said, "well, you have to go on by yourself. But I'm not really by myself." So he took out his Bible, say, "I have strength in this. And if this don't react quick enough"—speaking of his Bible—he had this gun. And he say, "But you moving forward, and all you have is *you*. So I'm more concerned about you, than about myself." Say, "But even much more than that, son,"—say, "I'm just so glad that you're here; so glad that all of y'all are here. And so death don't really mean nothin to me. I'm just so glad that I was able to *see*." And he's the one who used to tell me, "You know, you really a church. You know all of y'all are church."[69]

Such experiences changed CORE activists profoundly. Particularly, the relationships that they developed with other activists provided emotional support, intellectual stimulation, and, among the most commited, examples of love and courage. Many activists consciously experienced the liberating and heady process of emotional and psychological growth as a result of the collective experience. This sense of growth and change would make them profoundly disillusioned about the limited political changes that the movement's sacrifices produced. By the late-1960s, and in the 1970s they would become disillusioned precisely *because* they had grown so very much. And the source of that growth was the collective experience.[70]

Lolis Elie contended that the movement "made us much bigger and better than we would have conceived of being." As a young lawyer in 1960, Elie had conventional goals: he hoped to become a prosperous attorney, and enjoy a life of middle-class stability and comfort. The movement redirected his life. He grew especially close to Oretha Castle, who became a "little sister," and to Richard Haley, who became a "big brother" and mentor after he settled in New Orleans in 1964. Elie was empowered and inspired by the young people of the CORE chapter, and by close relationships with his partners Robert Collins and Nils Douglas. The relationships within the movement, and the emotional and intellectual growth he experienced as part of the collective effort, "got me out of the cave" of Plato's allegory. In 1988, Elie dated a significant transformation of his life to 1963. In that year, James Baldwin's *The Fire Next Time* was published, and Elie and his friends read and discussed the book, as they had also read and discussed the works of W. E. B. DuBois. When Baldwin visited New Orleans on a fund-raising tour for CORE, Elie talked at length with the writer, and was impressed by the range and power of his intellect. Elie and his colleagues began to see themselves as an intellectual and political community, different in consciousness and orientation from the "normal anti-intellectualism" of New Orleans:

There was a community, we were getting together, we had our own community, in effect. . . . At this time, my law firm, Collins, Douglas and Elie, on Dryades Street—we were the very center of political, intellectual and social activity. . . . In the afternoon, we used to bring out the bottles—we used to drink black Jack Daniels and Haig & Haig Pinch—so every evening people would congregate. CORE was in our building, and all sorts of people were passing through.[71]

Elie described this period as an experience of "spiritual growth," due to his relationships with Oretha Castle, Richard Haley, his law partners, and the young people of the chapter. He described his colleagues as "mild-mannered people. They inspired me a lot." Lombard and Haley, especially, provided intellectual stimulation, and heightened Elie's evolving sense of himself as an intellectual. It was, he insisted, "the collectivity" that produced his sense of personal development.[72] Richard Haley, especially, taught Elie that "there is something more important than any of us, an eternal light." For Elie, CORE became a second family: "my close friends said, 'let's play out our high side. Let's strive to become better human beings.' "[73]

Rudy Lombard also found the movement a catalyst for his own development. "The movement made me what I am . . . you couldn't ask for a better way to come of age," he said in 1988. He especially valued the relationships he developed: "there's nobody in the world I respect more than them." He spoke of his colleagues as being closer than a family to him. With them, he read works by Martin Luther King, Jr., Frantz Fanon, and Malcolm X. Reading Baldwin's *The Fire Next Time* "had an enormous impact" on Lombard. But above all, the movement gave Lombard an opportunity for personal growth through the collective experience. CORE, he said,

gave us a vehicle for confronting the things we were supposedly to fear the most. And it has been a hallmark of my life. I don't have many fears, and haven't had any since the 1960s. It demonstrated an opportunity to grab hold of whatever it was you were fearful of—individually and collectively. Also, I think, to find out who you are, under adverse circumstances—if you have anything you can admire about yourself. And the other thing is, if you understand what that was about, it will stand you in good stead. . . . It was an incredible context in which to mature as a person, and I would say that extraordinary people came to terms with themselves there, and discovered America there. And all of their illusions about how great this place was, I think, were put to the test and should have been dissolved. I think you came away with some courage and a profound understanding of the nature of the society in which you have found yourself and which you are forced to deal with if you choose to stay in it.[74]

Through the early and mid-1960s, New Orleans' CORE leaders became a close-knit group within the regional CORE and SNCC activists. Alice Thompson and Doratha Smith found a role model in the strong-willed Oretha Castle. Elie and Lombard deeply admired Richard Haley and Jim McCain, an older black field secretary. Richard Haley also served as an older brother to Doratha Smith, who worked with him in the CORE Southern Regional Office in New Orleans in 1964. Haley married Oretha Castle in the late 1960s. Matt Suarez, though never a believed in non-violence, found a political mentor and "best friend" in Oretha Castle. Jerome Smith found that his relationships with Lombard, Dave Dennis, Matt Suarez, Ike Reynolds, and the Thompson sisters were strengthened by the dangerous tasks they undertook in Mississippi. Doris Jean Castle found her own relationships to the "CORE family" strengthened during the 1960s—precisely because these relationships fused trust and solidarity with personal survival and persistence in the face of adversity and danger.[75]

In a very different way, Tom Dent found a close sense of solidarity and bonding with his colleagues in the Umbra group in the years between 1960 and 1964. In Umbra, young black writers like Dent, Ishmael Reed, Steve Cannon, Calvin Hernton, and David Henderson tried to combine avant-garde literary techniques and politics in writings that reflected the unique perspective and idioms of black Americans. Many in the Umbra group, like Dent, tended to be cultural nationalists in perspective—to celebrate distinctively black speech and expression for its difference from mainstream white culture. The Umbra poets were refugees from their own pasts, and came together to create both a new black idiom and themselves. They needed each other, Dent later said, because "we needed that mutual support that came from severing ourselves ... from the limitations and expectations and restrictions of our backgrounds."[76] For Tom Dent, becoming a writer was a means of transcending his upper-middle-class background, and of reconnecting himself with the black experience that he had first encountered in his father's mother, "Gran." But this process was painful. His parents could not accept his decision to leave graduate school, and the rewards, honors, and comfort of membership in the black educational and political elite. The senior Dents could not understand their

eldest son's choice to pursue his seemingly perverse, hand-to-mouth vocation. Thus, Tom Dent, like others in Umbra, found in the group an
alternative community. He formed close and intense friendships with his
peers in Umbra.[77]

Dent was a pivotal figure in Umbra—a writer who could also mediate
between the greatly varying artistic visions and personalities of the often
chaotic group; an editor who could channel the energies of his colleagues
into publication and production. Several of the Umbra poets became his
"lifelong friends." Both Umbra, and the Free Southern Theater, which he
would join as an administrator and playwright in 1965, were "the deepest
experiences that I have ever had—and I think this is true of all of us, but
I know its true of me—that those are my most profound relationships."
In a poem about Umbra, he wrote,

> But we were naked then
> and we stripped our souls
> easy as the sun rose
> and what went on
> in that tenement prison
> was something in us
> bursting free like
> a flash fire [78]

The phrase "But we were naked then," means "that when you are that
intimately involved with others that you are hiding nothing," said Dent.
At the same time that he was working so closely with the Umbra poets,
he also worked for the NAACP Legal Defense Fund as a public information
officer. In that capacity, he came into close contact with the events of the
civil rights movement in the South—traveling in Mississippi with field
secretary Medger Evers before Evers' assassination in 1963, and working
under attorneys Jack Greenberg and Constance Baker Motley in the New
York offices of the Inc. Fund. But it was the fusion of art and politics
within the relationships formed in Umbra that changed Dent's life, much
as CORE and the Southern movement transformed the lives of many of
his colleagues from New Orleans. Umbra and the movement worked these
changes because they combined intellectual stimulation, personal growth,
and boundary-testing within the context of a collective experience. Both
Dent and New Orleans' CORE leadership found in their differing movement cultures a means to reconnect and more strongly identify with black
working-class and folk traditions—traditions that all had been prepared, by

education and opportunities of upward mobility—to leave behind. Dent would find this experience enhanced and enlarged when he joined the Free Southern Theater in 1965—a movement theater that made its home base in New Orleans.[79]

These experiences of growth fostered in Dent, Elie, Lombard, Jerome Smith, and Doris Jean Castle a disillusionment with the political and social system. When compared to their own intense experiences of self-development within the collective context, the civil rights movements' victories of 1964 and 1965 seemed inadequate and meager. Continuing white violence, perceptions of white control of CORE and the NAACP, and growing, class-based perceptions of political and economic power fueled the CORE members' disillusionment with the immediate goals of the civil rights movement. Ultimately, however, the cause of their disillusionment was not so much objective events or the nature of the changes that they could see, it was that they had outgrown the goals that they had initially sought, and had outgrown the assumptions of the system that offered them legislative victories like the Civil Rights Act of 1964 and the Voting Rights Act of 1965. Relationsips within Umbra and the movement had fused intellectual growth, political analysis, personal closeness, and, in the case of those on the movement's front lines, danger and terror. What survived those experiences was an individual and collective sense of self that found the much-heralded victories of the Second Reconstruction too late, and inadequate. It was a sense of self that identified with the condition of the black masses, whose lives were changed only minimally by the legalistic victories of the movement.

White violence provoked disillusionment among many advocates of non-violent social change. Even though he remained an advocate of interracialism and non-violence within CORE, Rudy Lombard found his faith eroded by the costs of the struggle:

In the year of the March on Washington [1963], I thought we were giving up too much; too many people were getting killed for what little we were getting. I felt very sensitive about being involved with something that risked so much. Too many people were getting brutalized—and that was the way it was going to *be*. *That* changed me. I didn't want to *do* that anymore. . . . You lose your naivete. You lose your innocence after awhile. . . . You come down to basically a power situation . . . you realize a point that, that's where it is. Eventually, you find out a lot about yourself. You realize that you're not . . . you don't have what Martin Luther King wants you to have. You don't want to fight all that adversity and still love people.

It's too much to ask. . . . If you respect anything at all, you respect power, because you have to, 'cause you're forced to.[80]

Lombard's movement experiences taught him that "Nobody ever *intended* for us to be equal . . . no white person is ever gonna live by a decision *you* make. [And] you don't *control anything*—not even your own cultural expression."[81]

Lolis Elie also dated his sense of disillusionment to 1963—the year in which he felt such a sense of intense growth and realization. He "really did not discern a change in the attitude of white people," he said in reference to racial integration.[82] Part of his disillusionment came from his perception of white control within the movement:

There came a point where, everywhere one looked, on almost every project, whites were in charge. And blacks began to resent that, and to wonder whether they [white people] could take orders from black people. And the answer was *absolutely no*. . . . Once this was perceived, we began to take another look at nationalism.[83]

Elie was drawn then to the teachings of Elijah Muhammad of the Nation of Islam. Elie's nationalism was reaffirmed by his dealings with New Orleans' white elites between 1962 and 1964. As a negotiator for the Citizens' Committee, he dealt with men who made the effective economic decisions for the city—and for whom nobody ever voted. He came to see blacks and poor whites in a similar and oppressed relationship to capitalistic power.[84] Over the next five years, as legal barriers to racial equality fell, Elie was aware that, "in all fairness, I'd seen more changes than I expected to see in my lifetime, but, on the other hand, those changes were unsatisfying."[85]

Doris Jean Castle, too, experienced both growth and disillusionment in the movement. One of her most telling moments of disillusionment occurred at a fund-raiser in New York City in 1964, where she worked to raise money for CORE. At a party held at a wealthy painter's house, CORE fund-raisers made a pitch for money to buy two-way radios for fieldworkers doing voter registration and community organizing work in the Freedom Summer project in Mississippi. Most CORE partisans had privately concluded that James Chaney, Andrew Goodman, and Mickey Schwerner, who had disappeared earlier that summer, were dead. Fundraisers suggested that, had the three had a two-way radio in their car, they might still have been alive. Castle remembered,

that something as insignificant as a two-way radio could have made the difference between them being alive and not alive. It really, really overwhelmed me. I could not deal with that. Here was all of this *money*, all of this *wealth*, all of this *power*, and here was people prostituting themselves for a donation, if you will, which, the best you could say for it, was no sacrifice at all. I mean, it was nothin. And here were three people—I mean, they were just *gone*. They were as insignificant as the two-way radios . . . that was one of the most horrible feelings that I ever had in the civil rights movement.[86]

The moment was searing for Castle because it made her feel the vulnerability of the civil rights movement in America. It made her question her colleagues' romanticism: "we did feel that because our cause was so righteous, we, too, by inference, were righteous." Within the flow of money and pledges during the evening, she perceived that the lives of the three missing workers "were about nothing, and the *ideals* were about even less" in the interpersonal politics of the event.

Her greatest sense of disillusionment came during the Selma to Montgomery march for voting rights in 1965. The violence of whites during the march convinced her that "it really had not come no farther than five years before. I mean, nothing had changed." Despite her belief that "we are all brothers," she remembered feeling that there was "no hope" for the whites who attacked the marchers: "there just ain't no hope for 'em. And I think King really was the last hope."[87]

Similar contradictions between personal growth, movement solidarity, and continuing white violence and federal apathy fed a growing sense of disillusionment in Oretha Castle, Jerome Smith, and Matt Suarez. For Oretha Castle, the conservatism of New Orleans' black community was a source of continual frustration. Even though she was part of the Citizens' Committee's leadership, she felt that the Committee's achievements, while necessary, were very limited. As a part-time student, she was CORE chair between 1961 and 1964. In 1964, she devoted a year to directing CORE's project in Monroe, Louisiana, one of the dangerous outstate communities. There, she said,

It was very clear that the kinds of activities we were involving ourselves in—in the way of direct action—were grossly inadequate in terms of building and developing a really politicized base that would be needed to impact whatever would take place.

For Castle, the visible changes that the movement produced—the Civil Rights Act of 1964, the Voting Rights Act of 1965, the ending of segregation—"were not nearly as important or significant as the kind of spiritual and internal change that developed within people—how black people came to see themselves as a people."[88] Similarly, Matt Suarez found his own commitments to the effort of building the Mississippi Freedom Democratic Party, and his own personal involvement in the movement, eroded by the seemingly unchanging terrors of white violence. In 1988, he stated, "I don't like people anymore," and described himself "in retreat" from the world of politics, a retreat that had become more insistent since the late 1960s.[89]

Jerome Smith's disillusionment was publicly voiced in an emotional three-hour meeting with Attorney General Robert F. Kennedy on May 24, 1963. Writer James Baldwin had organized a meeting of prominent blacks with the attorney general to discuss the black alienation that Baldwin had written about in his essay, "Letter from a Region in My Mind," which had recently been published in the *New Yorker*. Smith, who was in New York for medical treatment for head injuries that he had received when beaten by whites at McComb, Mississippi, began to speak. The encounter shocked Kennedy; and the meeting lasted three hours.[90]

The pacifist, Gandhian Smith stated that he was nauseated to be at the meeting, and that he was close to renouncing non-violence. When Baldwin asked if he would go to war for the United States, Smith shouted, "Never! Never! Never!"[91] Smith recalled that he saw the meeting as "an extension of my service, but it was no more different that me walkin' on a picket line, goin to jail, or sittin on a corner, explaining to somebody about our purpose." He was at the meeting because he was part of the struggle, and he saw the meeting with Kennedy as "nothing special. There was no specialness to it." But he saw the attorney general, and the forces that he represented, as men addicted to power. "I just simply thought, and still do, that when you are addicted to power, and when you have all the creature needs, that that addiction to power can blind you to madness, and what I told him then, that he would not understand until he understood that madness was color blind." Smith remembered that

I told him it was nauseating for me to even be there 'cause I just thought it was a hoax and a joke. I thought it was about power. I didn't think it was real. Unless he was willing to alter the structure of Wall Street, unless he was willing to have his children walk where I was walkin', I told him that I thought I had some strong feelings as to why a woman could have children with him. 'Cause there was nothing human. When you become addicted to power, you surrender your humanity.... And if Wall Street and his money is more important that the sufferings of all of these blacks in the streets, then I had questions about his whole being.[92]

The tumultuous personal changes that activists experienced in the field stood in sharp contrast to the relatively peaceful changes that black leaders and their white counterparts negotiated in New Orleans. Locally, New Orleans' CORE was led by a "backbone" of women after 1962, according to chapter secretary Doratha Smith. The three Thompson sisters, Ruthie Wells, and Doratha and Carleen Smith formed a very close group, and particularly admired their long time chapter chair, Oretha Castle. In 1964, the chapter initiated actions to desegregate the local theaters, forming chain pickets around Loew's theater, getting arrested repeatedly. Oretha and Doris Jean Castle, and the Reverend Avery Alexander filed a suit to desegregate the lunch counters at Schwegman's markets, and Callie Castle, the women's grandmother, became a plaintiff in a suit to desegregate Charity Hospital.[93]

The local chapter, however, found itself hamstrung by several developments. The Citizens' Committee's leadership frowned upon spontaneous and autonomous activism—as seen in the *Weekly*'s response to the NAACP Youth Council pickets on Canal Street between 1963 and 1965. Also, the chapter lost many of its dynamic leaders due to CORE and SNCC's decisions to focus on Voter Education Project (VEP) campaigns in Mississippi and Louisiana in the summers of 1963 and 1964. Many of the strongest local activists took field positions with CORE and then COFO, and so worked outside the city during the crisis years of 1963 and 1964. Additionally, the Southern Regional Office, located in New Orleans, was staffed by CORE leaders who were unsure about their commitments to either New Orleans' CORE or to the autonomous field organizations.[94]

Richard Haley contended that New Orleans' CORE had lost much of its strength by the time that he arrived in 1964. The purge of white members in 1962 had dampened the enthusiasm and energy of the group, and "many of the most effective" CORE members "felt a certain anger with the New Orleans black community. They felt that this was one of the more conservative communities in the country." Activists felt that from the sit-ins through the dime store picketings "they had gotten at great cost very slight support from the black community." It was difficult for the chapter to generate enthusiasm within the community. Additionally, voter purges discouraged activism in voter registration drives. "In a situation like that, which appears to be fragmented, there needs to be somebody to come in and take charge, in a dynamic way," he said. But as Southern Regional director, Haley deferred to the Citizens' Committee's leadership within

New Orleans, and so became a witness and facilitator of the quiet, rather than dramatic changes made by the black leadership within the city.[95]

By 1964 and 1965, the national CORE organization was torn by black-white conflicts, by increasing financial problems, and by splits between the field staffs in the South and the national office. While Lombard, Elie, and Haley appeared to be committed to interracialism in 1963 and 1964—even as they were becoming politically radicalized—the national CORE came to be split on the issues of black nationalism versus a continuing commitment to an integrated society; between the philosophical and intellectual commitment to non-violence and cries for black power and armed self-defense. Many of the leaders from the New Orleans chapter came to doubt CORE's viability as an organization; several in the field staff were clearly exhausted by the cumulative strain of their experiences since 1960.[96] During the 1965 national convention in Durham, North Carolina, a number of CORE members voted to support a resolution aganst the Vietnam War. Matt Suarez was one of them. Although James Farmer and others in the national leadership privately opposed the war, they felt it unwise to visibly anger the Johnson administration by making a public resolution. The motion was tabled, and in the wake of that conflict, Matt Suarez resigned; thirteen other staff members resigned in one day, and another ten to fifteen in the next two months. "That kind of finished CORE up in the South," he said in 1969.[97] Since late 1964, Rudy Lombard, Dave Dennis, and Oretha Castle had criticized the growth of the organization's national structure, which had mushroomed since the days of the Freedom Rides. As field secretaries and members who worked with local communities, they favored decentralizing and democratizing the organization. With the organizational changes of 1965, which included cuts in the budget of the field staff, and a growing prominence of the black power advocates within CORE, many field personnel resigned. By 1966, Jerome Smith, Dave Dennis, Richard Haley, and Rudy Lombard had left the organization.[98]

With the demise of the organization they had known in 1960 and 1961, New Orleans' activists returned to school and to work for various War on Poverty organizations. They expressed their movement-based radicalism in work with community organizations and cultural projects. Oretha Castle, Doratha Smith, and the Thompson sisters returned to Southern University to complete their degrees; Dave Dennis returned to Dillard, and Matt Suarez took a degree in political science from Tulane. Doris Jean Castle went to work as a fund-raiser for George Wiley's National Welfare

Rights Organization, and then returned to New Orleans to work in social service agencies. Jerome Smith returned to New Orleans in 1966, and in 1969 organized Tamburine and Fan, a youth center and educational program modeled on the movement's Freedom Schools. Rudy Lombard finished his doctorate at Syracuse. In 1966, he and Smith co-coordinated an African-Afro-American Conference in New Orleans. The objective of the conference was to "better understand and celebrate our cultural and historic ties to Africa."[99]

Within New Orleans, the moderates of the Citizens' Committee had triumphed. New Orleans' blacks won the rights guaranteed by the Civil Rights Act of 1964 and the Voting Rights Act of 1965 with a minimum of violence. After 1966, New Orleans' black community was clearly on its way to political power that would be realized by 1970. But the young idealists who had brazenly led the city's direct-action campaign, and who had provided much of the leadership for the movement within Mississippi and Louisiana, had grown beyond the changes that moderation, and mainstream politics could provide. Their continuing contribution to the city would lie at the intersections of culture and politics—in the Free Southern Theater, in the Congo Square Writers' Union, in political organizations, and in celebrating and supporting black art, cooking, and music. These were the cultural resources that all had come to revere more deeply through their movement experiences, and they were the rich possessions of New Orleans' black community.

S I X

"I Don't Know That I Would Feel as Valuable to Myself as I Feel That I Am": After the Revolution

I N recalling their political experience twenty and thirty years after the events of the civil rights movement, each New Orleans activist told his or her story through incidents and actions that reveal the symbolic content of his or her experience. These memories represent large blocks of time or powerful experiences in their lives. They are recalled as events which revealed something important, or which provided a transition from one stage of development to another. Often, these memories function as keys to the *meaning* of their experiences, and, hence, to the meaning of their lives.[1]

Memories of activism are both constructions of events and statements about the identities of the women and men who relate them. These memories link past and present, and they justify the contemporary lives of the narrators. As constructions of events and identity, they reveal the impact of activism upon the lives of men and women who have achieved a sense of personal coherence and consistency—at least in part—through activism.

Psychologists have maintained that the purpose of psychoanalysis and therapy is the achievement of biographical coherence for the client. This involves the creation or re-creation of a satisfying life-story from fragmented experiences and memories.[2] Clearly, New Orleans' activists achieved a high degree of biographical coherence in their lives. Significantly, they use their political experiences as organizing devices for their life-stories. Their narratives of activism appear to have been projective and retrospective. From the themes within their narratives of 1979, individuals fashioned consistent futures, which they proceeded to live throughout the 1980s. By the late 1970s and 1980s, these people had also developed life-stories that emphasized the consistency and continuity of their lives, motivations, and commitments.

Thus, the interviews of the late 1970s and 1980s document the process by which people create meaning. Activists retained certain memories of political conflict because these episodes had a specific place in their self-constructs. Individuals judged specific memories as important because of what they illustrated about their characteristic method of problem solving, and what they revealed about their role in historical change. The memories explain why, how, and in what ways a man or woman confronted the segregated past, and the importance of activism in his or her life story.

In addition to its projective and retrospective function, memory functions as a third dimension of activism, a commentary on the past and present that justifies both. Activists use memory to give the passage of time, and their lives, coherence. In this process, extreme experiences become personal benchmarks that symbolize methods of conflict and resolution. The interpretation of experiences of racist discrimination, danger, and ostracism vary greatly, depending on the actor's race, political ideology, status in the community, gender, and sense of self. Like other remembered events, experiences of extremity become parts of each actor's self-construction, and thus justify the self-image of the individual who told the story in 1979 or 1988, when interviews were conducted.

The narratives link personal past and present in important ways, but they also serve as commentaries on contemporary behavior and politics. Often, the temporal comparisons indicate a decline or slippage from the days of a leader's prime. Albert Dent, for example, cited the behavior of a segregationist army general who found his attitudes on race changed by service with Dent on a race relations committee. Dent indicated that Troy Middleton had his attitudes changed as a result of following orders to serve on this committee—which Dent then compared unfavorably with Andrew Young's actions as ambassador to the United Nations. Middleton had been led to do and believe right by duty, and Young, the onetime SCLC leader, had ignored duty and created controversy.[3] In this interview, Dent, like other leaders of different commitments, found the past of his activism, for all of its denials, in some way superior to the present.[4]

Dent's story may well be the result of a generalized nostalgia for efficacy, a tendency to see the more intense and engaged periods of one's life as superior to the relatively quiescent present. Such nostalgia could be nothing more than a natural feeling of loss for the power of one's prime, and for the climate that allowed an individual to have an impact, to create change and shape a new order. The nostalgia for efficacy could also be a function of the very changed political climate of the late 1970s and 1980s. Perhaps one way to deal with a pervasive despair over national politics was to interpret both the individual and collective loss of efficacy as an product of a political and moral decline. Even the most optimistic of activists, like Rosa Keller, were genuinely grieved by the politics of the Reagan years. So, too, were members of the protest generation, particularly Rudy Lombard and Jerome Smith. But unlike Keller, they did not mourn the loss of a friendly political administration as much as they mourned the lost intensity of their years in struggle. This was a collective intensity that neither could adequately replace.

The First Generation: Integrationists

The social context of symbolic memories varied by gender and race. Whites involved in interracial activities in the 1950s were facilitators in method and goals. Dr. James Dombrowski and Albert D'Orlando were ministers, men who resembled New Deal reformers in orientation. They were white men well outside the circles of power in the city. Similarly, Rosa Keller and Helen Mervis were facilitators and reformers whose energies were first drawn to very familiar projects and institutions of women of their class—the New Orleans Council of Jewish Women for Mervis, and the YWCA and the League of Women Voters for Keller. The white activists would have been community reformers and leaders by virtue of their social status and placement, but became deviants in their political crusades because they were involved with blacks, and because racial integration had become their obvious and dissident goal. Hence, the whites' most difficult memories often involve the ostracism that they received from other whites because of their interracial commitments, and the ways in which their activism made them deviant.

By contrast, black leaders became activists through self-interest, and through the privileges of their independent status within the segregated system. Placement within the system determined the content of experiences and memories. Both Leontine Luke and Virginia Collins became leaders within the black PTAs in an effort to help their own children, and the race in general. Like Keller and Mervis, they were acting in socially sanctioned forms of female activism. But both women also consciously followed the examples of their preacher fathers, for whom political action was an important part of social and religious life. For Luke and Collins, gender dictated the forms that self-interested political action would take. But, in interesting ways, the black women leaders acted with a sense of continuity with their paternal pasts; Keller and Mervis acted within acceptable forms of female leadership, but the *content* of their political roles clearly contradicted paternal attitudes on race.

The structure of symbolic memories varied greatly among the leaders. For A. L. Davis, Albert Dent, and Revius Ortique, public life had brought numerous rewards. Davis served on the city council before his death in 1978, and Ortique was a judge in 1988. All three had been honored by the white and black communities with awards, commendations, and plaques. Dent and Ortique had achieved national recognition, serving on regional and national commissions. These men had been racial negotiators who had often met in secret with white elites. In interviews of the late 1970s and 1988, both Dent and Ortique stressed that aspect of their careers: it connected them to power, and gave them power as strategic leaders who were trusted by important segments of the white and black communities. Thus, their stories revealed how they acted to create and to control change. Their memories placed them where their abilities alone *would* have placed them in a discrimination-free world: in decision-making arenas with other men of power.

Albert Dent served on several race relations committees in the 1940s and 1950s, and was instrumental in bringing the Urban League to New Orleans. "My role in New Orleans, in getting things done, is to work quietly with the power structure," he explained. Significantly, his greatest remembered triumphs were those of personal conversion—changing the minds of influential whites by virtue of his example and character. While this private effort was clearly part of his public role as a leader, Dent took pains to create a more militant persona than the black man who was honored by whites. He explained his prohibition on student participation in the sit-ins and Freedom Rides in terms of a commitment to education, asserting that students needed to know the difference between attending college and protesting. This may have been an effort to counter charges that he was overly conservative, or too intimate with wealthy whites like the Sterns. Albert Dent's public presentation of self in late life mirrored the balancing act that he had perfected in his most active years—that of a privately militant, but urbane racial negotiator who was the confidant and friend of powerful whites.

For his work with numerous institutions and committees, Dent had received a roomful of awards and plaques by 1978. This recognition clearly meant a great deal to him. "I always thought the day would come when I would be a man in New Orleans—and not a black man," he said. His role as a racial negotiator had, in fact, become symbolic of his life, and he was eager to remind interviewers of the part he had played in important changes and decisions that preceded the famous confrontations of the civil rights era. Dent's victory had been supremely public, and his own life's achievement was "wrapped up in this campus"—Dillard University. "That's my museum," he said in 1979, gesturing to the white brick buildings constructed during his administration. "That's enough of a museum." Dent died in 1984.[5]

Revius O. Ortique, a civil court judge in 1988, echoed Dent in the themes of his story. As a labor lawyer in the 1950s, he had seen a connection between civil rights issues and labor issues when he began to "move against labor unions in equal employment opportunity" suits. Although he became a successful lawyer, Ortique remembered most vividly the victories of the 1950s and early 1960s—the McDonogh Day Boycott, his representation of the black community in Bogalusa in the mid-1960s, marching in the large civil rights demonstration in New Orleans in 1963, and negotiating with New Orleans' white elite. As one of the negotiators for the black Citizens' Committee, Ortique met frequently with members of the white economic elite to achieve the peaceful desegregation of New Orleans. He was incorporated into this decision-making elite in 1966, when he was made a member of the Metropolitan Area Committee (MAC), a group concerned with racial relations within the city. Ortique served as MAC's first black president in the early 1970s.

In 1988, Ortique's perspective mixed elitism with a shrewd understanding of the economic consequences of racism and discrimination. Thus, while he had acknowledged to black leaders at a school board meeting that some black children might not be able to compete with whites, he insisted that those who could compete should be encouraged and pushed and developed. Ortique realized that the racial frontier of the 1980s and 1990s was economic, rather than political.

In 1988, he admitted that activism was "like an opium" for him—"You accomplish one goal, then you move on to the next." He had served on two presidential commissions, and had received numerous awards and commendations from black and white groups, elite and poor. He felt that his own role had been "to make certain that white people understood that there is no in between, it's all the way. It's the total dream we dream"— equal rights, total participation in the larger culture. In his memories, Ortique's role was consistent: that of repeated challenges to, and incorporation within the elite. At 65, he had one more goal: to move on to a position on the Louisiana Supreme Court. He was pleased with his life: "I really can say I'm a happy person."[6]

Dr. Leonard Burns maintained his medical practice and a successful travel agency in 1988. He was then deeply involved in boosting the city's tourist industry, and in promoting black ownership and participation in this critical business. Even though tourism was New Orleans' primary economic activity in the 1980s, blacks did not own any major hotels. Burns saw the next frontier of the black struggle to be economic development.

Leonard Burns had participated in numerous civil rights and community organizations in the 1960s. As a member of the Citizens' Committee, he had negotiated with representatives of the white business community. As a member of the Urban League and the Community Relations Council, he interacted with the "white intelligentsia" to promote wide-ranging racial changes. He maintained warm relationships with individual whites he grew to know in these integrated settings. Sometimes, however, these interracial relationships caused resentment among some of his black peers—who accused him of spending too much time with whites, and not enough with blacks. In the mid-sixties, he used his Urban League connections to bring together emerging white political leaders and black civil rights leaders. The men would "sit at my house around the den and just sip a little liquor and tell lies, tell jokes, and then after they had gotten to know each other, on a social level, and on a friendly level, mixed blacks and whites, that they [the whites] would understand our point of view. They would listen to our stories, we would listen to their stories. And that did happen." In this effort and others, Burns was a social facilitator of civil rights efforts in the community—a man who put black and white elites together. During this period in the 1960s, he was also heavily involved in the national NAACP.

Like Dent, Burns believed in moral suasion, and in changing the minds of white elites. He frequently argued with the young members of CORE and the NAACP Youth Council over tactics, believing that it was better to "get the manager of the store to change" without "the picket, without the heat, without the hardship." In the 1960s, he worked with the local NAACP leadership to desegregate hotels, taxicabs, and the tourist industry. With each instance of desegregation, Burns felt gratified that "we have broken a barrier, we have scaled the highest hurdle, and eliminated this one step, to make it a much safer, easier, and more comfortable place for our children to live." He was glad that young blacks did not face the "embarrassment, the denial, and the ostracism" that segregation had imposed.

Leonard Burns seemed happiest when discussing his successes with his travel agency. The business had allowed him to see the world, and to introduce other blacks to exotic vacations, exquisite foods, and novel experiences. At 66, he believed that "I've made a very satisfying move across that stage" of life. "I've been educated. I've served my country in the Marine Corps, which I enjoyed. I got to test my strength, my ability, my tenacity, my weaknesses. I've married, had children, had houses, had businesses. Being a vagabond, I've traveled around the world. . . . I have loved, and I have had the pleasure of having the benefit of friends." He had had six very close friends, and treasured these relationships. Most gratifying for Burns, however, was the legacy of his years as an activist—"to have some of the seeds I've planted many years ago to come back and tell me, 'Hey, look, you helped me to do this. You guided me into this. You told me this, and I've done this. And I've succeeded.' " Burns warmed to this gratitude from others: "that's my payoff," he said.[7]

Leontine Luke's symbolic memories revealed conflict and reconciliation, through a harmonious blend of hard work, dignity, and preparation. Much like Dent and Ortique, Luke believed in a kind of moral meritocracy: that preparation, character, and diligence brought eventual acceptance and recognition. Like Oralean and Joyce Davis, she expressed pride that New Orleans' leadership had desegregated the city without the assistance of outsiders.[8]

In 1979, Luke worked part-time as a support enforcement officer for the district attorney's office, a job that she had held since 1966. She had served on the March of Dimes board for 40 years, and was proud that she had integrated a number of boards and committees "because I was accepted. People were accepted in the neighborhoods because of who they were, their character and their ability, and that's the way New Orleans was made up." Though she remembered favoring "most demonstrations," she felt that several of the more dramatic confrontations of the 1960s were "not necessary." Like others of the first generation of black moderates, she opposed the black power movements of the mid- and late 1960s. She was "scared to death" when Black Panthers occupied several buildings and held a shoot-out with city police in the Desire Housing Project in 1970, because

I felt ... that the youth of our city was letting an organization like the Black Panthers come in and direct their movements. And I don't think that was right. Because I don't think that anyone can come in and tell you more about how to go about business in your home than you yourself—or your city.[9]

Luke's strongest memories of racial conflict and violence came from the school crisis of 1960–1961. During the crisis, white crowds harassed four small black girls as they entered two white schools in a working-class neighborhood in the Ninth Ward.[10] As an NAACP leader, Luke had worked with the black children who had desegregated two schools in the Lower Ninth Ward. She remembered the crowds who threw rocks and eggs at the children, and her own poor white neighbors who kept their children home rather than send them to school with blacks. She was scandalized by the willful ignorance of whites who chose illiteracy over integrated schooling.[11]

During the 1960s, Luke continued her work with voter registration and community organizing in her neighborhood. In 1979, she remained proud of the pin and certificate she received from a week-long session on nonviolence, held at Highlander in 1963. Her own devotion to education, hard work, and preparation was evident in the advice she gave to black students throughout the 1950s and 1960s. "I always tried to get them to remember, if a person wanted something, they had to prepare for it. You could be as smart as you want, or as you thought in your mind, but you had to have the proof." The "proof" meant a high school diploma, a college degree, and a voter registration card. If armed with those qualifications, and if able to pass examinations, young blacks would be "qualified" for the jobs for which they applied. Said Luke, "I told them the day would come when they wouldn't look at your face." But, she stated, achievement without active mentorship was meaningless: "you have to be able to give to someone else that that you have attained, because if you're educated and can't give it to someone else, you still can't do any good."[12]

Like Luke, Oralean Davis and her niece Joyce Davis were proud that New Orleans' desegregation had been achieved by local leaders, without the disruption provoked by outsiders. Perhaps obliquely, this was a reference to the agonies of Birmingham and Mississippi, where the SCLC and SNCC had staged some of the most dramatic public confrontations of the civil rights movement. Perhaps this was also an affirmation of the wisdom of the local leaders' moderate course—a course sometimes attacked by young militants.[13]

Oralean Davis recalled that her brother's church had been packed when A. L. mobilized his congregation for a protest or boycott. The Consumers' League, a black protest organization, and CORE often met in the New Zion Baptist Church after 1959, and Davis became an important leader in the Citizens' Committee. Oralean recalled that A. L. had not wanted "to be associates of white people, but to have the same privileges as whites." Her brother's most important white ally, she believed, was deLesseps S. Morrison, although his greatest political successes, which included a position on the city council, came in the 1960s, long after the Morrison era. According to his sister, the Reverend Davis was a mass movement leader who preferred negotiation to confrontation: there always was a "better way" than force. But Davis, as a moderate, had come under attacks from the young militants of the 1960s. According to Joyce Davis, black militants would assert that "those Uncle Toms [referring to Davis and the Reverend Avery Alexander] don't know what's happening," while both Davis and Alexander were actively negotiating with white elites. For Oralean and Joyce Davis, the civil rights movement and A. L. Davis' career were validated by the changes they had experienced: black leaders no longer had to meet "behind closed doors"—secretly—with white elites, but could openly conduct the business of politics and governance. Oralean Davis also saw her brother's work validated by the recognition that he attained in both the black and white communities—in the offices, awards, and plaques that accumulated before his death in 1978.[14]

In contrast, as a radical, Virginia Collins had highly different memories than did the more moderate black leaders. Her important memories were structured by the central conflicts of her ideology: elite exploitation of blacks, and a corresponding manipulation of white and black attitudes to ensure racial, rather than class conflict. Thus, she recounted periods of black and white cooperation, as in SCEF, coupled with official white interference and persecution. These were not unlike the memories of James Dombrowski, the former executive director of SCEF, and a radical like Mrs. Collins.

Collins had been highly active in mainstream civil rights efforts as a PTA leader, as an organizer for a massive voter-registration drive for the Coordinating Council of Greater New Orleans in 1963 and 1964, and as a community organizer for a War on Poverty agency in 1966. But she had, she said, remained a black nationalist in her political commitments. In 1958, she took part in a protest organized by the Universal Association of Ethiopian Women. The group petitioned the United Nations to protest a Louisiana law that pushed black voters off the welfare rolls. Collins and her colleagues insisted then that American blacks were "a nation in captivity." In the mid-1960s, Collins would become a leader of the Republic of New Africa, a nationalist group that wanted to gain a territorial homeland in the Southern states where the black population was most concentrated. As a nationalist, leftist, and community leader, she worked actively with SCEF in the late 1950s, and remained close to its supporters, and to the young militants in SNCC, through the 1960s.

In 1988, Collins' memories of her activism replicated her interpretation of American history and politics. When she became visibly involved in civil rights activities in the 1960s, the wealthy New Orleanians for whom she did private nursing canceled her contracts. She remembered vividly her experiences on picket lines. Although she had run workshops on non-violence "as a process, as a way of getting what you want," she was not non-violent herself:

I remember I was on a picket line at Selma, and I had one of these *strong* sticks, and I said, "Lord, if these people come here, I'm gonna have to die or something. I can't do this." Because they had been putting the hose on people and all that, and they was coming toward me. And I said, "Sonofabitch, I'll kill you," under my breath—and I had my stick just like this . . . and people just did nothin. The people said, "This woman crazy. She's not nonviolent, she crazy." But, I know I would've hit em.[15]

Her own activism involved considerable risks. During a period of months in 1965, segregationists bombed a number of buildings where integrated meetings were held, including the First Unitarian Church and D'Orlando's parsonage. During that period, Collins "got scared." One night, while sitting in her front room, she suddenly asked herself, "What if they throw a bomb here?" Momentarily, she left her study and walked to the back of her shotgun house. "And then I just collected myself," she said. "And I said, 'The hell with it. Nobody is gonna make me leave outta *my* house.' I say, 'If I die, I'll just be dead. But I'm asking God to look down on me. And I'm gonna stay here. And I've got guns and everything'— which I always did have."

Collins' radicalism deepened over the years. A year at the University of Wisconsin in 1967–1968 exposed her to cooperation among the white poor in Northern Michigan and fatalism among poor white farmers in the tobacco country of North Carolina. These experiences "showed me that we is all in the same boat—white, black, green, grizzly or grey. And the same man that had the black man down had everybody else down. It had nothin to do with what color you was." For Collins the federal government, and corporate capitalism were the oppressors of blacks and whites. Such corporate elites "worked overtime" to separate blacks and whites.

By 1970, Virginia Collins was thoroughly disillusioned with the results of racial integration in the public school system. "Just let the schools stay segregated. *Nobody* is getting educated the way things are now," she told a writer for the *Southern Patriot*. She contended that racist opposition to school integration had doomed the effort from the beginning. "People could have got together if they'd been left alone. Human beings can get together. That's why you have to get back to an examination of the system that has made it impossible for them to do so. That's the thing we have to fight now."[16] In 1971, Collins made a speaking tour with SCEF field-worker Carl Braden to organize support for her son Walter, who had received a heavy prison sentence after he had refused to be drafted for the Vietnam War.[17]

By the late 1970s, Virginia Collins became disillusioned about a number of her previous beliefs, particularly in her hopes that black political power could cure some of the "ills" of the black community. By 1988, she had become disillusioned about the prospects for political change through even grass-roots organization; she sadly recognized that few people remained as committed politically as she had been. Despite her pessimism about the government, and the economic system, Collins considered herself happy: "I enjoys life. I'm not a person that's grumpy. I don't think I ever was. So a little bit of something make me happy, feel good." She had returned to the Baptist church, where she taught a weekly Bible class.[18]

In contrast to the stories of the men, the memories of Rosa Keller and Helen Mervis revealed important facilitative actions, as did the narratives of Leontine Luke, Albert D'Orlando, and James Dombrowski. Of these individuals, Keller alone had real access to the white elite of the city, and her stories of facilitation—of bringing her "two worlds" together—often involved making the first and necessary introductions between black and white elites. For Keller and her peers, the greatest gains from civil rights efforts came from the relationships they established with black leaders. They also saw the changes in the national political system as significant, particularly the Civil Rights Act of 1964 and the Voting Rights Act of 1965. Because these women and men believed so strongly in the power of legal and political change, the legislative victories of the 1960s and the changed politics of the South were of enormous importance.

Rosa Keller remained an Urban League stalwart throughout the 1950s and 1960s. During this period, and others, she was ostracized by many of her old friends in upper-class white New Orleans, but continued to "walk in two worlds," those of the city's black and white elite. Like Albert Dent and Revius Ortique, Keller was eventually honored by organizations throughout New Orleans, in recognition of her work as a race relations leader and a community leader.[19]

In 1978, 1979, and 1988, Keller's memories were structured by themes of conflict and reconciliation, by the metaphors of knowing and unknowing. Keller maintained that her friends in the city's elite, which included members of her own family, had never known blacks as equals. Once the introductions were made—often, by Keller herself—the two groups could, and did recognize each other's humanity. Her own life in race relations had been both a "cause" and an "education"; prior to her Urban League experiences, she had known little of the deprivation that blacks faced, little of the violence inflicted upon blacks in the South. She was frequently shocked by the brutality of whites to blacks, including women and men of her own social class. In 1988, she took pains to emphasize her special status within the small civil rights community in the city. She was the only person with wealth and privilege who actively championed the cause of blacks, and she used her advantages consciously and consistently. But her descriptions of activism had an edge of desperation. Keller described herself as a "nice mother, and a nice grandmother," to a family she loved. Still, she saw herself first as a civil rights activist, asking, "What other cause would I have had?" She had never wanted a career on the society pages, and, she asserted, "If you spend your life playing bridge, or belonging to the garden club, I don't believe you can have a satisfied old age."[20]

Like Keller, Helen Mervis remained involved in the Urban League at both local and national levels in the 1950s and 1960s. Between 1962 and 1967, she headed the Community Relations Council (CRC), an organization that held educational forums on racial attitudes, discrimination, and integration to groups throughout the city. After her husband's death in 1967, she worked in a number of jobs—directing an interracial consortium between the three Catholic colleges in New Orleans, developing citizen-participation programs for the state and city governments, and finally, heading the city's Jewish Endowment in the 1980s. She had developed her fund-raising skills while working with the Urban League, and later with SOS. Like Keller, she lost friends due to her activism. Unlike Keller, she felt anger and frustration toward the "so-called leaders of the community," the traditional economic elite who were "so stiff-necked about race, and so tight in their pockets about any kind of help." For Mervis, activism brought rewards and personal growth: "It kept opening me up to new people, new experiences," she said. "I don't think very many people have the pleasure that that gives me."[21]

Through the Unitarian church, D'Orlando continued to promote racial integration. When a white student, also a church member, was arrested during one of the CORE sit-ins of 1960, the Unitarian church gave several thousand dollars toward his defense. During the school crisis of 1960–1961, the church raised almost $25,000 to assist groups fighting to integrate the schools. The Unitarians also gave money to help support the desegregation of Tulane University in 1961–1962. In the early and mid-1960s, D'Orlando also became active in the local ACLU. This activism, and the fact that integrated meetings were held at his church, was probably responsible for the bombings of the church and parsonage in 1965. Though terrified and angry, D'Orlando and his family were not injured; he continued to receive "rock-solid support" from his congregation. In 1988, retired and contemplative, he stated that he felt "privileged to have been in this part of the country" during the South's most significant social change. His activism had made him "much more concerned about what is happening," and had convinced him that "people *do* make a difference." He was pleased by the extent of black progress, but also wanted "change to continue. I want to see more acceptance among people; I want to see the country in better shape than it is now."[22]

James Dombrowski's symbolic memories resembled those of his white colleages in content, and those of Mrs. Collins in structure. In his own life and work, he was a facilitator and educator by temperament. Yet repeatedly, he experienced red-baiting and state repression due to his uncompromising stand on racism. In 1979, Dombrowski recalled the difficult times that he and others in SCEF experienced in the 1950s and 1960s. As early as the 1940s, he had grown impatient with the gradualists among race-relations liberals who temporized on segregation. "Sometimes you had to [make] a sharp break with the past," he explained. "First of all, you had to get rid of these [segregation] laws, to make it *legal* for people to be decent. When we started, we mustn't forget, there were these Jim Crow laws—and we were advocating something that was illegal." Dombrowski's activities with SCEF, and SCEF's support of SNCC, brought both local and national repression. He retired from SCEF in 1966.[23]

Like a number of other white activists, Dombrowski opposed the black movement toward separatism in the middle and late 1960s. "Logically, we're all one," he said, "You have to come together. It comes only from struggle, and our forces were at best very weak compared to the strength and resources of those who want to keep society as it is. So we have to have one another. For good or ill, we are all in the same boat together." In 1979, Dombrowski still believed one of SCEF's guiding assumptions from the late 1940s and 1950s—

that most people are decent, and will act decent, given the facts. If that were not so, democracy would go out the window.... But in a class-divided society like ours, the price that you have to pay to be decent is such that not too many are willing to do it. But the surprising thing is not how few there are, but how many, in the face of that threat.

At 82, Dombrowski retained a socialistic view of racial and economic divisions in America and in New Orleans. He saw a "monolithic" power structure opposing economic and social change. He hoped for a world at peace "with a modicum of equality." His own development had been influenced by books, teachers, and by the "religion of Jesus," not the in-

stitutionalized church, "where religious concepts are formalized and fro-
zen." As a radical, he believed that

we have to destroy this class-divided world, as a beginning. As we all know, people
who have everything they want, are the most unhappy. People that are in the
struggle to change things are, on the whole, much more happy than those . . . just
rusting.[24]

Dombrowski continued to live on Governor Nichols Street in the
French Quarter through the 1970s. He began to paint after he retired from
SCEF, and created vivid tropical scenes from lush colors. He loaned these
paintings to friends throughout the city. James Dombrowski died in 1983.

Specific historical conditions created the opportunities for civil rights
leadership and activism in the 1950s, and the women and men who became
interracial leaders were financially independent of segregationist power,
and tended to be facilitators and negotiators by temperament. This was
necessary because interracial cooperation was frequently a covert activity,
threatened by segregationist officials who equated black advancement and
integration with communism. A negotiator's style was also necessary because of the very real power imbalance between white and black leaders
of segregated communities. The black leaders of the 1950s, then, combined
a necessary racial diplomacy with a subtle use of protest in behalf of civil
rights, and strategically used their few white allies to achieve modest, but
visible gains in a decade of Massive Resistance and McCarthyism.

The Political Generation

The second generation had different memories than the activists of the
1950s. Although they had become young adults during the late 1940s and
early 1950s, they had entered activism as mature adults around 1960. At
this time, many were young professionals; Nelson, Landrieu, Collins, Elie,
and Morial were attorneys. These men had different expectations than
those of the first generation. Determined to fight segregation, they expected
it to be abolished in their lifetimes. And they were ambitious for political
office and for leadership positions. They were a more aggressive generation
than that of A. L. Davis and Albert Dent, and were no less determined to
prove themselves in the white-controlled political world, and to participate
in it on a basis of equality. These men sought, and took challenges that

the older integrationists could not. As attorneys, they often represented movement activists in dangerous situations. With the backing of the federal courts, they waged and won landmark civil rights cases. They then confronted the question that the movement had pressed in its community-organizing and voter-registration campaigns: whether or not to participate in electoral politics, to become part of the system that they had fought and gained the right to enter. On this question, the leaders of the political generation of activists resolved their lives differently. Three became political leaders in New Orleans.

The white liberals who were part of this generation in 1960 included a few attorneys like Landrieu and Nelson, and the white women who joined SOS. This generation of women were mentored by older leaders like Helen Mervis and Rosa Keller. Ann Dlugos, Peggy Murison, and Betty Wisdom found in SOS a cause and a logical extension of their liberal convictions. For these three women, SOS was part of a community activism expected of upper-middle-class and upper-class women. After the school crisis, the women remained involved in community work, but Dlugos and Murison remained principally involved in their earlier interests, and did not become more involved in interracial work. Wisdom did, and became a political ally of Dutch Morial in the late 1970s.

The women of SOS recalled vivid incidents of public violence and harassment. These shocked them into an awareness of class differences within the white community. But they also remembered great warmth and friendship from those on the embattled SOS board, from people who collectively took an unpopular stand, and grew closer through the crisis. For these women, SOS represented an extreme episode in their political lives, a period when their own liberalism and values were severely tested.

The men of this generation had different kinds of memories. As lawyers, they fought segregation through the legal and political systems. Hence, their most vivid memories included scenes of political drama, at negotiating tables or in courtrooms, or in public forums and debates. For both blacks and whites, civil rights work was sometimes isolating, and occasionally dangerous. Yet the rewards were clearly visible by the mid-1960s: an increasing black vote, and growing black political power in the city, and throughout the South. Thus, each man made a choice as to whether or not he would pursue a political career. Their interviews, and the trajectories of their lives reflect the importance of this choice, and their initial choices to champion the black revolt.

In 1988, Moon Landrieu was eight years out of office. He had served as mayor of New Orleans from 1970 to 1978, and as secretary of the Department of Housing and Urban Development in 1979–1980 under the Carter administration. In an interview, he spoke of his life in terms of tumultuous developments: his quiet boyhood in New Orleans followed by his conversion to an integrationist perspective at Loyola University, to his trial by fire in the state legislature in 1960, followed eventually by terms in the city council, and his years as mayor. He felt that his first term in the legislature helped his political career. "It matured me," he said.

There's nothing like going through that kind of personal crisis that ... there's nothing else that gives you that kind of backbone of self-assurance.... You're getting slaughtered every day, but somehow you're not dead, you're not bleeding. And you've developed an attitude about things. I managed for the most part to subordinate my self-interest, and did what was right, and it's a philosophy that has carried me throughout my political career, in facing tough decisions. *Just do it!* And because I got re-elected, it more than fortified me.[25]

Landrieu was proud of his terms as mayor, and proudest of having brought blacks into city government in meaningful ways. "We *moved* the system, we *moved* the system from an all-white system in which there was nobody [black] above the broom and mop level, we *moved* it." And his young administration did this by constant pressure, much of it initiated by Landrieu himself. "We moved it aggressively, beyond most people's wildest imaginations, beyond mine, to be honest with you." As both mayor and HUD secretary, Landrieu believed that he "ran a good race."

At 57, Landrieu had just finished putting his ninth child through college. His daughter Mary served as state treasurer, and several of his other children had become lawyers. He was happy with his marriage and his family, and described his life as "fortunate." But Moon Landrieu was restless. He still wanted to be president, but could not see how this would happen. And he longed for something public and important to occupy his energies. "You miss the applause. I haven't really—I've done very well—but I haven't really found anything that satisfies me as much as running a city." He stated that "most politicians, I think, certainly those who fall into my mode, are public performers, you know. We're speakers, we're entertainers, we're policy-makers, and when you're not in a position to do those things, there's a certain sense of loss about it."

Landrieu had fond memories of his family, particularly his deceased father. His mother—"a tough German woman"—still lived with Moon and

Verna. Landrieu acknowledged having been pushed by his mother, who had selected his high school, then his college. In her old age, she was still ambitious for her son. In 1984, after considering running for the presidency, he decided that he would not. He told his wife, and then decided to tell his mother.

So I went and sat down with her. Mama's had a little stroke here and there, and she shuffles, but she's still a very tough gal. I said, "Mom, I've decided I'm not gonna do this presidential thing. Thought about it, and I pretty well decided not to do it." I didn't want to tell her *flatly*, kinda consult with her. Said, "I'd like to know what you think about it, how you feel about it." She said, "Well, how do you think I feel about it? When all of those other men are running for president, and my son's not?"

You know, I just started to giggle. I walked over to her and kissed her, and said, "Okay, Mama, see you later."

Landrieu laughed at this "ultimate guilt trip. Here's this kid that comes off of west Adams Street, we lived in a little bitty shotgun house. I slept in the store room. I'm not trying to give you an Abe Lincoln story, but here I got to be a lawyer, a mayor, I got to the Cabinet of the United States, and my Mama—'How do you think I feel? . . . other men are running for president, you know.' Nothing is good enough for mothers, for their sons, in any event."[26]

In 1987 and 1988, Dutch Morial was also restless. He was elected New Orleans' first black mayor in 1978, and served two tumultuous terms. Morial had inherited a city with severe financial problems. During the 1980s, much of the federal support that Landrieu had been able to use aggressively had been axed by Republican administrations. Morial had tried unsuccessfully to levy property taxes within New Orleans to raise revenue, and had been defeated by the city council at each attempt. Much of the white support that had sent him into office in 1978 had evaporated by the election of 1982, when he was elected with an overwhelming black turnout. Many of Morial's former white backers had found him "abrasive" while in office. Landrieu endorsed his white opponent in 1982.[27] Morial himself felt that he had been held to a different standard than had previous mayors because he was black. He also believed that his political opponents had controlled the press, which, in turn, presented a distorted view of his administration to the public. In 1984 and 1985, Morial tried to change the city's charter to allow himself to run for a third term. Both initiatives failed.

In the late 1980s, Morial was concerned that his own history, and that of his administration, be told fairly. "The greatest thing a public figure has is a sense of history, I believe. I just want history to be fair." He wanted the record of his administration recorded in some other form than the local newspapers. He also hoped to see Michael Dukakis get elected to the presidency, and actively worked to recruit blacks to the Democrat's camp. Prophetically, he saw a Dukakis election as "my last hurrah" as a Democrat: "it's probably my last shot at seeing a Democratic president."[28] Though only 58 years old, Morial was concerned about posterity, about his reputation, about the record that would be left after he died.

In October of 1987, he had spoken of his career as an activist. He had taken pride in "performing well," and admitted that his work had been his life. He had received great satisfactions from his accomplishments in office, and as an NAACP leader in the 1960s:

If you're an artist, you're painting, you see something, it grabs you. Solving a problem, seeing it unfold—you see the solutions coming about and you see how you're affecting people's lives, how they appreciate and feel good about what you're doing, come up to you and thank you, you know, they appreciate it. . . . We all need that.

It's the greatest satisfaction one can get—to know that you're appreciated for what you've done or [are] trying to do. You feel that people feel comfortable 'cause they hear you speak out for them when they can't speak out for themselves, or you're somebody that raises questions and gets answers, and they can't do it for themselves.[29]

He still felt that racism and discrimination were problems for blacks, although he acknowledged that much had changed in his lifetime. He referred to a speech made by Judge Robert Carter, in which the former NAACP attorney claimed that while *de jure* segregation was ended, the legacy of segregation was a lingering feeling of superiority among many whites. While Morial conceded that he was "not one to shout 'racism' for everything, 'cause I think that nihilism is bad, whether its black or white," he acknowledged that he had begun to "wonder" about Carter's statement,

because what happens, too, as a result of the *de jure* segregation, you're never put into an environment where you can even be considered equal, separate and apart from your race or religion or whatever the form of racism or discrimination might exist. So people never know you. So they perceive you in ways that are inaccurate, or get their information third-handed, and they conclude about one's character, ability, personality, without having any real exposure to the individual which they can base whatever combined objective-subjective judgment they want to make on the individual. So I guess there's still some elements of supremacy in some people's minds, and that gets to be racism.[30]

Morial was also concerned with developing successors, with motivating young people, with contributing to opportunities for young blacks. As NAACP president, he had often spoken to high school students and other young blacks, explaining the purposes and program of the NAACP, and urging them to apply themselves to the business of living and achieving. But in the late 1980s, his dominant concern was with the historical record. "Sometimes you look back and many times you see the people who appreciate what you've done, and the others who don't appreciate, and I guess you think that everybody should appreciate," he said.[31] When he died unexpectedly of heart failure on Christmas Eve, 1989, he was given a traditional jazz funeral, and 10,000 black and white citizens came to pay respects. Opponents, friends, and family eulogized the combative man whose aggressive leadership had offended many whites, and inspired his black followers.[32]

Robert Collins was senior partner of Collins, Douglas, and Elie from 1960 until 1971, when he was appointed as a judge of the Criminal District Court for the Parish of Orleans. He remembered his years with CD&E— his years in the movement—as taxing, sometimes frightening, and fulfilling. He recalled the night in Plaquemine when state troopers charged into crowds on horseback, and scoured the black community for James Farmer. His most frightening experience occurred in Poplarville, Mississippi. Collins and his partners had gone to the small town to arrange bail and trial dates for an interracial team that had tried to desegregate the bus station. During the trial, which was held informally in a fire station, the town's mayor, who also functioned as its judge, became worried by the hostility of the whites at the proceedings. He arranged to have the lawyers and their clients escorted out of town, and out of the state, by the state police. Only two years earlier, a mob of whites had lynched Mack Charles Parker, a black man accused of raping and murdering a white woman. Collins recalled

That was one of the most frightening experiences of my life, that one. 'Cause we really did feel very much threatened. You know, to be in a place where somebody had been lynched just a year before. That alone creates that atmosphere, where you don't know what can happen to you. Somebody could bomb your car. Somebody could shoot you. So many cases of people just found shot. People found shot, you know. People were shot and killed for trying to register to vote, let alone to try to go into a town like Poplarville, Mississippi. That was as racist a town as you'd find in all of America.

Collins and his partners were then "trying to push the [legal] system as far as it could go. Somebody had to do it. There were a lot of people who didn't have the courage, who weren't willing to make the sacrifice, and I guess we were just crazy enough to try it at the time." The three traveled all over Louisiana in the early 1960s, taking cases in Clinton, Vidalia, Monroe, Bogalusa, St. Francisville, and other places, filing school desegregation cases in several parishes. After 1964, CD&E received legal assistance from the Lawyers' Constitutional Defense Committee (LCDC) a project that sent lawyers South to help the few Southern civil rights attorneys handle the numerous cases that the movement produced. Collins found this exposure to lawyers from other parts of the country interesting and stimulating. In 1965, he and Nils Douglas organized the Southern Organization for Unified Leadership (SOUL) in the Ninth Ward, and Collins organized the Community Organization for Urban Politics (COUP) in the Seventh Ward in 1969. In 1972, Collins was appointed to the newly created position of magistrate judge of the Criminal District Court by Governor Edwin Edwards, whose candidacy both SOUL and COUP had strongly supported. In 1974, Collins was elected to an eight-year term. In 1977, President Jimmy Carter nominated Collins for the position of United States district judge for the Eastern District of Louisiana. His nomination was confirmed by the Senate in 1978. This made Collins the first black federal judge in the Deep South.[33]

In 1988, Collins was happy with his work as a federal judge: "I don't have any wants other than what I'm already doing now. But from the standpoint of what I want from America, is perhaps the creation of a more just society than we have." Opportunities for blacks had changed, he acknowledged. "There are now opportunities for people who are aggressive and smart, and in the right place at the right time." But the persistence of the black underclass worried him, as did the the high crime rates among blacks. "How do you explain the fact that blacks are—what?—12 percent of the population, and yet you have all these people committing crimes, spending time in jail. I have to attribute it to an unjust system. I don't think that the community is really addressing it."[34]

In 1988, Lolis Elie practiced law in New Orleans, and maintained a passionate interest in arts and cultural projects in the black community. He remembered fondly his years with CORE, especially the early and mid-

1960s. During this time, he read several books by psychologist Abraham Maslow, including *The Psychology of Being*, and concluded that he and his friends in CORE had been able to become "self-actualized" people through the movement. His closest friends from those years included Richard Haley, Oretha Castle Haley, Rudy Lombard, and Tom Dent, as well as his partners Robert Collins and Nils Douglas. All were members of the extended "CORE family" in New Orleans, and maintained warm friendships with each other in the years since the 1960s. Elie attributed his leadership ability during his years with the Citizens' Committee to his CORE colleagues:

It was really these people, my ability to sit with them, by the time I got to a meeting with the Citizens' Committee, I knew I would be the clearest thinker in the room because I had a collective which was *not* the Citizens' Committee.

Throughout his life, Elie was drawn to defend blacks who were willing to risk their lives to achieve freedom, especially blacks who resisted white oppression. He had initially been impressed by the courage of the young people in CORE, who went into dangerous Southern jails, and confronted violent whites with non-violent tactics. By the mid-1960s, he grew more impressed by the philosophy of the black Muslims, and with Muslim spokesman Malcolm X. Viewing the white violence inflicted upon protestors in the South, Elie began to appreciate the need for armed self-defense of black communities. He admired the Deacons for Defense and Justice, a group of blacks from Bogalusa, Louisiana, who armed themselves in response to Klan violence. In 1965, Collins, Douglas and Elie represented the Deacons in their negotiations with members of the governor's race-relations council, and the Bogalusa city council. Elie vividly recalled an early meeting when

The city council had agreed to meet privately with the Deacons for Defense, or with representatives of the Deacons. So I wanted to know something about what the ground rules were gonna be. And I said, "The first thing I want to know is whether we're going to call each other 'mister,' or whether we're gonna be on a first-name basis." Well, [the white negotiators] didn't think that had any relevance— "What difference does that make," they said. Some years later, A. Z. Young [a leader of the Deacons] told me that that experience of having those people to have to call him "Mister" and for him to look at them in the eyes was the great experience of his life at that point. The thing that struck me, I say, here is a man who is willing to risk his life, but he is intimidated by what he's going to call someone.[35]

A similar conviction led Elie to defend a group of Black Panthers after a Panther-police shoot-out in 1970. The Panther defense was an extension of Elie's work for CORE and the Deacons: all represented black defiance and resistance. The Panther defense involved self-sacrifice. It was a momentous decision, and Elie believed that it effectively ended his chances for a political career. But the Panther defense was also a consistent part of Elie's personal development, his very personal rejection of the world of black political success. By the late 1960s, Lolis Elie had become disillusioned with racial integration, and had been unable to see significant changes in attitude among the masses of whites. He had also become wary of the very success of his law firm's political activities. When Collins and Douglas led SOUL and Collins led COUP, Elie felt that the black political organizations were determining CD&E's political decisions. This he could not tolerate. With great disappointment, Elie left the firm. "I quite honestly haven't been interested in law except to earn a living since then," he said in 1988. "As a lawyer, that was the substance of my legal life." He had to find a new direction for his professional life, and organized a public interest law firm with two former LCDC lawyers and former CORE field secretary Dave Dennis.

Elie's decision to represent the Panthers was part of a complex series of changes. "I knew, I knew that I could not represent the Panthers and curry favor with the white folks at the same time," he said. Less materialistic than he had been, and more radical, Elie made major changes in his life in the volatile years of the early 1970s. He took time off to read and re-evaluate his life, and drew farther away from the burgeoning successes of the black political organizations that CD&E had spawned.

In 1979 and 1988, Elie kept a distance from electoral politics. In 1979, he described himself as a black nationalist in orientation, adhering to the Muslim doctrine that "the collective white man is an evil person" whose "preferred method of conflict resolution is violence."[36] He believed that the leaders of the black movement had been too much influenced by the "integrationists" of the black elite, who were controlled by the wealthy whites who funded the NAACP and CORE. Elie saw American society divided by race and class, with the poor of all races oppressed by a heartless capitalism.

In 1988, Lolis Elie was more temperate in his judgment of whites, but just as despairing about the condition of the black masses. He was disillusioned with the successes of black politics in New Orleans. The Morial administration, and then the Barthelemy administration, convinced him that he had "grossly overestimated and misunderstood ... the nature of the black people who were gonna seek political power. And there is really no correlation between their vision of the world and my vision of the world." As in 1979, Elie counted individual whites among his close friends. He continued to see the world divided along racial and class lines, and controlled by an indifferent white elite.

Elie's greatest experiences were the friendships that he had forged in CORE. 1988 was a year of significant losses: his mother, and Richard Haley had died, and Oretha Castle Haley had died in late 1987. In a period of grieving, he was examining his spiritual values. "Basically, I'm an existentialist," he said, who lived in the "here and now." But grief, and growth, were making him analytical about his past and his future.[37] He missed Richard Haley, his "big brother" greatly: "he was someone who was teaching me that there is something that is more important than any of us, an eternal light." Elie emulated the apolitical Haley, who was without ambition for power within CORE and the movement. Elie's friendships with the Haleys and a few other intimates taught him to keep a moral account of himself. "You have to be accountable to your friends who are dead," said Elie. "Because it's bound to happen. They're gonna die depending on you." Although Elie regretted that he did not have more "material resources" as he neared 60, he felt that "to become a self-actualized person is worth almost any price."[38]

One of Elie's closest white friends was Jack Nelson, who ran a legal clinic at Loyola University's Law School in 1988. Nelson had taken a number of civil rights cases after *Lombard* and the Tulane suit. In 1963, Nelson represented the Houma Indians in a desegregation suit against the Terrebone Parish School Board, which resulted in the desegregation of the parish schools for Indian students. In 1967, he represented the black St. Augustine High School in a suit against the Louisiana High School Athletic Association, which desegregated interscholastic high school athletics in Louisiana. Between 1975 and 1977, Nelson represented Thomas Perkins, Jr., a black student at Harvard University, in his suit against the all-white New Orleans Athletic Club, which had refused service when Perkins had entered the club to buy a drink. Nelson won damages for Perkins from the club. Nelson ran unsuccessfully for a judgeship on the Criminal District Court in 1972.[39]

Nelson described his career in civil rights causes as a calling. In the late 1950s and early 1960s, he had felt "that I was in some way being invited or asked to represent these people so that they could live a dignified life." As a "man of faith," he liked to believe that it was "providence," or "a calling" that brought him to the movement,

You don't analyze callings. You either go or you don't. And so I didn't say, "Well, wait a minute, is this good or bad for me?" It appeared good. Not good in a recognized sense, but good in a sense that after it was over, I felt that I had accomplished something with *my life*. That I used a profession, at least the skills that were taught to me, as a student, to enter a profession to alleviate pain. I was aware of that. And I still am. And that is a very satisfying thing. . . .

There has to be a commitment, you have to be committed to something, and do it. I don't know, I just came on at a time in history when things fell into place for me. And I was needed, I responded, I don't understand why, I just did. And that was it. And I'm gonna go on.

Even though Nelson had experienced ostracism during the Tulane suit, and had lost an election that he thought he should have won, he believed that the discomfort endured by whites was miniscule when compared to that of blacks. He spoke of Lolis Elie. "He's a man that, if he'd been white, would've really gone places, politically, legally, economically. But you know, no matter what happened to me, Lolis suffered many times worse." He made comparisons:

It's the frustration. I could submerge myself in a culture that offered me a lot of comfort. I could become invisible in the white world by going to New York, or . . . but where could a black go in the 1950s? . . . I could return at night to a white, middle-class, upper-middle-class neighborhood, air-conditioned, but where could the black go? Regardless of our political views, I could stop at every fillin station between here and Memphis and *piss*. He couldn't. So, when I hear some white fella talkin about how much he's suffered, what he did, this, that, and the other, man, you wouldn't wanna change, I tell you.

The ostracism, the missed political career, the lack of many conventional rewards had hurt Nelson, but he persisted in his crusade out of a conviction that he—and the blacks—were right. He also had a sense of his own mortality, and of the historical moment. "One of the things I was blessed in having was the ability to be able to make a decision as if I was seated on my coffin," asking himself, "let's say I'm 75 years old: now what would I want that decision to be? I can't redo it. I can only do it once, and now. And for some strange reason, that became involved in my decision-making process. And I began to see later that this was the right thing to do. We may not understand it now, we would understand it later."

Throughout the 1960s and 1970s, he had had a sense of making history, of being in the heart of historical change. All of his work he had done as a solo practitioner, not as a lawyer for CORE or the NAACP or the ACLU. He felt that it was important for some men to initiate changes as individuals, partly as an inspiration to others who would come after. But more importantly, he said,

I changed *my* life. And, rather than trying to change the world by using this person, that organization, I probably started to change my life, being influenced, and accepting advice of people that I had begun to develop respect for, and that I had respect for. And, you know, I said, wait a minute, I gotta change. And I changed, and then everything just came naturally.

Nelson felt great satisfaction in knowing that he'd made a material contribution to the lives of blacks. When he saw a black student walking across Tulane's campus, or learned that a black had won an all-state athletic contest, he felt a sense of accomplishment. This was part of the power of legal change: "the power to change social custom quickly, without the need for violence."[40]

Nelson's sense of power as an attorney was linked to his need to act as an individual, rather than as part of one of the movement organizations of the 1960s. In 1979, he had contended that "individual development" and "individual security" were what the civil rights movement was originally "all about." He contended that organizations did not sufficiently empower people to act alone to change their lives or the social order. As an individual, Nelson had changed both. And, he advised me:

You ought to put a section in your thesis about the feeling of alienation among all of us, how little control we have over our own lives. I think that it's really important that people get a sense that you *can* change something. . . . What happens is, when organizations come in, they perpetuate a feeling of insecurity. . . . I mean, hell, you die alone.[41]

In 1988, Nelson continued to affect change as an individual, teaching some seventy law students a year about civil rights and individual rights. And, as a practicing Catholic, he felt that prayer was the most important influence in his life.[42]

Although she had been committed to public education, Ann Dlugos, like many of her friends, had sent her son to a private school after full-scale integration became a reality in their district. "None of us really believed that there would be mass integration," she said in 1978. But, she allowed that she "didn't want my son to go to Sophie B. Wright High

School, even if it had been all-white." Most of her friends placed their children in private schools. "I had a very bright 7-year-old. I wanted him to have the best education he could possibly have." She struggled with guilt feelings before concluding that her son should not suffer for her liberal political convictions.[43] In 1988, Dlugos was still politically active with the League of Women Voters, and was concerned about the proliferation of nuclear arms, and the prominence of political action committees (PACs) in national politics. She had been active in the League's human relations work, and had worked on school board campaigns for liberal candidates. Some of her closest friends were women she had met in SOS. Of her own civic activism, she said, "It's been fun, interesting, fulfilling. I haven't done a lot, but I've done as much as I wanted."[44]

In 1988, Harry B. Kelleher was 79. The school board testimonial, the Citizens' Committee negotiations, and the early years of the MAC were important parts of his life of civic leadership—leadership that included service on many of the corporate and philanthropic boards in the community. He praised highly the leadership of the black community during the tumultuous years of the 1960s, but rather casually affirmed, in his low, gravelly voice, the power of the men he represented. New Orleans, he acknowledged, was "an oligarchy," with the power centered in a handful of businesses and banks. "We had the levers of power," he explained.[45] It was a power that had been forced to move, and to change, by the black community, its leaders, and by the federal government. Kelleher's long memory encompassed several generations of life in New Orleans, from his grandmother's Civil War stories to the more recent development in the downtown. Many of his friends were gone. The most important, Darwin Fenner, had died in 1979. A day did not pass that Kelleher did not miss him.[46]

The leaders of the political generation were poised to take advantage of the opportunities that a bi-racial electoral politics offered in the 1960s. As lawyers and professionals, they staked their careers on legal and political change, and on the eventual victory of blacks in the civil rights struggle. Their life-trajectories and interviews reflect this continuing focus on the public world of electoral politics as a measurement of success and of racial progress. Even when those politics were judged negatively, as by Lolis Elie, the centrality of the electoral contest, and its public products, remained unchallenged. The focus on electoral politics was in part a result of the men's socialization as lawyers. All in some ways sought to achieve political goals through the legal system, and several were able to advance those goals through public office. For the political generation, the convergence of ambition and opportunity made electoral politics, and public office, both the reward and the end product of political change. Their narratives reflected their historical placement and their achievement of the movement's most basic political goals. In an interesting deviation, the narratives of Nelson and Elie suggested that the rejection of electoral politics— or, in Nelson's case, a lack of success in that effort—was to some extent a product of personal development. Although both were politically astute and ambitious men, neither seemed to desire a political career at critical junctures in their lives. Political success became a casualty of each man's sense of moral necessity. Elie and Nelson seemed to substitute internal journeys of spiritual and moral growth for the public activity of politics, and to credit that growth to decisions that turned them from a viable political life.

The Protest Generation

The third generation of New Orleans' activists often found the post-movement years disappointing. Disillusioned with and cynical about the political process, few possessed the requisite ambition or the faith to make political careers for themselves. They despaired of meaningful change through the political process, and were disappointed by the successes of black politics in New Orleans. In middle age, they remained highly interested but ambivalent about politics, and often yearned for the collective intensity of their pasts.

Gender did not structure the memories of the protest generation in the same way that it had structured the memories of the two preceding generations. Perhaps that was because on the Freedom Rides and voter registration campaigns, and in other protest efforts, the women of CORE often shared dangers similar to those experienced by the men. Doris Jean Castle Scott's recollection of the terror of the Freedom Rides did not involve any less danger than did Rudy Lombard's experiences in Plaquemine, or the dangers that Matt Suarez or Jerome Smith experienced in Mississippi communities. Although several writers have discussed and examined the sexism of the civil rights movement, New Orleans' CORE members did not address this as a major issue in their movement experiences. Perhaps this is because the women of the "CORE family" are black, and had different experiences than the white women who joined SNCC and CORE. Perhaps, too, it is because the strongest leader of the local chapter was a woman—the strong-willed and dynamic Oretha Castle, who combined community leadership, motherhood, and a rich family life during her years in the movement.[47]

While gender did not significantly differentiate the memories of the CORE members from those of their predecessors in New Orleans, the very extremity of many of their experiences did. The young partisans of CORE and SNCC assaulted the worst bastions of white supremacy and segregation. They made Freedom Rides into rigidly segregated and dangerous small towns in rural Louisiana and Mississippi, and registered black voters in parishes and counties where few, if any, blacks had voted since Reconstruction. They charged into their crusade with the belief that their cause was just, and that God was on their side, as Doris Jean Castle Scott said. And they connected in life-changing ways with rural black Southerners, many of whom lived in a poverty and oppression that their own families had only recently escaped. Within the movement, they were also exposed to national luminaries, politicians, black intellectuals, and white liberals. This array of experiences combined extremes in jarring and discontinuous ways, and provided the CORE leaders with opportunities for psychological and emotional growth. This growth occurred at a particularly volatile time in most of their lives, their young adult years, when the world seemed open with possibilities for transformation.

The possibilities for transformation were perhaps implicit in the politics of protest, a very unconventional politics for young women and men who had been groomed for college and middle-class achievement. The very assumptions of CORE—that the means of non-violence were as important as the ends of social change—made the tactic of direct action a test of one's character, courage, and resolution. Taking direct action into often violent communities and life-threatening circumstances, the young activists came to experience an individual and collective transformation, but this change was not replicated in the society around them. They recalled their collective experience in the movement as a period of unmatched intensity and development, a time of danger and great closeness with their colleagues. Like war veterans, few found this sense of intensity or purpose in their post-movement lives. And like some veterans, they longed for a return to those years of personal transformation and social upheaval.

In the 1980s, Richard Haley worked as an administrator for Louisiana's State Department of Education. He had held several administrative positions since leaving CORE. In 1969, he was director of resource development for Total Community Action (TCA) the local agency of the War on Poverty. In 1979, he headed a minority consulting firm and shared offices with Lolis Elie and Rudy Lombard. At that time, the soft-spoken, contemplative Haley focused on the unfinished and undone business of racial justice: the crippling poverty of much of black New Orleans. A former integrationist and idealist, he acknowledged that since his years with CORE,

what I have become *resigned* to as of now is that the establishment rolls merrily on. It would appear that the only way to make in-depth changes in the structure would be to attack the structure with sufficient power. To be able to achieve a position where you can speak from strength, and say, 'we propose.' ... About the only thing in which I have unshakeable faith in human relations and politics is the avarice and covetousness of man for power. The only idealists that I can remember having run across are people on the out, who have nothing to lose, or a *few*, on the in, who, for personal reasons, feel as though they have nothing to gain.[48]

Haley's movement experiences had changed him. He had experienced the erasure of racial and class differences with others in the struggle, and had also experienced the ferocious hostility of violent whites. He had grown and developed within the movement:

For once, I wanted to take a risk. It was generated by the excitement of the situation, by the attitudes and personalities of the students. ... I knew that there had to be a time, sooner or later, when you have to risk something. It meant a certain element of personal development that has changed my point of view. It also meant opportunities for a number of other individuals, and afforded them opportunities to develop in a way that they never would have, otherwise. It was an opening for individuals [who were] crying for opportunities, for miniscule changes in overall patterns of human relations. The changes were miniscule, but they were seeds whose volume and direction we have no way of knowing.[49]

Oretha Castle married Richard Haley in 1967. In 1978, she was deputy administrator at New Orleans' Charity Hospital, the facility that her grandmother Callie had sued years earlier. In evaluating the movement, she stated that the basic social changes—while necessary—were essentially "cosmetic." Her greatest gains from the movement were those of consciousness and awareness, and a closeness and understanding that she shared with her fellow activists. For Oretha Castle Haley, the movement's battle was a struggle for human dignity in this country—to be able to exist, to function, to be what you are ... and it's still pretty much the same. I don't think the nature of the struggle has changed at all. I don't think it's changed since slavery.

Despite the changes in black consciousness, and in her own personal consciousness, however, the movement did not change America enough. According to Oretha Castle Haley, the movement unmasked the "problem behind the problem" of segregation:

This country is a deeply racist country. In some ways, I think that is the root ... the economic system, and, in some ways, the political system builds on and translates that. The *root* problem of this country is that it's racist to the core. Every day, this country is becoming more and more regressive, with the economic system becoming more and more oppressive.[50]

In 1987, Oretha Castle Haley operated the Learning Workshop for pre-school children, and headed minority student recruitment at the LSU medical center. She had managed the successful campaigns of parish school board member Gail Glapion and city councilwoman Dorothy Taylor, but had not chosen to run for office herself. She had been active in a number of community crusades since her years in CORE. She died of cancer in the fall of 1987. Her husband Richard died in the spring of 1988.

Like Lolis Elie and Rudy Lombard, Doris Jean Castle Scott deeply missed her sister and Richard Haley. In 1989, she was a night admissions supervisor at Charity Hospital in New Orleans. Although her sister had continued to organize community politics in the years that followed the 1960s, Scott dropped out of almost all political involvement after her sister's death. During their years in the movement, Scott said that she had developed a role with her sister that paralleled her sister's role in New Orleans' black community. Oretha saw herself as an enabler for that community, and Doris Jean saw herself as a enabler for Oretha. Scott was a worker, rather than a leader. "Things that had to happen—I was more ready to do those things than to plan and strategize," she said in 1989.[51]

Her memories of the movement provided stark contrasts between her own fear and her retrospective awareness of danger, and moments of crushing disillusionment. She recalled vividly the Freedom Ride into Mississippi, and spending her nineteenth birthday in Parchman Penitentiary; she also recalled her fears and feelings of protectiveness for her older sister Oretha. She recalled moments that made her realize the complexity of the movement's crusade: the eventual kindliness of two jailers at Parchman—

deeply religious men who believed in segregation because they thought that God had ordained it. And Scott recalled her own complex motivations: that she wanted black people to be free of the indignities and constrictions of discrimination, but did not desire "the obliteration of melting black people into the overall American society."

I don't believe that I ever felt that what the civil rights movement should have been about was the integration of the races. I think that I recognized and I feel that the unlikelihood of that as well as I guess the unwelcomeness of it was something I've always held very very strongly and very close to myself. . . . I never felt that we should want to be like white people.

Neither could she totally accept the ethos of black nationalism and black power. "There was a lot of the philosophy of blackness, of black awareness, black identity that I obviously and certainly am in wholehearted agreement with. But just on a practical level, there was a lot wrong with it, in being a viable alternative to what we had." She related the build-up of government and police repression in the late 1960s to some of the black power rhetoric: "it was armed warfare on their part. We didn't have a *damned* thing. We didn't have the first tank." Additionally, she could not accept the "blanket indictment of the whole of America, the American people, as being typified by the George Wallaces, or on a more polished level, by the Ronald Reagans and Richard Nixons."

At the same time, she admitted that the late 1960s had been a period of great despair for activists like herself. After the death of Martin Luther King, Scott went to a meeting at Oretha's house "at which we seriously, *seriously* entertained trying to identify a white person that we could kill that would hurt white people as much as the death had hurt black people." The group could not think of anyone other than Senator Everett Dirksen, "and that sonofabitch died the next week." They talked assassination due to the "frustration at that particular time. . . . King was the only somebody who was saying 'please, let's give it a chance. Let's try again.' Everybody else was saying 'Burn. Kill'—and we had no reason not to. You had no reason not to."

Doris Jean Castle Scott returned to New Orleans in 1967. She never completed her degree at SUNO, but worked at a variety of social service jobs, some related to the War on Poverty in the late 1960s and early 1970s. She felt that the movement changed her life. Had she not been part of it, she believed that she would probably have lived the life of a middle-class professional: married, with several children, a comfortable home. "But I don't know if I would have been as valuable to myself as I feel that I am, because I did experience what I experienced in the civil rights movement. . . . I don't think that I would have had the opportunity to grow out of myself both inwardly and outwardly. And by grow, I guess I can only define that by saying that everything I have come to know, I have come to understand that I was decisional about it."[52]

In 1979, Rudy Lomard expressed an angry disillusionment with his hopes of the movement years. He believed that the major gains won by the movement had not changed the circumstances of most black people. "That other stuff was just cosmetic," he said. "Anything of any real value in this society is still controlled by whites." Lombard had earned a doctorate in urban planning from Syracuse University, and worked at a number of business projects in New Orleans and in Los Angeles. In 1979, he shared a suite of offices with Richard Haley and Lolis Elie. He produced a cookbook from the recipes of the city's great black chefs, and was involved in a number of cultural projects.[53]

In 1988, Lombard worked with a financial investment firm, with white partners, and owned part of a business in Los Angeles. His memories of the movement contrasted his sense of personal growth with the often dangerous situations that those in CORE and SNCC confronted. He remembered the terrifying night in Plaquemine, Louisiana, in 1963, when police attacked black marchers with cattle prods and tear gas, and hunted for James Farmer through the black community. He also remembered an evening spent getting Reverend Joe Carter out of jail in West Feliciana Parish, Louisiana. And he remembered Mississippi in the summer of 1964. Lombard and several others from SNCC and CORE worked in Philadelphia after Schwerner, Goodman, and Chaney disappeared, and were harassed by the lawmen who had orchestrated the Klan murders.

The movement had changed his life, and Lombard regretted that young people did not have this context in the late 1980s. The collective experience had been "an education" for him, "better than school." Within the movement, he had the opportunity to meet "the most incredible human beings, which is an education you can't buy, you can only discover as you struggle against things which oppress you. I think people who are noble, and who are worth knowing and loving, find those situations and gravitate toward them. That is the quality they put into their lives, that is an opportunity for them to refine their values, their aesthetics, and everything else." Lombard said that the movement had made him what he had become.

Lombard believed that those who had experienced the movement could not be fooled by the dominant political culture, or the media: "you know Rambo is a fraud. . . . And you listen for all the clues that tell you what the real motivations and circumstances are about the country that you claim as your own." People grew up in the movement, Lombard said. It gave them a sense of their own history, versus the official distortions of the educational system, and the culture. Through CORE and SNCC, he met blacks and whites—"incredibly gifted and intelligent people"—"who didn't buy into this, who wouldn't accept it at face value, who knew about the lies and distortions, and who were free of giving of themselves and that information."

He acknowledged that many people were "done in" by the movement, and had consequently found the years after the 1960s difficult. The movement's optimism "became an illusion," and many could not grow and adjust in the diminished political world of the 1970s and 1980s. Many former activists "can't *stand* the absolute way people indulge in the status quo now, and accept so many mediocre things." Rudy Lombard found the pervasive passivity of much of the public frustrating. "I don't understand passivity, and non-aggressiveness, and not willing to take risks, and worrying about being safe, being so compromised, being abused, and oppressed in a neo-colonial fashion. I don't buy into that. I don't understand it." He realized that people from the 1960s could not be expected to carry the changes of the civil rights years forward, but was saddened by the lack of continuity between his generation and those that had followed. He found local and national politics depressing. "Evil is profoundly more enduring, it seem to me, than good. But you can understand that people be disappointed."[54]

In 1986, Lombard ran for mayor of New Orleans, opposing black candidates Sidney Barthelemy and William Jefferson. He had earlier opposed efforts of the incumbent black mayor, Dutch Morial, to change the city's charter and seek a third term. In the 1986 campaign, Lombard attacked the concentration of black political power in New Orleans, and charged that his black opponents ignored the real needs of the poor black community. He denounced the state of public education, the conditions in many of the city's public housing projects, the high rates of teenage pregnancies within the city, and the alleged corruption of city officials.[55] Lombard also asserted that "those of us who struggled, who made real sacrifices in the cause of civil rights, never intended for power to rest in the domain of a privileged few." Commentators dismissed Lombard as a "wild card" and a "gadfly." He received 1 percent of the vote.[56]

Lombard's candidacy was clearly an act of protest, an expression of his conviction that the blacks who held public office were "betraying the movement, betraying the very things we had fought for." But his own experiences convinced him that having been an activist carried no special status within the black community. "I don't think it endears you to anybody. I don't think it endears you to blacks; if you let 'em, they'll treat you like trash." And while he was troubled by the fact that men like Morial and Barthelemy had inherited the gains that the movement produced, he was aware that "you can't make a commitment to the movement expecting that there's gonna be reciprocity. You can't do that. Life robs you of any such possibility."

Lombard was glad to have been a part of the civil rights struggle. "I thought that it was important to be counted among the number of people who stood up to this terrible system we describe as segregation. . . . It's important to me now to keep on struggling." He did not claim to be happy:

How can I be? I don't see how any sensitive, conscious person can claim too much happiness. There are too many evil things going on. And I'm disappointed 'cause it didn't turn out like we intended. An enormous price was paid. [James] Baldwin said, 'Well, the price is paid, all we have to do is claim our crown.' Well, the *claiming* is difficult as hell. In your own psyche, you can know what the truth is, and you can love yourself, and you can know that he was wonderful and there were people like him. Not as eloquent, talented in a different way. But he *existed*. We can make an affirmation about that. We knew he knew and understood it. And we've had great moments. But we're still oppressed. We still have to struggle. We have to vindicate his suffering. He was despised, and held in contempt by the culture that created him.[57]

Matt Suarez worked on Rudy Lombard's campaign in 1986. Twice, he had run unsuccessfully for political office in the late 1960s and in the early 1970s. He had also worked on other campaigns in the intervening years, but he found politics time-consuming, and his wife disliked the amount of time it took from the family and from their business. Suarez had wanted Lombard to become mayor: "I would have done anything to see him mayor," he said. "But even in his campaign, he was still not ready to do it. He was approaching the campaign as a reformist." Lombard refused to solicit votes from those he considered "political prostitutes," according to Suarez, who despaired of the "very high moral plane" of Lombard's approach. But Lombard's attitude was endemic among his friends in the CORE family:

There is nothin that we have been able to come together and do except move in behalf of a cause. Because within that circle of friends, there is enough talent and resources to probably build a major industry. But they would never come together to make money, right? I mean, that's just unthinkable, right? . . . But now, if the gong rings, and there's a cause out there, they'll all gravitate, and they off and running.

Suarez had wanted the CORE contingent to run candidates when he returned to New Orleans in 1966. But no one in the group wanted to get involved in electoral politics at that time. In 1988, Suarez believed that the city's black political leadership was the inevitable result of the abdication of political responsibility by those like the former CORE activists. But Suarez's friends were still moralists, and still absolutists in temperament; they sought political justice rather than political power.

Suarez had mixed memories of his movement years, particularly 1963 and 1964, which he spent in Mississippi. He felt that the most significant thing that CORE and SNCC did in Mississippi was to organize the Mississippi Freedom Democratic Party (MFDP) in 1964. While marching, demonstrating, and registering voters were all valuable activities, Suarez believed that "building your own political party and having an educational system so that people *understand* what the political apparatus of this country is, and how it functions, was the most important thing we could've done in Mississippi."

The work was rewarding, but very frustrating. Suarez fondly remembered a black Mississippian who very effectively conducted voter registration classes—and who could neither read nor write himself. He often felt frustrated by the passivity of many black Mississippians, until he realized its source: the local blacks knew that the young organizers of CORE and SNCC would leave after a summer, or even a year, but that they would remain within the most rigidly segregated and dangerous state in the union.

Suarez also remembered beatings, violence, and terror, in Laurel, near and in Canton, and near other small communities. He learned to adapt to the constant fear of violence, and to the threat of trouble. Nevertheless, some experiences unnerved him. The most frightening occurred near the town of D'Lo, Mississippi. Suarez, who then operated as a "free-lance troubleshooter" out of the Jackson office, was called to pick up some movement people who had been arrested near D'Lo. Suarez sped to the location, and was beaten by a highway patrolman on his arrival. Suarez was then told to get John O'Neal, a SNCC activist, out of a jail two blocks away:

It was up on a hill, and all you could see was this little light that set on a post at the top of the hill. Looked like way down there. And they told me to go down there and get him. The police told me, go down to the jail, and check him out, and get him out of jail. And I swear, that was the longest walk. I mean, that was like walkin to the gas chamber, right? I just knew I was being sent off to be killed out there, in the blackness of the night. But nothing happened. I walked there, got John out, we came back down.

O'Neal had been driving the group of workers who had been arrested, so Suarez was told to drive him back to Jackson. "And I was still so scared and shakin so bad from that walk up there, and walkin back with John, that we almost went off the embankment, went off the highway, driving back, because I had my foot to the floor, right? . . . But I was just racing, trying to get back. He was in jail, but I was scareder than he was, cause that walk through the darkness and up that hill I just knew meant the end, you know."

Such experiences bound Suarez more closely to his friends in the movement. The disappointing years of the 1970s and 1980s, however, soured him about humanity in general. He left Mississippi in 1965, and returned to New Orleans to work on a degree in political science. For several years, he was involved in consulting work with Head Start and other War on Poverty agencies. This was a "butterfly" existence. In 1988, Suarez and his wife operated a pre-school learning center. His family was the major source of his personal happiness. Suarez felt fulfilled by his work with the school's young students, but confessed that he didn't "like people anymore," and yearned for the opportunity to buy a farm in the country and to walk away from most people and obligations. He had felt this need for perhaps ten or fifteen years. He wanted this farm "bad, desperately bad," he said. "I am retreating."

Matt Suarez had become disillusioned by a number of experiences. The violence he encountered in the movement made him jaded about human nature. But, perhaps more importantly, he believed that "what I and my colleagues were attempting to do was completely misinterpreted." Black people, and society in general, "think that integration was the problem, or lack of integration, *segregation* was the problem. And that's *not* what I was fighting for." Suarez was fighting for "equality, justice, opportunity," the liberal, individualistic dream of most Americans. He wanted blacks not to be penalized, automatically, because they were black. However, "After it's all said and done, I still think we're in a foreign land, and that the situation, rather than getting better, is getting worse." He worried about the generation of young black males who felt so completely frustrated "that they will make the Watts riots and the Detroit riots look like child's play." While he despaired of these often violent young men, his work with pre-schoolers was a conscious attempt to reach the next generation, to teach children to reason and to judge for themselves before they were assimilated by the pressures of the street.

Suarez remained close to a number of his friends from CORE and SNCC. He saw John O'Neal, Rudy Lombard, and Jerome Smith in New Orleans; he had been close to Oretha Castle. Suarez also remained close to several people he came to know through CORE and SNCC in Mississippi. "I've developed some relationships that will be with me for a lifetime. You know, no matter where I go, or where they go, we're a thousand miles apart, we know, its almost like mental telepathy, right? That we're moving in the same direction, and if I call them in California, in Washington, in Canada, wherever they at, we're going to have basically the same approach to solving a problem." Several worked in similar fields: Oretha Haley, Suarez, and Jerome Smith worked with young black children, while Bob Moses of SNCC, and Ed Dubinsky, a former mathematics professor from Tulane, were both involved in teaching math to elementary school children. Said Suarez,

No matter where you're at, or where they're at, you know you're always pretty much going in the same direction. And when you shift, you know that they're all shifting, too, even though you haven't spoken about it. They're shifting, too, and if there's a problem, and they call you about the problem, it's just to touch base on something, because you know that y'all in agreement on the same strategy, tactics, everything.[58]

In 1988, Jerome Smith operated Tamburine and Fan, an educational and cultural program for black children in New Orleans. He taught children black history, African history, and the history of black struggles throughout the world. Smith saw this work as a continuation of his role in the movement. "I just see myself as a community organizer, you know," he said. "In CORE, they called us a field worker. I'm a field-worker. Then and now, that's how I see myself. No more, no less." Smith derived much happiness from his involvement with the children in Tamburine and Fan.

"But as Jerome on Jerome, just me . . . there's more a kind of sorrow song than a joy song."[59]

Smith had almost religiously fervent memories of the civil rights movement. He recalled the heroism of the Mississippi blacks, of the men who built the first community center an Canton, Mississippi, and who slept outside the building with their guns, guarding it against white attacks. He recalled the strength of indigenous communities, and the closeness he felt with his movement colleagues in CORE and SNCC. These relationships

gave you strength, a sense of not being alone. It gave you a confirmation; it certified the rightness of your purpose. It minimized your fear, helped you to overcome your fear. There was a collective strength, even when you were by yourself, that minimized your fear. Just the thought that whatever the action was, somebody would be there for you, and if they were not there then, they were on their way. Even if they were not, there was a comfort and a commitment and there was always the knowledge that you would be rescued or helped—and celebrated. Not celebrated in the public sense, but celebrated in the sense of knowing that we were like each other's saviors.[60]

Smith's most difficult times came in the post-movement years. At some point in the mid 1970s, he felt a sense of rupture with the momentum of his past, of "feeling lonely in the struggle for the first time." No one thing precipitated this sense of loss, but a cumulative sense of stagnation. He remembered

reaching moments when there was no one to call, like being in situations that would dictate trying to reach out, and you couldn't make the same kind of calls anymore. I mean, being smashed by the hurt of the loss of the heart. And then, the rapin' of the movement by the political forces . . . and just seeing a tremendous amount of indifference to what had gone on before from the adult community.[61]

Smith remained a radical critic of the political system. While he conceded that "a certain kind of improvement" had been made in the material lives of blacks, he felt that "the emotion of the times has not changed. The plantation is very much intact." He believed that blacks were still not accepted by the larger society:

the only time a black man could be accepted is when he allow his balls is off, when he become Uncle Remus. And ain't no different with Jesse [Jackson], 'cause once they discovered he was de-balled, he couldn't become president. And if he would've, if that possibility would have been real, I'm sure that he would be with King and Malcolm X. Because the country still do not accept the black man, 'cause the price of being that is death. And that has not changed. . . . I would prefer to have the strength of the mens who picked the cotton and was in chains and didn't get the social programs but had their manhood intact.[62]

The movement had changed Jerome Smith's life. It "certified the teachings" of his mother's house, and opened up new avenues of information and learning. But more importantly, it connected Smith more firmly to the daily struggles of the rural blacks, and gave him an awareness that his intellectual sophistication could not provide. He kept his identity as a movement person, as a "field-worker" who worked with children:

One of the things I rejoice in this moment is that I am able to walk in the streets where I started from. . . . Whatever the sophistication was, it did not take me from that. In my person, I can walk on any street I done been on, and I don't be troubled by the shadow.[63]

In 1988, Tom Dent administered the New Orleans Jazz and Heritage Foundation, a job that provided him with a steady income, but left him little time for writing. He had published two books of poetry since his years with the Free Southern Theater, and contributed articles and essays to national periodicals. He had begun to write a memoir of his return to New Orleans in the mid-1960s that would capture both his boyhood and his years with the FST. He had conducted taped oral history interviews with people involved in the civil rights movement in Mississippi, and with New Orleans and Acadian musicians. Dent hoped to begin a "Southern Journey" project that would document the effect of the movement through small Southern communities. He hoped to interview the black activists, and young people, to discover how much had changed.

Dent's years with Umbra and with the Free Southern Theater gave him his voice as a writer, even though he partly submerged his own creativity by the administrative work that he did in both ventures. His work with the Jazz Fest was an extension of this kind of administration, exhibiting as it did the creativity of the African diaspora in the New World. Dent was writing about New Orleans, about his childhood, about his oddly privileged black youth, but he had had to return to New Orleans to do this. He had needed to become re-engaged in his "love-hate" relationship with the city, and with his own past.

In New York, he had consciously chosen work that forced him out of his past, forced him into contact with ordinary black people. For a time, the "extremely shy" Dent was a cosmetics salesman for a black firm. He carried his small black box of make-up samples into the worst neighborhoods of Harlem, and was never harmed. He met valuable people on his journeys, even though he failed miserably as a salesman. One acquaintance, a woman who had worked at the Welfare Department, advised him to find work there. As a welfare investigator, Dent confronted some of the most deprived, and some of the saddest situations of his life. Daily, he became immersed in a world of misery from which his parents had tried to shield him. By the time he returned to New Orleans, he was ready to use these experiences in his own writing, as he developed an identity apart from his father through his work with the Free Southern Theater.

The Free Southern Theater was first an interracial, then all-black troupe that emerged from the civil rights movement in 1964. In 1964 and 1965, it toured communities throughout the Deep South, playing before black audiences that had never seen drama before. Their early material included *Purlie Victorious*, and *In White America*. In the later 1960s, the group used more black-authored material. In 1965, the FST settled in New Orleans, and "emerged as the first community theater in the south," according to Dent. It offered training workshops in theater and writing to the New Orleans community, and stimulated ongoing theater and literary projects in the community through the 1970s and 1980s. As the civil rights movement waned after 1966, the theater became more completely a New Orleans troupe.

When Dent returned to New Orleans in 1965, he noticed the FST, and became excited about it, and the possibilities it presented. "I could see it as the application of a lot of things I had learned, a lot of things I had seen," he said in 1979. "It really wasn't understood or appreciated by people in New Orleans." The theater "attacked the provinciality" of the city in ways that Dent appreciated. The FST was a "movement theater going into the black community. It challenged the ethos of America, of the South." Dent began hanging around the theater almost every day. In 1966 he became the group's associate director.

Very consciously, I'd been trying to find my own direction out of the shadow of my father, who [was] extremely well-known. . . . I knew that if I came back, I'd have to deal with that, with the perception people have of me as *his* son, without ever really *seeing* me. . . . I wasn't ready to walk back into *that* without some *very* good reason. The Free Southern Theater gave me something positive to do, and an identity. It gave me enough reason to put up with the other stuff.[64]

His work with the FST was productive in many ways. He saw the theater as a cultural effort in the South, as an attempt to move the black

South from a "cultural backwash" into something alive and culturally vibrant. New Orleans' black musical culture had long had an exceptional vitality, but other creative arts, by comparison, languished. "The atmosphere of black New Orleans, and the black South that I grew up in, was one which I had to leave, if I wanted to develop creatively." The theater, he felt, was a good device for "developing culture" because it combined other arts—rhetoric, music, dance, visual art, and speech. The FST combined the talents of a diverse, movement-oriented cast in a volatile, creative mix. The period was good for Dent, in part because the theater developed in the "crisis situation" of the civil rights movement:

The civil rights movement was an interesting period for so many people because it was a crisis period, and people transcended themselves. For writers and artists—it may happen a little while after that—the drive is to define what happened. With the added impetus of believing that such definition is important, and that's the difference.[65]

His years with the theater involved an "incredible struggle," just to keep the troupe alive financially, and to keep it operating. In the aftermath of this experience, Dent focused more firmly on his own writing, and on the questions of identity that the experiences of Umbra and the FST seemed to provoke. Central to this struggle was his effort to integrate all of his diverse experiences as legitimate parts of the American black experience, while maintaining a connection with the black culture from which his father and grandparents had come—and had left. Dent's "Southern Journey" project through the small southern towns was a way to connect with this culture, and with his own father's past:

I think the most difficult thing to do was to come to understand and to integrate into what I'm doing, my father's work and his own tendencies toward things. . . . This I could only understand through transcendence, and through a kind of historical—I have to understand where he came from to understand him. To go back beyond him. That's my way of doing it. . . . But that's always been the most difficult part, and you have to do that.[66]

Tom Dent's aesthetic struggle replicated the journeys of his colleagues in New Orleans' black protest generation. They were people who consciously maintained a connection with the black heritage that all were trained, by education and by opportunities for mobility, to escape. Through the movement, all had become conscious of their roots in black folk culture, and in the efforts of their immediate predecessors—the ambitious parents, teachers, and preachers who counseled hard work and racial uplift, striving and ceaseless struggle. In 1988, the women and men who had sat down at dime-store lunch counters, who had refused to move, and who had worked in poor black communities throughout the South, still saw their lives as struggle.

The CORE activists were inheritors of a particular historical moment that fused racial liberation with a worldwide generational youth revolt. They had been prepared for protest by both the opportunities offered by education, and by their awareness of the rising black revolt throughout the South of their childhoods. They had watched the Montgomery Boycott unfold, and had been inspired by the student protests of 1960 in Greensboro and in Baton Rouge. But several had also sought out New Orleans' indigenous black protest in Consumers' League picket lines. They had been drawn to unconventional politics at a time when protest was dangerous, and then spent several intense years in even more critical situations.

Electoral politics evoked ambivalent feelings from most members of this generational group. Their temperaments and experiences led them to equate politics with compromise and with corruption. Additionally, their movement-born suspicion of mainstream middle-class values left them alienated from the symbols of success that their predecessors found so valuable, and necessary for self-esteem. The movement had connected them with a black past and present normally denied by the upward mobility purchased with education and competence. By identifying the black struggle in essentially class terms, they had become alienated from much of their own recent past. They viewed the moderate victories won by the Citizens' Committee and their peers in other Southern cities as necessary and valuable, but also as inadequate and "cosmetic."

The movement had produced individual and collective growth, which had in turn produced marginality and alienation. Perhaps as a consequence, the members of the protest generation spoke of consciousness and self-development in ways that most of their predecessors did not. It was as though the self, and the memory of the collective experience, became a substitute for the disappointing compromises and dailiness of public life and middle-class complacency. This generation had self-consciously made history, and had felt themselves transformed in the process. Their individual and collective development had, however, equipped them badly for the years after the revolution, when they came to realize that American society had not changed nearly enough.

SEVEN

The Meanings of the Stories

*M*OST of the stories in this book were taped in November of 1978, in April and May of 1979, and in June and July of 1988. I conducted the first set of interviews as part of dissertation research on the desegregation of New Orleans' institutions. The interviews were frequently intense and dramatic. Many were emotionally moving. Albert Dent, with suppressed anger, described his experiences of denial as a boy and young man. Rosa Keller related the agonies that Skelly Wright and his family experienced during the school crisis of 1960–1961. Rudy Lombard remembered his intense idealism, and bitter disillusionment.

In subsequent years, I remained interested in the lives of the people who had related their political experiences. Particularly, I was interested in the long-term impact of activism on the lives of individuals. I hypothesized that the collective historical experience, and the timing and the nature of activism, had a powerful impact on both the way that people experienced interracial leadership, and the way in which they incorporated it into their lives. I was also interested in the stability, or the instability, of activists' stories. If in 1988, individuals told the same stories about important political and personal experiences that they had in 1978 and 1979, it might indicate that they had incorporated those experiences as part of their autobiographies, and that these life-stories, and the identities from which they were drawn, had remained consistent over the almost ten-year interval between interviews. Conversely, a different set of memories, and different meanings ascribed to similar stories, would indicate significant changes in an individual's life, and a different conception of his or her self.

Our life stories change over time; our autobiographies—and our conceptions of our lives—change as we age, and assimilate new experiences.[1] Alessandro Portelli has suggested that life stories exhibit complementary emphases on both change and stability: one changes, learns, and grows, but somehow remains the same.[2] Portelli's arguments stress the fluid and varied nature of experience over time, and suggest that personal narratives change with the addition of experience, age, or, in the case of New Orleans' leaders, with changes in national politics.

I returned to New Orleans in 1988, hoping to re-interview the women and men with whom I had first talked. I was curious as to which forces would dominate the stories of New Orleans' activists, and what the passage of almost a decade would have done to the intensity of many of their narratives. Eight years of a conservative national administration had constricted the federal funds upon which the city had depended in the 1970s. The city's poor black population lost ground economically during the 1980s. Tight municipal budgets were reflected in the neglect of streets and highways, and in the evidence of decay that contrasted with the city's image as a tourist attraction, a convention center. Between 1970 and 1980, New Orleans changed from a majority-white to a majority-black city. It had become the third-poorest large city in the country.[3] In 1985, 27 percent of the city's families lived below the poverty level, and almost half of the city's black families lived in poverty. Unemployment in the black community hovered at 25 percent.[4]

I wondered if recent changes in federal policies, and the deterioration of the local economy, would have affected activists' view of their own lives and accomplishments. I also wondered if age might have softened the anger that many exhibited in the late 1970s—the anger at segregation, at local elites, at continuing racism and injustice. I wondered, too, if the passage of time might have changed the sense of empowerment that many activists had described earlier—an empowerment that was rooted in individual and collective acts of social change.

When I returned to New Orleans in 1988, I was able to re-interview twenty of the original forty-six people with whom I had talked in the late 1970s, and eight people with whom I had not talked previously. A number of people had died, several had moved, and one elderly woman simply did not want to talk about the past. But roughly half did. Their stories showed a surprising consistency and coherence. They told the same anecdotes, often with little change in language. Urban League president Helen Mervis described the experience of fund-raising in black churches after the League was thrown out of the Community Chest in 1957. Lolis Elie remembered being impressed with the courage of the Deacons for Defense and Justice in Bogalusa and Jonesboro. Rudy Lombard recalled the terrifying night of police attacks in Plaquemine, Louisiana, in 1963. The twenty new interviews indicated that individuals had indeed incorporated their narratives of activism into their life stories, and that the meaning of these stories had remained stable. Civil rights leadership had remained an important part of their identities, and an enduring source of pride.

Almost always, stories of dramatic events, of danger, of crisis, and of growth revealed an important aspect of an individual's personal and social development. Women and men related their stories as a process of personal and political growth which shaped activist careers. They described their careers in varying terms of change and consistency—the change involved in becoming an activist, the consistency of purpose after the initiation into politics, and the personal changes that crises provoked. New Orleans' leaders experienced themselves as historical actors who had made contributions to history. They also saw themselves as individuals who had taken risks, made stands, and been vindicated by the political and social changes of the Second Reconstruction.

The oral interviews revealed a strong sense of biographical coherence among the narrators. Although they described their lives in ways that were consistent with their generational experience, their political beliefs, and their race, they all expressed a consistent sense of self, and a sense of satisfaction with their lives and efforts. This sense of biographical coherence may be rooted in two related aspects of their lives. First, the time in their lives at which activists told their stories is probably of great importance. Second, the structure of their stories provide an important key to the kinds of coherence that each generation achieved.

Oral narratives are both historical and psychological documents that should be evaluated by different criteria than are used to evaluate other historical evidence. Most historical documents are evaluated by their correspondence to some actual reality; their "truth" depends upon whether they give correct evidence about "what really occurred" at a given time and place. According to psychologist Donald Spence, the "narrrative truth" of personal testimony depends upon "continuity and closure and the extent to which the fit of the pieces takes on an aesthetic finality."[5] Narrative truth also depends upon coherence and upon the reliability of the account—upon the extent to which a story produces a meaningful explanation of an event or process.[6] Individuals tend to explain transitional junctures or crises in their lives in similar, patterned ways. If these accounts form a consistent and coherent explanation of personal change and development, we find the narrative reliable. Conversely, we find a narrator unreliable if he or she tells stories that do not cohere. We distrust his or her account because the pieces do not seem to fit, or because the motivations of principal actors seem unbelievable. When individuals produce narratives that do not represent a reality with which we are familiar, we distrust their stories.

The stories of New Orleans' activists displayed considerable consistency. The narrators drew meaning from retrospective accounts of their experiences, a meaning that projected them into the future. They also exhibited a strong identification with history itself, with the changes that they had helped to make. And all claimed a fidelity to the values that had inspired them to act, although these values were often modified by later experiences.

There are reasons for the consistency of self and voice in the numerous stories in this book. We live in a culture that prizes personal coherence. Even though many of us experience ourselves as several "selves," perhaps fragmented at particular moments in our lives, we strive for a sense of wholeness, a sense of completion to the development we experience. Even psychologists who posit the reality of such fragmented or "distributed" selves, affirm that human beings attempt to present themselves as developmentally coherent and whole.[7] We understand our lives as wholes by making them into comprehensible and comforting stories. Each "self" thus contains numerous personal experiences woven into a coherent story. This story—or this self—includes a past that anticipates its own future through the values and expectations that are projected at the moment of telling.[8]

One might expect political activists to produce narratives that display biographical coherence. First, the act of relating one's life pressures an individual to create a coherent developmental account of his or her experiences. Our personal stories are, after all, "implements for carrying out relationships. They are means of informing others of one's goals, one's history of those goals, and one's potential future." By telling our stories, we make ourselves socially intelligible to specific audiences. Accordingly, people with a sense of historical importance endow their narratives with more coherence than do those without an identification with public life and social change. In recounting their lives as historical narratives, activists communicate a culturally shared frame of reference as they relate widely validated experiences and achievements.[9]

In an interview, the self emerges as a relationship between the speaker and interviewer, a relationship that is " 'dialogue dependent' designed as much for the recipient of our discourse as for intrapsychic purposes."[10] This dialogue-dependent self can only communicate the meaning of his or her experiences by constructing a story that "contains both continuity and coherence."[11] In order to communicate a meaningful life, then, one must fashion a socially coherent and continuous self in an interview.

In the relationship of the oral history interview, political activists attempt to replicate their personal sense of historical importance in the record being taped. The interviewer represents a conduit to an official historical record. Since the interview is retrospective, the narrator is invited to present an archaeology of his or her own life, an archaeology which will show that motivations, actions, and results were consistent throughout the past. History itself adds to the retrospective determinism of the project; we generally tend to view historical change as somehow inevitable by the very fact of its accomplishment. So, too, narrators often see their own lives as inevitable in resolution, since they see themselves as having exhibited a consistency of motive and action throughout lived time. This is particularly the case if their beliefs and actions are sanctioned by historical change and by a national consensus.

The age of a narrator contributes to this tendency toward coherence and continuity. Some life-span psychologists have pointed to the years after age 45 as a period of increasing reflection and evaluation of one's life. Much life-reviewing occurs when individuals are in their sixties. At this point, evaluating and reviewing one's life can be "an essential part of the process of deriving meaning from existence." A personal search for meaning is often initiated by an awareness of mortality, triggered by the death of family members or friends, and by a sense of the body's own fragility and limits. At such mid- and late-life junctures, life-reviews can be therapeutic, as they allow individuals to integrate their experiences into a coherent whole. Additionally, the late-life years of the sixties and seventies are often periods of reconciliation for individuals. In these years, they often make peace with their pasts, and accept the outcome of their lives as, in fact, inevitable, and certainly irreversible.[12]

Almost all of the narrators of this study were in their forties, fifties, and sixties at the time of the interviews in 1978–1979 and 1988. Many were in their sixties; several were older. A number had experienced the death of colleagues, friends, and relatives. Most were at reflective and evaluative junctures in their own lives, and seemed willing to discuss the meaning of their lives and political crusades, and their feelings about their experiences. Many individuals seemed to use the interviews as opportunities to discuss the important events and accomplishments in their lives, and to elaborate on the meaning of their experiences. The events that they remembered often signified important actions, and equally important life-transitions. Frequently, political events and changes in the political environment had provoked important life-transitions. Repression created ostracism and sometimes danger; perceived radicalism precluded political success for James Dombrowski and Virginia Collins. The collapse of CORE, and the death of an organized movement, generated a search for an alternative political life among people like Lolis Elie, Jerome Smith, and Rudy Lombard. Alternately, the political environment of the late 1960s and beyond invited other life changes associated with political success and increased status for a number of activists. This happened for Robert Collins, Dutch Morial, Moon Landrieu, Revius Ortique, A. L. Davis, Rosa Keller, and Albert Dent. Among these narrators, biographical coherence was in part a product of historical change.

Within the context of both historical and personal changes, activists told their stories in patterns similar to others of their generation and political values. Their patterns were the product of similar historical experiences and long relationships. The three generations of activists created distinctive types of political careers within their personal and occupational lives.

Living the Struggle: Careers of Activism

The concept of a career of activism is important, because it combines a number of public and personal experiences. A career implies a long-term commitment to a course of action, to social goals, and to individual and collective values. A political career operationalizes an individual's social and personal values; it also allows a sense of efficacy to grow as a leader achieves important personal and group goals. A career also implies a progression in status and function as an individual develops and ages. Within this progression, values emerge successively as goals are pursued and attained, or lost. Individuals measure their personal success within careers by the degree to which they can convince themselves of their own feelings of progress, and the extent to which friends and others affirm the pace and meaning of their personal trajectories.[13]

We can understand activism as an important part of the "career set" that made up each individual's life. The career set encompassed each person's occupational, domestic, and recreational careers.[14] Within these segmented parts of each leader's life, activism served as part of an occupational career, or as part of a recreational career, if political work was an avocation rather than a vocation. Or a political career might begin as an occupational career that encompassed much more of a leader's life, only to be translated later into another occupation. This often happened with the protest generation, which moved from positions as community organizers to postmovement careers that replicated the values, if not the activities, of their experiences within the movement. Political careers had important developmental functions. The nature of these functions and the timing of each individual's engagement helped to determine the impact of the political career upon other areas of his or her life, and upon the life that emerged from an era of crisis and achievement.

Significantly, the collective historical experience of each generation, the timing of activism, and its nature helped to determine the function that political action performed in the lives of New Orleans' leaders.

First, the collective historical experience of each generation gave its members a distinctive worldview, and view of race. Large historical changes, like the Depression of the 1930s and World War II, had different impacts on how sensitive men and women were to race, politics, and poverty. Historical circumstances also affected the kinds of messages about race that parents gave to their children, and the examples of resistance and community leadership that they set. Most importantly, parental models schooled women and men in self-confidence and self-assertion, which were necessary qualities for those who would challenge a social system.

Second, the timing of activism was important. To some extent, mentorship determined the timing, and the character of activism. Mentors transmitted traditions of protest and leadership, and frequently provided opportunities for individuals to act. They often exerted a catalytic effect on individuals' lives.

Third, the nature of activism shaped individual and collective perceptions of significant change. Styles of activism generated specific strategies for achieving goals. The racial negotiator often had a far different perception of significant political change than did the "actionist" or "field-worker" of CORE, but the negotiators used the threat of direct action, and the young people's impatience, as an important bargaining chip in reaching their objectives. Thus, the timing and nature of activism interacted with historical change to produce distinctive styles of collective action, and distinctive political careers. The function that activism played in each individual's life determined the meaning of his or her career. Activism had a different function for each generation. Historical changes ordained different opportunities for political actors, and different meanings of racial liberation. Timing was important, because politics filled different functions in the life-stages of various leaders. These functions were largely consistent with the stages of adult development that scholars like Erik Erikson have studied. Particularly, the function of activism varied with the timing at which an individual began his or her political career.[15]

The first generation typically entered politics as mature adults with well-defined roles within the community. Activism gave these individuals opportunities to increase their power and influence. Activism also enhanced these leaders' sense of personal efficacy, as they battled a system that all considered unjust and oppressive. Although few saw immediate rewards for their often lonely efforts, they were later able to see long-term changes in their community. Thus, the woman or man who began a political crusade in his or her late thirties or early forties could later achieve personal and community goals on a broad canvas, as he or she moved within one or more racial communities. This leader usually felt a strong investment in the general community welfare, and made his or her appeals on that basis. Racial activism gave such women and men wider latitude for what Erikson has called "generativity"—"the concern for establishing and guiding the next generation."[16] Generativity and altruism were often primary motivations for the first generation. Most were themselves economically secure and comfortable, but pushed for changes that would benefit others beyond their families and immediate friends. Leaders of the first generation worked through established social and political institutions that shaped the lives of others. All maintained an interest in education, and in opening opportunities for young people in the community. Several of these women and men became mentors of activists in succeeding generations.

Individuals who entered political life in their late twenties and early thirties made activism a means of defining and supporting their careers and lives. Young lawyers became known to the larger community through activism, which frequently projected them into a future of bi-racial politics. Civil rights leadership filled personal needs that were specific to young professionals: it allowed them to focus their ambitions for social change through acceptable means, through the law and through political action. These leaders were often guided by influential mentors, and developed their own political roles in relation to those mentors, and to immediate possibilities within the community.[17] Typically, members of this generation used established institutions to challenge the discriminatory practices of state and local agencies. Lawyers and black organizations used the law and federal courts to attack discriminatory state laws, and white liberals organized Save Our Schools to oppose school closure. This generation saw the electoral process as a necessary key to black empowerment. They developed careers as activists with an eye toward eventual success in electoral politics.

Leaders who entered politics in the years of late adolescence or early adulthood had different needs and agendas. Adolescence and young adulthood are periods of ego consolidation. Young people attempt to separate from parents, and to find new role models and mentors. Political identities adopted during this "young adult transition" have long-term consequences. A compelling political experience can permanently alter an individual's values and beliefs.[18] The protest generation, which entered politics during this period of the young adult transition, had a different agenda than their elders because they were free of adult responsibilities, and because they became part of a mass movement, the black student revolt of the 1960s. The movement experience became a critical part of their identity formation, a crucible of their adult political lives. Leaders of this generation had fewer commitments to local institutions than did their elders. They joined a national organization, CORE, which only loosely directed the affairs of local chapters. They attacked segregation with the organized disruption of direct-action protest. Even the leader of the NAACP Youth

Council, though tied to the dictates of the national office, felt no obligation to obey the orders of the local hierarchy.

In the oral interviews upon which this book is based, individuals discussed and evaluated their political careers. Most judged their roles in historical change, and the success of the civil rights movement, by the values and goals adopted during their activist years. Leaders evaluated the present by the standards of the vision of politics that had initially inspired them. They judged their individual successes by the extent to which they had created lives that were continuous with their roles as activists. All felt it important to have the movement's achievements, and hence their own values and lives, affirmed by historical judgment and by the larger society.

A major component of an activist career is, of course, ideology. Leaders develop these ideas and beliefs from interaction with parental models, mentors, and peers, and from education. Political experience itself often generates changes in individual and collective ideologies, as campaigns are won or lost, and goals either reached or abandoned. Ideological identification, in turn, can determine an individual's class and status identity. Civil rights activism often altered social status and personal mobility. Leaders sometimes experienced harassment, terrorism, and ostracism. They also achieved wider visibility in the black community, or status in New Orleans' emerging bi-racial, civil rights community of the 1950s and 1960s. A number achieved political success and personal recognition. Individuals responded personally to these experiences in ways that were consistent with their initiation into bi-racial politics. Their symbolic class identities at mid-life reflected a consistency with the values of their activist years. Leaders' judgments about the American ethic of social mobility, about the value and centrality of electoral politics, and of the meaning of black advancement, were revealed in these symbolic identities. Activists who believed that black electoral success demonstrated the ultimate victory of the civil rights movement also maintained an unshaken belief in individual social mobility and in democratic liberalism—particularly when they had experienced considerable mobility and recognition themselves. Such individuals emphasized racial difference far less frequently than did those who maintained a symbolic class identity with the black working class and the black poor.

The First Generation: Integrationists

The first generation was profoundly influenced by the Depression of the 1930s and by World War II. James Dombrowski and Virginia Collins were both drawn to the Southern Conference on Human Welfare in 1938, and both witnessed the impoverishment of black and white Southerners. Helen Mervis was attracted to left-wing politics as a student in the 1930s, as was Albert D'Orlando in the 1940s. Rosa Keller found the example of Nazi genocide a terrifying conclusion to unbridled racism, and joined the Urban League in part because of her fears. Revius Ortique and Leonard Burns both served in the military.

Within New Orleans, mentors shaped the direction and tone of this generation's activism. Class and status provided specific opportunities for mentorship and for political involvement. Racial diplomats became prominent according to the institutions they represented, and the resources they could tap. Institutions of philanthropy and uplift played a significant role in the lives of Albert Dent, Rosa Keller, Leonard Burns, Revius Ortique, and Helen Mervis. All were involved in the Urban League, or with Dillard University. Will Alexander, a New Deal Farm Security administrator, had been a mentor to Albert Dent. Keller was mentored by community activist Gladys Cahn, and by J. Westbrook McPherson of the Urban League. Betty Goldstein introduced Helen Mervis to the Urban League, and Albert Dent and A. P. Tureaud had served as mentors to Revius Ortique. Leonard Burns found mentors in *Louisiana Weekly* publisher C. C. DeJoie, and a doctor who urged him to get involved in community organizations to help build his practice. Virginia Collins and Leontine Luke both had preacher fathers as political mentors and role models.

The nature of the activism that these individuals undertook was a product of socialization, historical context, and the timing of activism in the life-course. This generation undertook activism as a constituent part or by-product of adult careers. James Dombrowski's activism defined his career as director of SCEF. For women like Mervis, Keller, Luke, and Collins, activism became an unpaid career that emerged from volunteer projects. For Luke, Collins, and Mervis, activism also led to occupational career opportunities which replicated the roles that the women had filled as community leaders. Burns, Ortique, and Dent operated as racial negotiators, in part because of their status within the community, and in part because of their freedom from local economic and political pressures.

Civil rights activism complemented and enhanced the roles that the first generation had developed in New Orleans, in part because of its nature and its function within their lives. Five became racial negotiators. Their political work became a way to produce widespread changes for the city's black population, and to make interpersonal changes among the city's elite. Racial negotiators felt that the latter often produced changes in the city's public and private institutions. Activism became a way for blacks to achieve political status within their community, and for whites to achieve an alternative status within the developing bi-racial political community in the city.

Not surprisingly, the work of this generation was premised on very progressive assumptions. They genuinely believed that if individuals were given the correct facts about race and prejudice, that they would then change their behavior and institutions. Thus, this group placed great emphasis on *knowing* the racial Other, or of becoming known by him. The impulse was educational, the methods diplomatic. The radical SCEF held community forums and published the *Southern Patriot* to document the costs of racism; Mervis later formed the Community Relations Council to educate whites and blacks about racial issues. When educational methods and diplomacy failed, the black community leaders responded with lawsuits, and by organizing boycotts—a low-risk, but dignified refusal to participate in demeaning rituals of discrimination.

In retrospective assessments of their lives as activists, New Orleans' leaders indicated that their political lives had satisfied a number of personal needs. They had widened their network of close friends and relationships, having endured difficult periods of ostracism and harassment over the 1950s, and, in some cases, the 1960s. Radicals like Dombrowski and Collins found their opportunities circumscribed and their hopes frustrated by extremist and moderate responses to their political commitments. All, however, felt to some extent vindicated by the historic changes that the movement had produced. All expressed deep satisfaction with their political careers, and a sense of having taken risks, and created history. Even James Dombrowski and Virginia Collins claimed this sense of serenity and achievement, although both were greatly disappointed with the national government, and with capitalism itself. All endorsed the ideals of interracialism that had made them integrationists in the 1950s.

The Political Generation

The second generation was shaped by World War II and the postwar world. Many came into middle-class professions as a result of the GI Bill, and the prosperity of the late 1940s and 1950s. Their ideas of race and opportunity were expanded by the war and its aftermath: black lawyers like Robert Collins, Ernest Morial, and Lolis Elie attended newly desegregated law schools. Their service in the military gave them new social experiences, and exposure to new environments that they used to measure progress in New Orleans. Law offered these men both an independent living, and a way to make changes in the condition of blacks. The *Brown* decision, especially, promised a new era in black opportunity, and in race relations in the South. Also, importantly, the era of Massive Resistance demonstrated the extremism of the forces of racial repression. It made these men far less optimistic about the efficacy of racial diplomacy than were their elders.

Similarly, white liberals were changed by the war and its aftermath. John P. Nelson, Jr., Moon Landrieu, and Ann Dlugos were devoutly religious Southerners, who found it difficult to believe in both Christianity and segregation. All three had been raised in families which stressed social responsibility, and which had given them self assurance and a strong sense of personal security. The war years brought changes for all three. Nelson first encountered educated and cultivated blacks in his service in the army. He found a resolution to his own turbulent feelings about the war and race in Louis Twomey's classes at Loyola University. Moon Landrieu's feelings on race were changed by his years as an undergraduate and then law student at newly integrated Loyola University. Ann Dlugos' ideas on race and segregation were influenced by her Sunday school teachers, and by professors at Sophie Newcomb College. For religious, moral, and political reasons, these three were opposed to the campaign of Massive Resistance in the 1950s. All felt confident that the federal government would prevail.

As young adults, this generation cultivated lasting relationships with important mentors. Attorney A. P. Tureaud was a valuable mentor for Ernest Morial; Jack Nelson became a mentor and friend to Lolis Elie. Nelson himself found a mentor and ally in Father Twomey. Moon Landrieu had Chep Morrison as a mentor, and Ann Dlugos was inspired by Mary Allen. These mentors transmitted values and styles of leadership. Tureaud was a member of the city's Creole elite, and reinforced Morial's tendencies toward elitism, individualism, and political moderation. Twomey and Nelson believed that law was an instrument of social change, that it should be used to obtain both political and religious ends. For Lolis Elie, this orientation complemented the spiritual emphasis of his later mentor in CORE, Richard Haley. In Chep Morrison, Moon Landrieu had an important example of both success in bi-racial politics, and of a failure of will. Morrison had been a very successful mayor with a bi-racial constituency until he refused to take a stand for school desegregation during the school crisis of 1960–1961, or for racial liberalism during the gubernatorial campaign of 1959. Mary Allen taught Ann Dlugos to express her political values in community activism—much as Dlugos' mother had.

Electoral politics and legal change became benchmarks of racial progress for this generation, and an important part of their evolving political identities. This was due to the centrality of electoral politics and court decisions in defining national and local racial issues in the 1950s, and to the driven, ambitious nature of the young attorneys. Most of these leaders were sure that the federal government would win its battle with segregationist state politicians. Additionally, they were aware that an unfettered black vote would dramatically alter urban politics in the South. From his first years in practice, Moon Landrieu set out to build a bi-racial constituency. Collins, Douglas, and Elie began to organize black voting organizations after the passage of the Voting Rights Act of 1965. Nelson himself ran for office twice. The timing of political socialization, the rapidly changing historical context, and their own positions as attorneys gave this generation a belief in and commitment to electoral politics and the law as means of racial liberation and personal success. At mid-life and beyond, their lives remained defined by their continuing acceptance of, or rejection of this equation.

Due to the timing of activism, and the professional status of the individuals involved, civil rights work functioned as a training ground for electoral politics, and as a method of career-building. In the early years of the 1960s, this work was often risky. Collins and Elie occasionally found themselves in terrifying situations, confronting judges or local police who displayed little respect for federal law, or for the rights of blacks. Nelson took unpopular cases, and lost the two elections in which he ran. Yet as an education, the civil rights movement offered enormous challenges, and heady achievements. To the young attorneys, it seemed that everything could be resolved by law and politics, and their lives were part of that resolution. Activism fused moral absolutes, professional aspirations, and local and national political goals. This generation had a sense of being empowered by the legal system, and by national political changes which sanctioned their personal and political crusades.

Even white liberals like the women of SOS viewed their activism as part of a political process that aimed to change electoral politics—which, they believed, could change their social system just as surely as could the law. Ann Dlugos, Peggy Murison, and Betty Wisdom—three of the younger women prominent in SOS—saw their efforts as part of a campaign to change local and regional politics. For each woman, SOS was a continuation of earlier political work in the League of Women Voters, the Independent Women's Organization, and the American Civil Liberties Union.

Because activism defined both professional and political lives, the men of this generation described their choices in terms of their success in or their rejection of a career in politics. Those who did not seek political office, or who failed in the effort, as did Nelson and Elie, refocused their life objectives accordingly, in ways that were consistent with the values that they had brought to and developed in their activist lives. Both men had invested their crusades with a religious meaning; the movement had ignited their shared sense of moral absolutism. Both made choices that seemed to preclude successful political careers. Yet they interpreted their choices in terms of the personal and spiritual growth that each had achieved on his moral journey. In their mature years, both Nelson and Elie found an ultimate meaning in the spiritual gains that had come, at least in part, from renouncing or losing the movement's most visible reward—a successful political life.

Not surprisingly, the men of this generation expressed a more enduring sense of racial difference, and class issues, than did most members of the first generation. Additionally, their views of black progress were less optimistic than were those of their elders, although these politicians, attorneys, and community activists had seen their faith in electoral politics vindicated by the changes of the 1970s and 1980s. Most had come to realize the economic limits of recent political change. Black and white activists were sadly aware that the economic situation of the black poor in New Orleans had worsened since 1970. They also knew that black mayors and city officials could do very little to alleviate the deprivation that haunted many of the city's depressed neighborhoods.

The Protest Generation

The young people drawn to direct-action protest had grown up in the postwar era of boycotts and rising black militancy. They came from working-class black families in which their parents had encouraged both personal achievement and ambition, and resistance to segregation. Jerome Smith and Rudy Lombard had emulated their fathers' examples of physical resistance to segregation; Doris Jean Castle saw in her parents and grandmothers examples of pride and dignity. A number of the CORE members were first-generation college students when they became involved in the Consumers' League's boycott, and then the black student movement.

They joined the movement at a critical time in their lives—the transition to adulthood. Then, individuals are particularly susceptible to momentous changes in ideology and life direction. To join a large social movement at this juncture was life-transforming. The Castle sisters, Jerome Smith, Rudy Lombard, and Matt Suarez found new role models and mentors in people like James T. McCain of CORE and the Reverend A. L. Davis in New Orleans. They conducted dangerous, often frightening protests both inside New Orleans and "in the field" beyond, in Mississippi, Louisiana, and in other Southern states. They experienced extremes in human closeness and in danger. They also developed considerable political skills as they organized communities, working with the poorest black farmers, with local leaders, and with movement luminaries. The movement experience, and the relationships they developed in it, changed their lives. Many CORE leaders became radicalized and disillusioned by their experiences. They also asserted that they had grown in life-changing ways.

The movement had a transformative effect because it caught the young activists at a particularly vulnerable period in their lives, a period of identity-formation and consolidation. The movement separated them from their peers in New Orleans and gave them a new community of reference. It also gave them careers as political activists in the service of black liberation. It connected them to the experiences of working-class blacks in ways that their own projected lives as college-educated blacks would not have.

The activist career was a transformative experience because it fused many aspects of the young leaders' lives into an interconnected network of meaning. Friendships, political goals, personal growth, and racial liberation were all enmeshed in the movement experience. The movement gave the activists life-direction and values in crucial formative years of their lives—the period between 1960 and 1966, when the political world of Southern black people changed dramatically. The intensity of this experience generated a sense of accelerated development in many activists, and a sense of tremendous accomplishment. The years after the movement offered nothing so intense or so collectively compelling. People like Rudy

Lombard, Jerome Smith, Matt Suarez, and Lolis Elie felt the loss very keenly.

The young people had entered the campaign against segregation with euphoric hopes. They had ventured into some of the most hostile white communities, and some of the most dangerous areas to do community organizing and voter registration. And they began this with a faith that their direct-action campaigns would change the attitudes of whites, and that their efforts in community organizing would help generate long-lasting changes in the condition of black people. Continuing white violence, and sluggishness at the national level eroded these hopes, and disillusioned many former idealists.

Activist careers created within the movement had to be refocused, or redirected in the late 1960s, 1970s, and 1980s. The strength of the movement experience was evident in the way in which the CORE partisans fashioned lives and careers that were consistent with the values of their youth. Like many of the white activists who ventured South during Freedom Summer of 1964, the black student activists of New Orleans largely fashioned careers in the social services, in the arts, and in the helping professions.[19] Thus, their careers as organizers and "field-workers" set a blueprint for their later lives, but one that had to be recast and redirected as they returned to school, began to work, and did or did not create families.

Significantly, this generation maintained a strong sense of working-class identity. Although most came from working-class families, their education and jobs would normally have placed them squarely in the ranks of the black middle class. The movement, however, had fused their own expectations of personal success with the fortunes of the black working class and the black poor. They had hoped for personal and collective transformation. At mid-life, the CORE leaders continued to measure social change by the progress, or lack of progress, among the black poor. They remained angry about racial injustice, and expressed a continuing ambivalence about the value of electoral politics in producing meaningful social change. Like their elders in the community, the former militants expressed a sense of personal coherence and consistency throughout their careers of momentous and sometimes disruptive change. Unlike the moderates, they felt that their lives had been almost miraculously transformed by the process of making history.

The former CORE leaders retained this sense of personal transformation because it was the product of a collective experience from which they had gained a sense of collective identity. Their sense of growth, of change, and of achievement was linked to this collective identity, and to the conviction that they had made history for blacks by being part of a genuine mass movement. At mid-life and later, their sense of symbolic class identity remained rooted in the collective experience, because that experience had enlarged their hopes, and had joined them to something larger and more inspiring than their individual selves.

The Retrospective Structuring of Lives

In the late 1970s and in 1988, New Orleans' leaders shaped personal narratives that were consistent with their generational experience. To a large extent, this was due to the historically specific styles of activism that each generation undertook. The 1950s had been marked by the ascendance of the racial diplomat, although this kind of leader was joined—and challenged—by the race man in the late 1950s and early 1960s. The race man represented a switch from an older, class-oriented style of interracial leadership to a mass-oriented leadership that was unafraid to confront white elites. The race man was, in turn, pushed by the students in CORE, who were not afraid to risk arrest and prison to obtain their rights.[20]

Each generation described episodes of personal and political crisis in characteristic patterns. These crisis situations became emblematic of their personal styles of racial leadership, and symbolized their relationship to historical change. Such experiences retrospectively became moments of self-definition and often functioned as transitional experiences for narrators. Crises variously signified a change from one set of beliefs to another, or they functioned as learning, or even as conversion experiences. Because these experiences often fused personal and political experience, they stood as moments when activists felt themselves connected to history.

Activists related these experiences with great intensity and emotion. Their memories indicated that activism had become a resource for defining the past, and for continuing self-definition. Interviewed at mid- and late-life, individuals described their lives, and the trajectories of their careers, by political experiences that served as personal benchmarks of transition, crisis, and change. Retrospectively, these experiences appeared to be building blocks of their mature selves. Activists achieved a sense of coherence through the memory of change and crisis.

Within the first generation, the attacks on the NAACP of the 1950s, the school crisis of 1960, and the voting struggles of the 1950s and 1960s provoked intense emotional memories. McCarthyism and massive resistance created a tense and dangerous environment for advocates of racial change. Albert Dent remembered his quiet management of library desegregation, and his secret role in carrying donations to the NAACP offices in New York. Rosa Keller recalled the furor aroused by her petition to the school board in 1955, by the Urban League crisis of 1957–1958, and by the school crisis of 1960–1961. James Dombrowski recalled the SISS investigations, Albert D'Orlando remembered the HUAC hearings, and John P. Nelson remembered his unsuccessful race for the school board. McCarthyism and Massive Resistance fused in the 1950s, creating a repressive environment for anyone who advocated racial integration. The leaders of the 1950s experienced harassment as political and social ostracism and red-baiting. For radicals like Dombrowski and Collins, this kind of harassment continued into the 1960s.

Activists of the 1950s used boycotts, lawsuits, and negotiations to achieve black goals. They remembered achievements as moral and political victories. Revius Ortique recalled the sweeping success of the McDonogh Day Boycott; Leonard Burns remembered the trickster victory of desegregating the municipal auditorium, and the use of the indigenous Mardi Gras celebration to launch the protest of Carnival Blackouts. Rosa Keller and Albert Dent found satisfaction in the achievement of library desegregation, and Keller in the integration of city buses. Such victories validated the individualistic visions of this group of leaders. These successes demonstrated that individuals could change history, and that federal laws could alter the racial practices of their city.

The victories of the 1950s combined private, class-based leadership with mass mobilization for relatively safe forms of protest. The narratives of the first generation reflected a mix of privileged initiative and mass arousal. Leaders' stories also revealed the tightly drawn circles of interracial activists of this era. Albert Dent and Rosa Keller knew each other through Dillard's Board of Trustees, and through Keller's service on the board of Flint-Goodridge Hospital. Keller, Ortique, Burns, and Mervis interacted through the Urban League. Keller, Mervis, and Nelson were leaders of Save Our Schools. And Keller helped to finance the desegregation of Tulane, which Nelson then argued. Significantly, Virginia Collins, Albert D'Orlando, and James Dombrowski were all aligned with SCEF.

Because their political identities and actions were so firmly directed toward public evidence of change, the moderates of this generation took the evidence of such changes as proof that their crusade had been won. Black political leadership, integrated public schools, and open public facilities represented major victories and changes. This generation also took seriously the accolades, awards, and honors that their community and others gave them for their interracial leadership. The moderates found meaning in the public recognition of their activism; it sealed their importance in history. Somewhat conversely, radicals James Dombrowski and Virginia Collins saw such public successes as evidence that not much of significance—i.e., economic institutions—had in fact been altered. For them, meaning was a function of action itself, and of the goals and hopes that each had nurtured over long lives in struggle. For Collins, this struggle was tied to the work of her predecessors, to the "slave girl" grandmother who had become educated, and to her black nationalist father, the Garveyite preacher. Collins found a continuing meaning in her family tradition of opposition and resistance.

Second-generation activists functioned as political leaders and legal advisers in the constitutional and legal battles of the early 1960s. Accordingly, the arena of power included the closed rooms of the city's elite, the courtrooms of the federal system, and the decision-making councils of a mass movement. The second generation found itself acting in the service of and representing the black student movement and community groups that brought blacks into electoral power in the late 1960s. The battles they fought were legal and political, and the dangers they experienced were sometimes those of the movement itself—threats from armed troopers in Plaquemine, Louisiana, or a hostile mob in Poplarville, Mississippi.

Ernest Morial took civil rights cases as A. P. Tureaud's junior partner. John P. Nelson, Jr., ran for the school board, served on the board of SOS, and took the *Lombard* case when the sit-ins began. Robert Collins and Lolis Elie represented CORE, and Elie had, with Morial, served as legal adviser to the Consumers' League during the boycott of 1959–1960. As a freshman legislator, Moon Landrieu publicly voted against legislation to uphold and extend racial segregation in Louisiana. Ann Dlugos, Betty Wisdom and Peggy Murison attempted to both change local opinion and resolve the school crisis through SOS. The women testified at legislative hearings on school closure, and had attempted to publicize the disastrous effects of closing public schools. Wisdom and Murison had volunteered to drive and walk white children into the two embattled schools in the Ninth Ward, and had been exposed to mob violence and harassment.

This generation experienced crisis and its resolution through the law and the political system. Their careers and lives were validated by both legal and political victories and by historical change itself. Landrieu emerged from the crisis of 1960–1961 as a successful politician and mayor; Robert Collins became a federal judge. Lolis Elie became a negotiator for the Citizens' Committee while he and his partners took cases throughout Louisiana. John P. Nelson successfully argued *Lombard* before the Supreme Court in 1963, and saw Tulane desegregate that year. Dutch Morial had a meteoric career as a local NAACP president and political leader, and served two terms as New Orleans' first black mayor. The victories remembered were both political and legal: negotiations with the white elite of New Orleans, working with the Deacons for Defense and Justice in Bogalusa, defending CORE workers within and outside New Orleans. All of these men felt pride in the changes that they had helped to create. Their careers as activists had been visibly validated in both their personal and political lives. For the women of SOS, the eventual integration of the city's public schools occasioned some ambivalence: guilt in Dlugos' case for educating her son in a private school, and a mixture of guilt and regret on Murison's part for keeping her children in a public school where, she felt, they received an inadequate education.

This generation derived meaning from the public acceptance of their crusade, and from its results. They differed from the sometimes isolated crusaders of the first generation in both their ambition and in their forthright search for power. The lawyers' careers were based on wide-ranging public changes in racial status. Federal legislation mandated these changes in 1964 and 1965, with the Civil Rights Act and the Voting Rights Act. Afterwards, new black political organizations like SOUL and COUP backed liberal white and black candidates for public office. Morial, Collins, Elie, and Nelson had sought to push the law and legal system to its limits to guarantee effective enfranchisement for blacks. In the changes of the 1960s, they saw their hopes both realized and limited. Thus, the meaning of their experience was bittersweet. They had achieved much, but had seen their successes severely limited in the last twenty years. By 1988, the meaning of their crusades was, in fact, historic. Though they remained engaged, the historic moment of hope had vanished.

In 1988, Robert Collins continued to find meaning in his life as a judge.

Dutch Morial found validation in his accomplishments as mayor, and in his role as a spokesman for the voiceless and the powerless. Landrieu was validated by his concrete accomplishments: "we *moved* the system." For these men, achievement had a material, practical, public meaning that resided in the possession and use of power. Conversely, historical changes converged with tumultuous personal experiences for Jack Nelson and his friend Lolis Elie. Both men responded by turning inward, and by specifying more closely the targets of their political concern. For both men, meaning had a largely spiritual dimension that included achievements in the public world, but was not defined by them. The meaning of their efforts rested in the spiritual and personal transformations that each had experienced, and had seen in others. Thus, the public achievements of the civil rights era remained sources of affirmation and pride, but did not constitute the meaning of their lives in history.

The third generation had sought to transform the world of blacks, first through direct action, and second, by community organization aimed at voting rights and political representation. They had emerged as leaders of the sit-ins in New Orleans, and later worked in Louisiana, Mississippi, and in other places with CORE. Many became disillusioned by the extremes of hope and disappointment that they experienced in their efforts. They also became cynical about electoral politics. All found meaning in what they had hoped to do in the movement, and meaning in the experience of struggle. This was at once a private and communal sense of meaning, a shared discourse among former activists who remained friends in mid-life.

The events that they remembered juxtaposed personal growth with great danger and sacrifice. Jerome Smith and Doris Jean Castle recalled the terrifying Freedom Rides. Rudy Lombard remembered police attacks in Plaquemine in 1963, and harassment and danger in Philadelphia, Mississippi, in 1964. Matt Suarez remembered brutal beatings, fear, and a sense of accomplishment in building the Mississippi Freedom Democratic Party.

In the late 1970s and 1988, the protest generation retained an oppositional consciousness to both recent history and to the successes of black politicians in the 1970s and 1980s. Their continuing ambivalence about electoral politics reflected a fundamental distrust of power itself, and an unwillingness to effectively engage in political life for the sake of power. Their own impulses remained transformative at mid-life, rooted in the great transitions that they had experienced as activists. Accordingly, their sense of meaning was individually structured by both collective and intergenerational themes of struggle and resistance—to their connections with fellow activists, and with family histories that stressed dignity and opposition to common conditions of oppression. The evocation of family traditions, and of a collective identity were perhaps necessary alternative psychic supports for women and men who had made and experienced great changes, and who remained largely alienated from the political world surrounding them. Distrusting the accolades of power, cynical about politics, they found their vision of themselves reinforced by family predecessors, and by the vibrant cultural traditions of the larger black community that still lacked power, and wealth.

New Orleans' activists found meaning in the hopes that had inspired them during their periods of greatest political efficacy. During such periods, they had felt most connected to history, having become part of the historical process through personal action. Retrospectively, activists endowed those hopes and actions with a personal meaning that gave coherence and consistency to their narratives, and gave a sense of continuity to their lives. At mid-life and beyond, memories of activism became personal narratives of fulfillment and reconciliation, stories that united the present to the past. Perhaps this is because activism itself became a means of establishing and sustaining hope, and thus sustaining a coherent sense of self.

Notes

1. Introduction

1. Beverly Hendrix Wright, "New Orleans: A City That Care Forgot," in Robert D. Bullard, ed., *In Search of the New South: The Black Urban Experience of the 1970s and 1980s* (Tuscaloosa: The University of Alabama Press, 1989), 45–74.

2. Virginia R. Dominguez, *White by Definition: Social Classification in Creole Louisiana* (New Brunswick, N.J.: Rutgers University Press, 1986), 91–182.

3. *Ibid.*, 205–61.

4. Sterling Stuckey, *Slave Culture: Nationalist Theory and the Foundation of Black America* (New York: Oxford University Press, 1987), 59–61; John Blassingame, *Black New Orleans, 1860–1880* (Chicago: University of Chicago Press, 1973), 1–22.

5. Blassingame, *Black New Orleans*, 17–21.

6. *Ibid.*, 201–10.

7. Huey L. Perry and Alfred Stokes, "Politics and Power in the Sunbelt: Mayor Morial of New Orleans," in Michael B. Preston, Lenneal Henderson, Jr., and Paul L. Puryear, eds., *The New Black Politics: The Search for Political Power* (New York: Longman, 1982), 223–24; Daniel C. Thompson, *The Negro Leadership Class* (Englewood Cliffs, N.J.: Prentice Hall, 1963), 1–32.

8. See Pierce Lewis, *New Orleans: The Making of an Urban Landscape* (Cambridge, Mass.: Ballinger, 1976), 40–77; see also Martha Ruth Mahoney, "The Changing Nature of Public Housing in New Orleans, 1930–1974," M.A. Thesis: Tulane University, 1985.

9. Gary B. Mills, *The Forgotten People: Cane River's Creoles of Color* (Baton

Rouge: Louisiana State University Press, 1977); Blassingame, *Black New Orleans*; John H. Rohrer and Monroe S. Edmonson, eds., *The Eighth Generation Grows Up: Cultures and Personalities of New Orleans' Negroes* (New York: Harper & Brothers, 1960).

10. Tom Dent, "Mardi Gras Eve/1968," *Exquisite Corpse*, vol. 6, no. 1–4, January–April 1988.

11. *Ibid.*, 21.

12. Thompson, *The Negro Leadership Class*, 124–25.

13. Lolis E. Elie, "Niggertown Memories," *Black River Journal*, New Orleans, 1977.

14. *Ibid.*

15. Thompson, *The Negro Leadership Class*, 123–25.

16. Tom Dent, "St. Joseph's Day Celebrations or the Origins of Super Sunday," *New Orleans Tribune*, March 1986, pp. 14–15.

17. Thompson, *The Negro Leadership Class*, 2–70.

18. Karl Mannheim, "The Problem of Generations," in Karl Mannheim, *Essays on the Sociology of Knowledge*, edited by Paul Kecskemeti (New York: Oxford University Press, 1952), 276–322.

19. See Ron Fraser et al., *1968: A Student Generation in Revolt* (New York: Pantheon, 1988); Jack Whalen and Richard Flacks, *Beyond the Barricades: The Sixties Generation Grows Up* (Philadelphia: Temple University Press, 1989); Doug McAdam, *Freedom Summer* (New York: Oxford University Press, 1988); Sara Evans, *Personal Politics: The Roots of Women's Liberation in the Civil Rights Movement and the New Left* (New York: Knopf, 1980).

20. See David C. Rubin, ed., *Autobiographical Memory*, (Cambridge, Mass.: Harvard University Press, 1986).

2. Overcoming Massive Resistance

1. By "progressive", I am referring to people who were to the left of the Cold War liberals who dominated organizations like the Urban League. These included Albert D'Orlando, pastor of the First Unitarian Church, who had been a member of the American Student Union while in college in the 1940s, and Dr. James Dombrowski, who directed the Southern Conference Educational Fund (SCEF) in the 1950s and early 1960s.

2. Kim Lacy Rogers, "Organizational Experience and Personal Narrative: Stories of New Orleans' Civil Rights Leaders," *Oral History Review*, vol. 13, 1985, 23–54.

3. Thompson, *The Negro Leadership Class*, 88–96.

4. Mrs. Leontine Goins Luke, Interview by Kim Lacy Rogers, 22 May 1979.

5. *Ibid.*

6. Virginia Young Collins, Interview by Kim Lacy Rogers, 11 July 1988.

7. See Hollinger F. Barnard, ed., *Outside the Magic Circle: The Autobiography of Virginia Foster Durr* (Tuscaloosa: The University of Alabama Press, 1985), 116–70.

8. Jack Peebles, "Subversion and the Southern Conference Educational Fund" M.A. Thesis, Louisiana State University of New Orleans, 1970, 1–8; Aldon Morris, *The Origins of the Civil Rights Movement: Black Communities Organizing for Change* (New York: The Free Press, 1984), 120–39.

9. Virginia Collins to Rogers, 11 July 1988.

10. *Ibid.*

11. *Ibid.*

12. Virginia Y. Collins (Sr. Dara Abukari), Interview by Glenda B. Stevens, 31 August 1979.

13. *Ibid.*

14. Oralean Davis, Interview by Kim Lacy Rogers, 19 May 1979; Monte Piliawsky and Paul J. Stekler, "From Black Politics to Blacks in the Mainstream: The 1986 New Orleans Mayoral Election," *The Western Journal of Black Studies,* vol. 15, no. 2, 1991, 114–21.

15. Tom Dent, Interview by Kim Lacy Rogers, 31 October 1987.

16. Wilma Dykeman and James Stokley, *Seeds of Southern Change: The Life of Will Alexander* (Chicago: University of Chicago Press, 1962), 59–68; 174–96; Morton Sosna, *In Search of the Silent South: Southern Liberals and the Race Issue* (New York: Columbia University Press, 1977), 20–41.

17. Albert Dent, Interview by Kim Lacy Rogers, 12 November 1978.

18. *Ibid;* John Pope, "Albert Walter Dent Dies Sunday at 79," *Times-Picayune,* February 13, 1984, pp. 1, 4.

19. Judge Revius O. Ortique, Interview by Kim Lacy Rogers, 1 July 1988.

20. *Ibid.*

21. Dr. Leonard Burns, Interview by Kim Lacy Rogers, 8 July 1988.

22. *Ibid.*

23. Dr. Leonard Burns, Interview by Kim Lacy Rogers, 14 May 1979.

24. Rosa Freeman Keller, Interview by Kim Lacy Rogers, 9 November, 1978.

25. Rosa Freeman Keller, Interview by Kim Lacy Rogers, 28 November 1978; Rev. Albert D'Orlando, Interview by Kim Lacy Rogers, 27 July 1988; Helen Mervis, Interview by Kim Lacy Rogers, 1 July 1988.

26. Kim Lacy Rogers, "Humanity and Desire: Civil Rights Leaders and the Desegregation of New Orleans, 1954–1966," Ph.D. Dissertation, University of Minnesota, 1982, 27–73.

27. Keller to Rogers, 9 November 1978.

28. *Ibid.*

29. Rogers, "Humanity and Desire," 31–38; Rosa Freeman Keller, Interview by Kim Lacy Rogers, 8 April 1988; Virginia Collins to Rogers.

30. Mahoney, "The Changing Nature of Public Housing in New Orleans," 66; Keller to Rogers, 9 November 1978.

31. Keller to Rogers, 8 April 1988.

32. *Ibid.*

33. *Ibid.*

34. Mervis to Rogers, 1 July 1988.

35. Helen Mervis, Interview by Kim Lacy Rogers, 7 May 1979.

36. D'Orlando to Rogers.

37. Arthur Kinoy, *Rights on Trial: The Odyssey of a People's Lawyer* (Cambridge, Mass.: Harvard University Press, 1983), 216–17.

38. Peebles, "Subversion," 9–10; Dombrowski to Rogers.

39. Peebles, "Subversion," 10–11.

40. Dombrowski to Rogers.

41. See Barnard, *Outside the Magic Circle*, 171–209.

42. Rogers, "Humanity and Desire," 75–81.

43. J. Skelly Wright to Chuck and Rosa Keller et al., Friday [n.d.], Rosa [Free-man] Keller Collection, Amistad Research Center; see also, Rogers, "Humanity and Desire," 78–81.

44. J. Skelly Wright, Interview by Glenda B. Stevens, 9 December 1979; Harry B. Kelleher, Interview by Kim Lacy Rogers, 8 May 1979; Judge John Minor Wisdom, Interview by Kim Lacy Rogers, 10 June 1988.

45. J. Skelly Wright, "Address on the Presentation of the Papers of Alexander Pierre Tureaud," Amistad Research Center, 1975; J. Skelly Wright, Speech, 8 December 1979, Amistad Research Center; Jack Bass, *Unlikely Heroes* (New York: Simon & Schuster, 1981), 17–53, 112–35.

46. Sidney Tarrow, *Struggling to Reform: Social Movements and Policy Change during Cycles of Protest* (Ithaca, N.Y.: Center for International Studies, Cornell University, 1983); Bert Klandermans and Sidney Tarrow, "Mobilization into Social Movements: Synthesizing European and American Approaches," in Bert Klander-mans, Hanspeter Kriesi, and Sidney Tarrow, eds., *From Structure to Action: Comparing Movement Participation across Cultures* (Greenwich, Conn.: JAI Press, 1988), 2–30.

47. "Supreme Court Unequivocal Ruling Is Hailed as Second Emancipation," *Louisiana Weekly*, May 22, 1954.

48. Albert Dent to Rogers.

49. Numan Bartley, *The Rise of Massive Resistance* (Baton Rouge: Louisiana State University Press, 1969).

50. Neil R. McMillen, *The Citizens' Council: Organized Resistance to the Second Reconstruction, 1954–1964* (Urbana: University of Illinois Press, 1971); Earlean Mary McCarrick, "Louisiana's Official Response to Desegregation," Ph.D. Dissertation, Vanderbilt University, 1964, 14–33.

51. McCarrick, "Louisiana's Official Response," 1–27, 30–81, 117–21.

52. Thompson, *The Negro Leadership Class*, 90.

53. Bartley, *The Rise of Massive Resistance*, 82–123.

54. *Ibid.*

55. Peebles, "Subversion," 18–76; Virginia Collins to Rogers; see also Jack M. Bloom, *Class, Race, and the Civil Rights Movement* (Bloomington, Ind.: University of Indiana Press, 1987); see also Kinoy, *Rights on Trial*.

56. "United Clubs Announce Date for UNCF '54 Ball," *Louisiana Weekly*, January 30, 1954; Burns to Rogers, 14 May 1979.

57. Burns to Rogers, 14 May 1979.

58. Bloom, *Class, Race, and the Civil Rights Movement*, 1–17, 87–119; Elizabeth

Jacoway and David R. Colburn, *Southern Businessmen and Desegregation* (Baton Rouge: Louisiana State University Press, 1982), 1–14, 82–97.

59. Dr. Leonard Burns, Interview by Kim Lacy Rogers, 13 July 1988.

60. *Ibid.;* "United Clubs Announce Date for UNCF '54 Ball."

61. Burns to Rogers, 14 May 1979.

62. "Urge End of Bias McDonogh Day Parades," *Louisiana Weekly*, January 23, 1954; Judge Revius O. Ortique, Interview by Kim Lacy Rogers, 9 November 1978.

63. "Three Groups Unite to Protest McDonogh Day Discrimination," *Louisiana Weekly*, February 6, 1954.

64. Ortique to Rogers, 1 July 1988.

65. "Solid Front Snubs McDonogh Day Bias," *Louisiana Weekly*, May 5, 1954; Ortique to Rogers, 9 November 1978; Luke to Rogers.

66. Ortique to Rogers, 9 November 1978.

67. Edward F. Haas, *DeLesseps S. Morrison and the Image of Reform: New Orleans Politics, 1946–1961* (Baton Rouge: Louisiana State University Press, 1974), 26–83, 249–80.

68. "A Firm Rebuttal to a Stupid Smear," *Southern Patriot*, vol. 12, March 1954; Peebles, "Subversion," 18–30.

69. *Ibid.*

70. Barnard, *Outside the Magic Circle*, 254–73.

71. Dombrowski to Rogers.

72. Peebles, "Subversion," 18–37; Dombrowski to Rogers.

73. Dombrowski to Rogers.

74. *Ibid.*

75. "Groups Ask Facilities Be Opened to All," *Louisiana Weekly*, March 6, 1954; "No Reason for Discrimination," *Louisiana Weekly*, March 13, 1954.

76. Albert Dent, Interview by Glenda B. Stevens, 15 September 1979.

77. *Ibid.*

78. Rosa Keller, Unpublished Mss., Rosa [Freeman] Keller Collection, Amistad Research Center.

79. Keller to Rogers, 9 November 1978; Keller, Unpublished Mss.

80. "Library Board 'Defers Action' on Bias Protest," *Louisiana Weekly*, April 3, 1954; Collin B. Hamer, Jr., Head, Louisiana Division, City of New Orleans Public Library, to author, February 7, 1980.

81. A. J. Chapital, Sr., "President's Annual Report," November 1, 1954–November 30, 1955, New Orleans Branch NAACP, 28–210, Presidential Reports (Annual) 1951–1955, NAACP Papers, Earl K. Long Memorial Library, University of New Orleans.

82. Albert Dent to Stevens.

83. "N. O. Petition Proves Decency's Strength," *Southern Patriot*, vol. 13, October 1955; "Challenge School Board Defiance," *Louisiana Weekly*, September 17, 1955.

84. Keller to Rogers, 9 November 1978.

85. Bartley, *The Rise of Massive Resistance*, 130–35.

86. *Louisiana Weekly*, May 26, 1956; *Louisiana Weekly*, June 6, 1956; Keller to Rogers, 9 November 1978.

87. Helen Mervis, Interview by Kim Lacy Rogers, 18 November 1978.

88. "New Orleans Moves into Civil Rights Circles," *Louisiana Weekly*, January 12, 1957; "United Clubs Inc. Public Meet Feb. 21," *Louisiana Weekly*, February 23, 1957.

89. Burns to Rogers, 13 July 1988.

90. "Bus Desegregation Is Working Out Smoothly," *Louisiana Weekly*, June 7, 1958; Luke to Rogers, Oralean Davis to Rogers.

91. Ortique to Rogers, 9 November 1978.

92. "Minutes of the Board of Directors of the Urban League of Greater New Orleans, November 13, 1958"; Dr. Forrest LaViolette, "Rev. Albert D'Orlando, Pastor, Unitarian Church, Interview No. 1, July 8, 1959," "Notes on Leadership," Giles Hubert Papers, Amistad Research Center.

93. D'Orlando to Rogers.

94. Albert Dent to Rogers.

95. Pope, "Albert Walter Dent Dies Sunday at 79," pp. 1,4.

96. Albert Dent to Stevens; Tom Dent to Rogers, 31 October 1987.

3. Desegregating New Orleans' Schools

1. Piliawsky and Stekler, "From Black Politics to Blacks in the Mainstream," 114–21.

2. See Elizabeth Jacoway and David R. Colburn, eds., *Southern Businessmen and Desegregation* (Baton Rouge: Louisiana State University Press, 1982).

3. Judge Robert Collins, Interview by Kim Lacy Rogers, 8 June 1988.

4. *Ibid.*

5. *Ibid.*; Lolis E. Elie, Interview by Kim Lacy Rogers, 23 June 1988.

6. Lolis Elie, WWOZ, New Orleans, "The Civil Rights Movement Remembered," 16 January 1989.

7. Elie to Rogers, 23 June 1988.

8. *Ibid.*

9. *Ibid.*

10. Robert Collins to Rogers.

11. John P. Nelson, Jr., Interview by Kim Lacy Rogers, 22 June 1988.

12. John P. Nelson, Jr., Interview by Kim Lacy Rogers, 23 April 1979.

13. *Ibid.*

14. Moon Landrieu, Interview by Kim Lacy Rogers, 13 June 1988.

15. Ann Dlugos, Interview by Kim Lacy Rogers, 30 June 1988.

16. Frank Read and Lucy S. McGough, *Let Them Be Judged: The Judicial Integration of the Deep South* (Metuchen, N.J.: Scarecrow Press, 1978), 119–29; Haas, *Morrison*, 247–57.

17. Dlugos to Rogers, 30 June 1988.

18. Bloom, *Class, Race, and the Civil Rights Movement*, 111–15.

19. *Ibid.*, 114.

20. *Ibid.*, 114–17.

21. See Robert Coles, "New Orleans, 1960: 'As Bad as They Make It, the Stronger I'll Get,'" and Clare Jupiter, "New Orleans, 1979, 'It Was Worth It'," *Southern Exposure*, vol. 7, Spring 1979, 55–63. See also Rogers, "Humanity and Desire," 74–260.

22. Read and McGough, *Let Them Be Judged*, 118–19.

23. See Morton Inger, *Politics and Reality in an American City: The New Orleans School Crisis of 1960* (New York: Center for Urban Education, 1969).

24. *Ibid.*, 9–27; Read and McGough, *Let Them Be Judged*, 119–29.

25. Inger, *Politics and Reality*, 1–49; see A. J. Liebling, *The Earl of Louisiana* (Baton Rouge: Louisiana State University Press, 1970).

26. Liebling, *The Earl of Louisiana*, 131–244; Inger, *Politics and Reality*, 1–49.

27. *Ibid.*

28. See Liebling, *The Earl of Louisiana*.

29. Landrieu to Rogers, 13 June 1988.

30. *Ibid.*

31. Inger, *Politics and Reality*; Read and McGough, *Let Them Be Judged*, 139–41.

32. See Inger, *Politics and Reality*.

33. Keller to Rogers, 9 November 1978.

34. "Save Our Schools, Inc." [pamphlet, n.d.]; SOS Newsletter #2, August 23, 1960; SOS Newsletter #5, March 15, 1961; Publications Committee, SOS, "Our Stake in New Orleans Schools: A Study in Education and Economics," August 1, 1960; Articles of Incorporation of Save Our Schools, Inc., April 25, 1960; Save Our Schools (SOS) Papers, Amistad Research Center; also see Inger, *Politics and Reality*, 1–50.

35. Ann Dlugos, Interview by Kim Lacy Rogers, 12 November 1978.

36. Dr. Henry Mitchell, interview, "The Civil Rights Movement Remembered," WWOZ, New Orleans, 16 January 1989.

37. "Dryades Street Hires Negroes," *Louisiana Weekly*, April 30, 1960 "Consumer League Efforts Responsible for 30 Jobs," *Louisiana Weekly*, May 14, 1960.

38. Dr. Henry Mitchell, interview, "The Civil Rights Movement Remembered" "Consumers' League Moves to 'New Front' in Job Fight," *Louisiana Weekly*, July 30, 1960; " 'Fight for Jobs' Report Made by Consumers' League," *Louisiana Weekly*, August 13, 1960.

39. "Collegians Join Pickets," *Louisiana Weekly*, April 23, 1960; "Democracy in Action," *Louisiana Weekly*, 21 May 1960.

40. Elie to Rogers, 23 June 1988.

41. Lolis E. Elie, Interview by Kim Lacy Rogers, 10 November 1978.

42. Ruth Despenza, "Statement, September 10, 1960," "Report of James T. McCain, New Orleans, Louisiana, September 8 through September 25, 1960," Papers of the Congress of Racial Equality, (CORE Papers), State Historical Society of Wisconsin.

43. Gordon R. Carey, Field Director, to Local Contacts and Members of the Advisory Committee, 1960, "Report of James T. McCain, New Orleans, Louisiana,

September 8 through September 25, 1960," John Payton, UPI, "New Orleans, September 17," CORE Papers.

44. *Ibid.*

45. *Ibid.*

46. Nelson to Rogers, 23 April 1979.

47. "4 Sit-Ins to Appeal 60-Day Sentence," *Louisiana Weekly*, January 14, 1961.

48. Nelson to Rogers, 23 April 1979; John P. Nelson, Jr., "Answers to Questionnaire for Prospective Nominees for United States Circuit Judgship," 4 June 1977, John P. Nelson, Jr., Papers, Amistad Research Center.

49. "Report of James T. McCain," *State Times*, Baton Rouge, La., September 22, 1960. CORE Papers.

50. Inger, *Politics and Reality*, 50–55; Read and McGough, *Let Them Be Judged*, 142–45.

51. See Inger, *Politics and Reality*.

52. Luke to Rogers.

53. *Ibid.*; Inger, *Politics and Reality*, 33–45.

54. Inger, *Politics and Reality*, 33–45.

55. Luke to Rogers.

56. Peggy Murison, Interview by Kim Lacy Rogers, 1 May 1979.

57. Betty Wisdom, Interview by Kim Lacy Rogers, 16 November 1978; Wright to Stevens.; Jack Bass, *Unlikely Heroes*, 112–35; Nelson to Rogers, 23 April 1979.

58. Betty Wisdom to Rogers, 16 November 1978.

59. Nelson to Rogers, 23 April 1979.

60. Landrieu to Rogers, 13 June 1988.

61. Inger, *Politics and Reality*; Llewellyn Soniat, Interview by Kim Lacy Rogers, 1 June 1988; Keller to Rogers, 9 November 1978.

62. Inger, *Politics and Reality*, 50–75; Haas, *Morrison*, 270–82.

63. Inger, *Politics and Reality*, 63–68; Harry B. Kelleher, Interview by Kim Lacy Rogers, 8 May 1979.

64. Joseph B. Parker, *The Morrison Era: Reform Politics in New Orleans* (Gretna, La.: Pelican Press, 1974), 116–32.

65. Betty Wisdom, "Letter from a New Orleans Mother," *Nation*, November 4, 1961, 353, 364; Betty Wisdom to Rogers; Kelleher to Rogers, 8 May 1979.

66. "Jail Two More Core Pickets," *Louisiana Weekly*, April 29, 1961 "State Police Arrest 9 in 'Peaceful Picketing,' " *Louisiana Weekly*, March 11, 1961; "Ministers joined CORE Pickets at Woolworths," *Louisiana Weekly*, December 2, 1961.

67. Kelleher to Rogers, 8 May 1979; Lolis Elie, Interview by Kim Lacy Rogers, 15 November 1980.

68. Read and McGough, *Let Them Be Judged*, 157–62; Mrs. Ethel Young and Arthur J. Chapital, Jr., to "Co-Worker," May 21, 1962; A. P. Tureaud to Orleans Parish School Board, January 20, 1962; Daniel E. Byrd to Messrs. Marshall and Tureaud, August 11, 1961, A. P. Tureaud Papers, Amistad Research Center.

69. Read and McGough, *Let Them Be Judged*, 154–62; "Ruling 'Disaster' to New Orleans," *New York Times*, April 7, 1962; Claude Sitton, "Opponents of Court Base

Hopes on Change of Judges," *New York Times*, April 7, 1962, Clippings Files, Amistad Research Center.

70. Read and McGough, *Let Them Be Judged*, 156–62; Inger, *Politics and Reality*, 67–69.

71. "School Boycott Fails in Louisiana," *New York Times*, April 12, 1962; Read and McGough, *Let Them Be Judged*, 140–62.

72. Stuart Scheingold, *The Politics of Rights: Lawyers, Public Policy, and Political Change* (New Haven: Yale University Press, 1974), 120.

73. "La. Unit OKs 1217 More School Grants," *States-Item*, October 2, 1962, Save Our Schools (SOS) Papers, Amistad Research Center; Ed Planer, "Louisiana: The Expensive Way to Fight Integration," *Reporter*, September 18, 1963, Clippings Files, Amistad Research Center. See also, Lewis, *New Orleans*, 75–96, 101; Perry and Stokes, "Politics and Power in the Sunbelt," 223–25.

4. *"Would New Orleans Burn?"*

1. Burns to Rogers, 14 May 1979.

2. Davis to Rogers; Luke to Rogers; Kelleher to Rogers, 8 May 1979.

3. See Steven E. Barkan, *Protestors on Trial: Criminal Justice in the Southern Civil Rights Movement and the Vietnam Antiwar Movement* (New Brunswick, N.J.: Rutgers University Press, 1985); see also Kinoy, *Rights on Trial*.

4. Collins to Rogers; Ernest "Dutch" Morial, Interview by Kim Lacy Rogers, 30 July 1988.

5. Landrieu to Rogers, 13 June 1988.

6. Kelleher to Rogers, 8 May 1979; Rosa Freeman Keller, Interview by Kim Lacy Rogers, 7 May 1979.

7. Ernest "Dutch" Morial, Interview by Kim Lacy Rogers, 30 October 1987.

8. Charlotte Hays, "The Life and Times of Dutch Morial," *Figaro*, November 16, 1977.

9. Morial to Rogers, 30 October 1987.

10. Morial to Rogers, 30 July 1988; Hays, "The Life and Times of Dutch Morial," p. 7.

11. Arthe Agnes Anthony, "The Negro Creole Community in New Orleans, 1880–1920: An Oral History" Ph.D. Dissertation, University of California, Irvine, 1978; Laura Foner, "The Free People of Color in Louisiana and St. Dominque: A Comparative Portrait of Two Three-Caste Societies," *Journal of Social History*, vol. 3, Summer 1970, 406–30; Luke to Rogers; Suarez to Rogers; Lolis Elie, Interview by Kim Lacy Rogers, 12 July 1988.

12. Harry B. Kelleher, Interview by Kim Lacy Rogers, 9 June 1988.

13. Kelleher to Rogers, 8 May 1979.

14. *Ibid.*

15. *Ibid.*

16. See Charles Y. W. Chai, "Who Rules New Orleans: A Study of Community Power Structure," *Louisiana Business Survey*, vol. 16, no. 5, 1972, 2–11; Ortique to Rogers, 9 November 1978; Elie to Rogers, 15 November 1980.

17. Kelleher to Rogers, 8 May 1979.

18. Bloom, *Class, Race, and the Civil Rights Movement*, 166–67.

19. Morris, *The Origins of the Civil Rights Movement*, 239–50.

20. August Meier and Eliott Rudwick, *CORE: A Study in the Civil Rights Movement, 1942–1968* (New York: Oxford University Press, 1973), 213–328; Taylor Branch, *Parting the Waters; America in the King Years* (New York: Simon & Schuster, 1988), 451–561, 673–802; George Lipsitz, *A Life in the Struggle: Ivory Perry and the Culture of Opposition* (Philadelphia: Temple University Press, 1988), 93–116.

21. Bloom, *Class, Race, and the Civil Rights Movement*, 215–24; see also Steven E. Lawson, *Black Ballots; Voting Rights in the South, 1944–1969* (New York: Columbia University Press, 1976), 250–352.

22. Jacoway and Colburn, *Southern Businessmen and Desegregation*; see also Bloom, *Class, Race, and the Civil Rights Movement*, 214–24.

23. Burns to Rogers, 13 July 1988; Thompson, *The Negro Leadership Class*, 104.

24. Kelleher to Rogers, 9 June 1988.

25. "State Police Arrest 9 in 'Peaceful Picketing'," *Louisiana Weekly*, March 11, 1961; "Right to Picket Sought," *Louisiana Weekly*, March 18, 1961; "CORE Pickets Say 'Jail No Bail' after Arrests," *Louisiana Weekly*, April 22, 1961; "Jail 2 More CORE Pickets," *Louisiana Weekly*, April 29, 1961 "State Acts to Curb Voter Registration," *Louisiana Weekly*, November 11, 1961; "Ministers Joined CORE Pickets at Woolworth," *Louisiana Weekly*, December 2, 1961.

26. New Orleans CORE, "Summary of Activities 1961," CORE Papers.

27. Kelleher to Rogers, 8 May 1979.

28. "New Orleans, 1961, Summary of Activities, 1961," Lolis Elie to Mr. Richard Haley, June 6, 1962, CORE Papers; Kelleher to Rogers, 8 May 1979; Elie to Rogers, 15 November 1980; Ortique to Rogers, 9 November 1978.

29. Kelleher to Rogers, 8 May 1979.

30. "N.O. Lunchcounters Quietly Desegregate," *Louisiana Weekly*, September 15, 1962.

31. Kelleher to Rogers, 9 June 1988.

32. Kelleher to Rogers, 8 May 1979.

33. Ortique to Rogers, 1 July 1988.

34. Revius Ortique, Interview by Glenda B. Stevens, 21 November 1979.

35. Ortique to Rogers, 9 November 1978.

36. Ortique to Rogers, 28 November 1978.

37. Ortique to Rogers, 9 November 1978.

38. *Ibid.*

39. Ortique to Stevens.

40. *Ibid.*

41. Elie to Rogers, 15 November 1980.

42. Elie to Rogers, 10 November 1978.

43. Lolis E. Elie, Interview by Kim Lacy Rogers, 22 May 1979.

44. Elie to Rogers, 22 May 1979; Kim Lacy Rogers, " 'You Came Away with Some Courage': Three Lives in the Civil Rights Movement," *Mid-America*, vol. 71, no. 3, October 1989, 175–94.

45. "Selective Buying Campaign Postponed," *Louisiana Weekly*, March 30, 1963 "Canal Street Stores Will Hire Negroes," *Louisiana Weekly*, April 4, 1963 "Report Progress with Canal Street Stores," *Louisiana Weekly*, May 11, 1963.

46. "Schiro's Remark Stirs Speculation," *Louisiana Weekly*, June 22, 1963.

47. "Strong Position Is Urged to Avert Racial Strife Here," *Louisiana Weekly*, July 27, 1963; "20 Leadership Groups Back Ministers' Stand," *Louisiana Weekly*, July 27, 1963; "No Mass Demonstrations Here Because of 'Communication,'" *Louisiana Weekly*, July 27, 1963.

48. John E. Rousseau, "Asks Promises of Good Faith To Be Fulfilled," *Louisiana Weekly*, August 8, 1963; M. Marcus Neustadter, Jr., "City Starts Action on 6 Point Plan," "6 Point Petition Not Unreasonable," *Louisiana Weekly*, August 17, 1963; "Now Is The Time To Move Forward," *Louisiana Weekly*, August 24, 1963 "Long Record of Peace to Be Maintained," *Louisiana Weekly*, August 13, 1963.

49. "Peaceful Demonstration Seeks End of Segregation," *Louisiana Weekly*, October 5, 1963.

50. *Ibid.*

51. Morial to Rogers, 30 October 1987.

52. Kelleher to Rogers, 8 May 1979.

53. "City Council Hears 18-Point Rights Petition," *Louisiana Weekly*, October 12, 1963.

54. John E. Rousseau, "Canal Street Needs Positive Answers," *Louisiana Weekly*, September 7, 1963; John E. Rousseau, "Committee Clarifies Position on Canal Street," *Louisiana Weekly*, September 14, 1963 "Too Many Chiefs, Not Enough Indians," *Louisiana Weekly*, September 28, 1963.

55. "3 'Sit-Ins' Sue City Gov't.," *Louisiana Weekly*, February 8, 1964.

56. Kelleher to Rogers, 9 June 1988.

57. Elie to Rogers, 15 November 1980.

58. See Chapter 5.

59. Robert Penn Warren, *Who Speaks for the Negro?* (New York: Random House, 1965), 28–43.

60. Elie to Rogers, 15 November 1980.

61. Morial to Rogers, 30 July 1988.

62. Kelleher to Rogers, 8 May 1979.

63. Harry B. McCall to Kim Lacy Rogers, Personal Communication, 26 March 1980.

64. Keller to Rogers, 28 November 1978.

65. Elie to Rogers, 15 November 1980.

66. "Freedom Marchers Gain Three Out of Five Objectives," *Louisiana Weekly*, October 10, 1964.

67. Elie to Rogers, 22 May 1979.

68. Keller to Rogers, 28 November 1978.

69. Cheryl V. Cunningham, "The Desegregation of Tulane University," M.A. Thesis, University of New Orleans, 1982, 1–20.

70. *Ibid.*; Keller to Rogers, 28 November 1978.

71. Keller to Rogers, 28 November 1978.

72. Cunningham, "The Desegregation of Tulane," 16; Nelson to Rogers, 23 April 1979.

73. Nelson to Rogers, 23 April 1979.

74. John P. Nelson, Jr., Interview by Kim Lacy Rogers, 28 July 1988.

75. Kim Lacy Rogers, "Lawyers' Stories: White Attorneys and the Black Civil Rights Movement," paper presented at the Sixth International Oral History Conference, Oxford, September 13, 1987; Judge John Minor Wisdom to Rogers; Bass, *Unlikely Heroes.*

76. Nelson to Rogers, 22 June 1988.

77. Keller to Rogers, 28 November 1978.

78. Cunningham, "The Desegregation of Tulane," 68–69.

79. Keller to Rogers, 28 November 1978.

80. Cunningham, "The Desegregation of Tulane," 76.

81. *Ibid.*, 78–84.

82. *Ibid.*, 85.

83. *Ibid.; The Tulane Hullaballoo,* 12 December 1962, Tulane University Archives.

84. Keller to Rogers, 28 November 1978.

85. Irwin Klibaner, *Conscience of a Troubled South: The Southern Conference Educational Fund,* 1946–1966 (New York: Carlson, 1989), 200–207.

86. Virginia Y. Collins, Interview by Glenda B. Stevens, 31 August 1979; Dombrowski to Rogers.

87. Walter Collins, Interview by Kim Lacy Rogers, 17 May 1979.

88. See Bloom, *Race, Class, and the Civil Rights Movement,* 155–85; Frances Fox Piven and Richard A. Cloward, *Poor People's Movements: Why They Succeed, How They Fail* (New York: Pantheon, 1977), 181–263.

89. See Klibaner, *Conscience of a Troubled South,* 202–7.

90. *Ibid,* 202–3.

91. *Ibid,* 204.

92. *Ibid,* 204–5.

93. *Ibid;* see also Peebles, "Subversion."

94. Collins to Stevens; Peebles, "Subversion," 55–58.

95. Elie to Rogers, 10 November 1978.

96. Barkan, *Protestors on Trial,* 41–52.

97. Ernest Goodman, "The NLG, the FBI, and the Civil Rights Movement: 1964—A Year of Decision," *Guild Practitioner,* vol. 38, no. 1, Winter 1987, 1–17; Bass, *Unlikely Heroes,* 286–96; Elie to Rogers, 12 July 1978; Robert Collins to Rogers, 8 June 1988.

98. See Lawson, *Black Ballots,* 130–36; 227–29; "Can't Do the Job Alone," *Louisiana Weekly,* October 12, 1963.

99. Daniel C. Thompson, Interview by Kim Lacy Rogers, 23 May 1979.

100. "Jail 90 in Picketing of Vote Registration Office," *Louisiana Weekly,* September 28, 1963; "Vote Registrar Denies Bias," *Louisiana Weekly,* October 5, 1963.

101. Collins to Stevens.

102. Erika Munk, "The New Orleans Scene," *Reed,* vol. 4, no. 1, December 5, 1963, pp. 3–4.

103. "Thousands Jam Vote Registration Office," *Louisiana Weekly*, August 29, 1965.

104. Piliawsky and Stekler, "From Black Politics to Blacks in the Mainstream."

105. *Ibid.*, 16–17; see also James Chubbuck, Edwin Renwick, and Joe E. Walker, "The Emergence of Coalition Politics in New Orleans," *New South*, vol. 26, Winter 1971, 16–25.

106. Robert Collins to Rogers; "Biography of Judge Robert F. Collins," Author's Collection.

107. Landrieu to Rogers, 13 June 1988.

108. Piliawsky and Stekler, "From Black Politics," 17–18; Tom Dent, "New Orleans versus Atlanta: Power to the Parade," *Southern Exposure*, vol. 7, Spring 1979, 64.

5. *"Terror and Solidarity"*

1. Jerome Smith, Interview by Kim Lacy Rogers, 8 July 1988.

2. Jerome Smith, Interview by Tom Dent, 23 September 1983, Mississippi Civil Rights Oral History Collection, Amistad Research Center.

3. Smith to Rogers, 8 July 1988.

4. Doris Jean Castle Scott, Interview by Kim Lacy Rogers, 19 January 1989.

5. Oretha Castle Haley, Interview by Kim Lacy Rogers, 27 November 1978.

6. Oretha Castle Haley, Interview by James Mosby, 26 May 1970, Civil Rights Documentation Project, Moorland-Springarn Research Center, Howard University.

7. Castle Scott to Rogers.

8. Dr. Rudy Lombard, Interview by Kim Lacy Rogers, 7 June 1988.

9. Dr. Rudy Lombard, Interview by Kim Lacy Rogers, 9 May 1979.

10. Lombard to Rogers, 7 June 1988.

11. Oretha Castle Haley, Interview by James Mosby, 26 May 1970; Lombard to Rogers, 7 June 1988; See James Farmer, *Lay Bare the Heart: An Autobiography of the Civil Rights Movement* (New York: Arbor House, 1985), 67–133.

12. Matt Suarez, Interview by Kim Lacy Rogers, 20 June 1988.

13. Matt Suarez, Interview By Tom Dent, 31 July 1977; Thomas C. Dent Papers, Amistad Research Center.

14. Elie to Rogers, 12 July 1988.

15. Richard Haley, Interview by Kim Lacy Rogers, 25 April 1979; Meier and Rudwick, *CORE*, 90–92.

16. Richard Haley to Rogers, 25 April 1979; Meier and Rudwick, *CORE*, 106, 113; James Baldwin, "They Can't Turn Back," *The Price of the Ticket: Collected Nonfiction, 1948–1985* (New York: St. Martin's/Marek, 1985) 215–28.

17. Richard Haley to Rogers, 25 April 1979.

18. Baldwin, "They Can't Turn Back," 226–27.

19. Richard Haley, Interview by Kim Lacy Rogers, 9 May 1979.

20. *Ibid.*

21. Tom Dent to Rogers, 31 October 1987.

22. *Ibid.*

23. Dent, "Mardi Gras Eve/1968."

24. *Ibid.*, 20–23.

25. Tom Dent, Interview by Kim Lacy Rogers, 25 June 1988.

26. See Ronald Fraser et al., 1968: *A Student Generation in Revolt* (New York: Pantheon, 1988), 1–60.

27. Morris, *The Origins of the Civil Rights Movement*, 129–34.

28. *Ibid.*; Lombard to Rogers, 9 May 1979.

29. Doug McAdam, *The Political Process and the Development of Black Insurgency*, 1930–1970 (Chicago: University of Chicago Press, 1982), 125–45.

30. Clayborne Carson, *In Struggle; SNCC and the Black Awakening of the 1960's* (New York: Oxford University Press, 1981), 1–30; Seth Cagan and Philip Dray, *We Are Not Afraid: The Story of Goodman, Schwerner, and Chaney and the Civil Rights Campaign in Mississippi* (New York: Macmillan, 1988).

31. Matteo Suarez, Interview by Robert Wright, 11 August 1969, New Orleans, Civil Rights Documentation Project.

32. Richard Haley, Interview by Robert Wright, 12 August 1969, Civil Rights Documentation Project.

33. Rogers, "You Came Away With Some Courage."

34. Alice Thompson, Interview by Kim Lacy Rogers, 25 July 1988; Doratha Smith-Simmons, Interview by Kim Lacy Rogers, 27 July 1988; Jerome Smith, Interview by Kim Lacy Rogers, 8 July 1988.

35. Ruth Despenza, "Statement, September 10, 1960"; "Report of James T. McCain, New Orleans, September 8 through September 25, 1960," CORE Papers.

36. *Ibid.*; Gordon R. Carey, Field Director, to Local Contacts and Members of the Advisory Committee, 1960; John Payton, UPI, "New Orleans, September 17" CORE Papers.

37. Oretha Castle Haley to Rogers.

38. Meier and Rudwick, *CORE*, 115–26.

39. McCain, "Mass Meeting: Rudy—Statement from Jail" [1960] CORE Papers.

40. "Rudy's Statement at City-Wide Meeting," CORE Papers.

41. Meier and Rudwick, *CORE*, 115–16.

42. Castle Scott to Rogers.

43. *Ibid.*

44. Suarez to Wright, 11 August 1969.

45. Oretha Castle Haley to Rogers.

46. Lombard to Rogers, 7 June 1988; Oretha Castle Haley to Mosby, transcript pp. 14–15; see also "Xavier, Dillard Deny 'Sit-Down' Classes," *Louisiana Weekly*, March 20, 1960; "Xavierites Answer University Critic," *Louisiana Weekly*, March 26, 1960; Richard Haley to Rogers, 9 May 1979; Davis to Rogers.

47. James Farmer, *Lay Bare the Heart*, 195–205.

48. Castle Scott to Rogers.

49. Smith to Rogers, 26 July 1988.

50. Castle Scott to Rogers.

51. Suarez to Wright.

52. Oretha Castle Haley to Rogers.

53. Oretha Castle Haley to Mosby.

54. *Ibid.*

55. Richard Haley to Rogers, 25 April 1979.

56. Richard Haley to Rogers, 9 May 1979.

57. Meier and Rudwick, *CORE*, 222.

58. Lombard to Rogers, 9 May 1979.

59. Farmer, *Lay Bare the Heart*, 246–54.

60. Elie to Mosby, transcript pp. 13–14.

61. *Ibid.*, 15.

62. Lombard to Rogers, 9 May 1979.

63. Lombard to Rogers, 7 June 1988.

64. Meier and Rudwick, *CORE*, 215.

65. Richard Haley to Rogers, 9 May 1979.

66. *Ibid.*

67. Smith to Rogers, 8 July 1988.

68. Smith to Rogers, 26 July 1988.

69. *Ibid.*

70. Rogers, "You Came Away with Some Courage."

71. Elie to Rogers, 23 June 1988.

72. *Ibid.*

73. Elie to Rogers, 12 July 1988.

74. Lombard to Rogers, 7 June 1988.

75. Smith to Rogers, 26 July 1988; Castle Scott to Rogers; Doratha Smith-Simmons to Rogers, 27 July 1988; Alice Thompson to Rogers; Suarez to Rogers.

76. Michel Oren, "The Umbra Poets' Workshop, 1962–1965: Some Socio-literary Puzzles," in Joe Weixlmann and Chester Fontenot, eds., *Studies in Black American Literature*, vol. 2, *Belief v. Theory in Black American Literary Criticism* (Greenwood, Fla: Penkeville, 1986), 200.

77. Tom Dent to Rogers, 31 October 1987; Tom Dent to Rogers, 25 June 1988.

78. Tom Dent, "Ten Years after Umbra (for David and Calvin)," *Magnolia Street* (New Orleans: Tom Dent, 1976), 21.

79. Tom Dent to Rogers, 25 June 1988; Tom Dent, Interview by Kim Lacy Rogers, 20 July 1988.

80. Lombard to Rogers, 9 May 1979.

81. *Ibid.*

82. Elie to Rogers, 23 June 1988.

83. Lolis Elie, Interview by Kim Lacy Rogers, 24 April 1979.

84. Elie to Rogers, 15 November 1980.

85. Elie to Rogers, 23 June 1988.

86. Castle Scott to Rogers.

87. *Ibid.*

88. Oretha Castle Haley to Rogers.

89. Suarez to Rogers.

90. Cagan and Dray, *We Are Not Afraid*, 310–11.

91. *Ibid.*

92. Smith to Rogers, 26 July 1988.

93. Ed Hollander to Marvin Rich, August 5, 1964; Doris Jean Castle, "CORE on Canal Street," [March 1964]; Richard Haley to Mr. Bernard Diamond, May 10, 1964, CORE Papers.

94. Richard Haley to Rogers, 9 May 1979.

95. *Ibid.*

96. Meier and Rudwick, *CORE*, 404–8.

97. Suarez to Wright.

98. Meier and Rudwick, *CORE*, 394–98, 404–8.

99. "African, Afro-American Slated Here May 6 to 8," *Louisiana Weekly*, Saturday, May 7, 1966, p. 3.

6. "I Don't Know That I Would Feel"

1. Joseph M. Fitzgerald, "Autobiographical memory: A Developmental Perspective," in David C. Rubin, ed., *Autobiographical Memory* (Cambridge, Mass: Harvard University Press, 1986), 123–33; see also Jerome Bruner, "Life as Narrative," *Social Research*, vol. 54, no. 1, Spring 1987, 11–32.

2. Donald Spence, *Narrative Truth and Historical Truth: Meaning and Interpretation in Psychoanalysis* (New York: Norton, 1982); Donald Polkinghorne, *Narrative Knowing and the Human Sciences* (Albany, N.Y.: SUNY Press, 1988); Erving Polster, *Every Person's Life Is Worth a Novel* (New York: Norton, 1987).

3. Dent to Stevens.

4. See the narratives of Lolis Elie in Chapter 3, and Rudy Lombard, Doris Jean Castle, and Oretha Haley in Chapter 4.

5. John Pope, "Albert Walter Dent Dies Sunday at 79," *Times-Picayune*, February 13, 1984, pp. 1,4; Dent to Stevens; Tom Dent to Rogers, 31 October 1987.

6. Judge Revius O. Ortique, Interview by Kim Lacy Rogers, 26 July 1988.

7. Burns to Rogers, 13 July 1988.

8. Oralean Davis and Joyce Davis to Rogers.

9. Luke to Rogers.

10. See Chapter 3.

11. Luke to Rogers.

12. *Ibid.*

13. Jerome Smith, interview, "The Civil Rights Movement Remembered," WWOZ, New Orleans, 16 January 1989.

14. Oralean Davis and Joyce Davis to Rogers.

15. Virginia Collins to Rogers.

16. Ann Braden, "The Case for Separate Schools," *Southern Patriot*, vol. 28, no. 8, August 1970, p. 6.

17. Ann Braden, "Tour Builds Support for Collins," *Southern Patriot*, vol. 29, no. 6, June 1971, pp. 1, 4.

18. Virginia Collins to Rogers.

19. Millie Ball, "Rosa F. Keller, Rights Activist, Wins Loving Cup," *Times-Picayune*, August 29, 1985, pp. 1, A–5.

20. Keller to Rogers, 8 April 1988.

21. Mervis to Rogers, 1 July 1988.

22. D'Orlando to Rogers.

23. Dombrowski to Rogers, Peebles, "Subversion."

24. Dombrowski to Rogers.

25. Landrieu to Rogers, 13 June 1988.

26. *Ibid.*

27. Keller to Rogers, 8 April 1988.

28. Morial to Rogers, 30 July 1988.

29. Morial to Rogers, 30 October 1987.

30. Morial to Rogers, 30 July 1988.

31. *Ibid.*

32. Frank Donze, "Second-Liners March Dutch Morial Home," *Times-Picayune*, December 27, 1989, pp. A–1, 8.

33. "Biography of Judge Robert F. Collins," Author's Collection.

34. Robert Collins to Rogers, 8 June 1988.

35. Elie to Rogers, 23 June 1988.

36. Elie to Rogers, 245 April 1979.

37. Elie to Rogers, 23 June 1988.

38. Elie to Rogers, 12 July 1988.

39. John P. Nelson, Jr., "Answers to Questionnaire for Prospective Nominees for United States Circuit Judgeship," Author's Collection.

40. Nelson to Rogers, 22 June 1988.

41. Nelson to Rogers, 23 April 1979.

42. Nelson to Rogers, 22 June 1988.

43. Dlugos to Rogers, 12 November 1978.

44. Dlugos to Rogers, 30 June 1988.

45. Kelleher to Rogers, 9 June 1988.

46. *Ibid.*

47. See Sara Evans, *Personal Politics*; Doug McAdam, *Freedom Summer*; Joyce A. Ladner, "A Sociology of the Civil Rights Movement: An Insider's Perspective," paper presented at the annual meeting of the American Sociological Association, Atlanta, Georgia, August 27, 1988; see also Alice Thompson to Rogers; Smith-Simmons to Rogers, 27 July 1988.

48. Richard Haley to Rogers, 9 May 1979.

49. *Ibid.*

50. Oretha Castle Haley to Rogers.

51. Castle Scott to Rogers.

52. *Ibid.*

53. Lombard to Rogers, 9 May 1979.

54. Lombard to Rogers, 7 June 1988.

55. Piliawsky and Stekler, "From Black Politics," 31–32.

56. *Ibid.*; Iris Kelso, "A Wild Card in the Mayor's Race," *Times-Picayune-States Item*, September 12, 1985, p. 31.

57. Lombard to Rogers, 7 June 1988.

58. Suarez to Rogers.

59. Smith to Rogers, 8 July 1988.

60. Smith to Rogers, 26 July 1988.

61. Smith to Rogers, 8 July 1988.

62. Smith to Rogers, 26 July 1988.

63. Smith to Rogers, 8 July 1988.

64. Tom Dent, Interview by Kim Lacy Rogers, 10 May 1979.

65. Tom Dent to Rogers, 25 June 1988.

66. *Ibid.*

7. The Meanings of the Stories

1. Agnes Hankiss, "Ontologies of the Self: On the Mythological Rearranging of One's Life-History," in Daniel Bertaux, ed., *Biography and Society: The Life-History Approach in the Social Sciences* (London and Beverly Hills: Sage, 1981), 203–9; Bertram Cohler, "Life Course as Narrative," in Paul B. Baltes and Orville Brim, Jr., eds., *Life-Span Development and Behavior*, vol. 4, (New York: Academic Press, 1982), 206–41.

2. Alessandro Portelli, " 'The Time of My Life:' Functions of Time in Oral History," *International Journal of Oral History*, vol. 2, no. 3, November 1981, 162–80.

3. Huey L. Perry and Alfred Stokes, "Politics and Power in the Sunbelt," 222–55.

4. Alan Katz, "Bleak Picture," *Times-Picayune*, May 4, 1986, p. 27.

5. Spence, *Narrative Truth and Historical Truth; Meaning and Interpretation in Psychoanalysis*, 31–32.

6. See Polkinghorne, *Narrative Knowing*, 137–52.

7. Jerome Bruner, "Autobiography and Self," in Bruner, *Acts of Meaning* (Cambridge, Mass.: Harvard University Press, 1990), 112–13.

8. Polkinghorne, *Narrative Knowing*, 150.

9. Kenneth Gergen and Mary Gergen, "The Self in Temporal Perspective," in Ronald P. Abeles, ed., *Life-Span Perspectives and Social Psychology* (Hillsdale, N.J.: Lawrence Erlbaum, 1987), 126–32.

10. Bruner, "Autobiography and Self," 110.

11. Vera Ingrid Tarman, "Autobiography: The Negotiation of a Lifetime," *International Journal of Aging and Human Development*, vol. 27, no. 3, 1988, 184.

12. Michael Romaniuk, "Review: Reminiscence and the Second Half of Life," *Experimental Aging Research*, vol. 7, no. 3, 1981, 320; see also Sharan Merriam, "The Concept and Function of Reminiscence: A Review of the Research," *Gerontologist*, vol. 20, no. 5, 1980, 604–8.

13. Donald R. Spence, "Some Contributions of Symbolic Interaction to the

Study of Growing Old," in V. W. Marshall, ed., *Later Life: The Social Psychology of Aging* (Beverly Hills and London: Sage, 1986), 107–23.

14. Donald R. Spence and Thomas D. Lonner, "Career Set: A Resource Through Transitions and Crises," *International Journal of Aging and Human Development*, vol. 9, no. 1, 1978–1979, 51–65.

15. See Erik H. Erikson, *Identity, Youth and Crisis* (New York: Norton, 1968); Marshall, *Later Life*.

16. Erik H. Erikson, *The Life Cycle Completed: A Review* (New York: Norton, 1982), 55–82; Erikson, *Identity, Youth and Crisis*, 138–39.

17. Margaret M. Braungart, "Aging and Politics," *Journal of Political and Military Sociology*, vol. 12, Spring 1984, 79–98.

18. Jerrold M. Post, "The Seasons of a Leader's Life: Influences of the Life Cycle on Political Behavior," *Political Psychology* vol. 2, nos. 3–4, Fall-Winter 1980, 35–49.

19. See McAdam, *Freedom Summer*.

20. Thompson, *The Negro Leadership Class*, 56–75.

Bibliography

Anthony, Arthe Agnes. "The Negro Creole Community in New Orleans, 1880–1920: An Oral History." Ph.D. Dissertation, University of California, Irvine, 1978.

Baldwin, James. *The Price of the Ticket: Collected Nonfiction, 1948–1985*. New York: St. Martin's/Marek, 1985.

Ball, Millie. "Rosa F. Keller, Rights Activist, Wins Loving Cup." *Times-Picayune*, August 29, 1985, pp. 1, A-5.

Barkan, Steven A. *Protestors on Trial: Criminal Justice in the Southern Civil Rights Movement and the Vietnam Antiwar Movement*. New Brunswick, N.J.: Rutgers University Press, 1985.

Barnard, Hollinger F., ed. *Outside the Magic Circle: The Autobiography of Virginia Foster Durr*. Tuscaloosa: University of Alabama Press, 1985.

Bartley, Numan. *The Rise of Massive Resistance*. Baton Rouge: Louisiana State University Press, 1969.

Bass, Jack. *Unlikely Heroes*. New York: Simon & Schuster, 1981.

Blassingame, John. *Black New Orleans, 1860–1880*. Chicago: University of Chicago Press, 1973.

Bloom, Jack. *Class, Race, and the Civil Rights Movement*. Bloomington, Ind.: Indiana University Press, 1987.

Braden, Ann. "The Case for Separate Schools." *Southern Patriot*, vol. 28, no. 8, August 1970, p. 6.

——— . "Tour Builds Support for Collins." *Southern Patriot*, vol. 29, no. 6, June, 1971, pp. 1, 4.

Branch, Taylor. *Parting the Waters: America in the King Years*. New York: Simon & Schuster, 1988.

Braungart, Margaret M. "Aging and Politics." *Journal of Political and Military Sociology*, vol. 12, Spring 1984, 79–98.

Bruner, Jerome. *Acts of Meaning*, Cambridge, Mass.: Harvard University Press, 1990.

——— . "Life as Narrative." *Social Research*, vol. 54, no. 1, Spring 1987, 11–32.

Bullard, Robert D., ed. *In Search of the New South: The Black Urban Experience of the 1970s and 1980s*. Tuscaloosa: University of Alabama Press, 1989.

Cagan, Seth, and Dray, Philip. *We Are Not Afraid: The Story of Goodman, Schwerner, and Chaney and the Civil Rights Campaign in Mississippi*, New York: Macmillan, 1988.

Carson, Clayborne. *In Struggle: SNCC and the Black Awakening of the 1960's*. New York: Oxford University Press, 1981.

Chai, Charles Y. W. " Who Rules New Orleans: A Study of Community Power Structure." *Louisiana Business Survey*, vol. 16, no. 5, 1972, 2–11.

Chubbuck, James; Renwick, Edwin; and Walker, Joe E. "The Emergence of Coalition Politics in New Orleans." *New South*, vol. 26, Winter 1971, 16–25.

Cohler, Bertram. "Life Course as Narrative." In Paul B. Baltes and Orville Brim, Jr., eds., *Life-Span Development and Behavior*, vol. 4. New York: Academic Press, 1982, 206–41.

Coles, Robert. "New Orleans, 1960: 'As Bad as They Make It, the Stronger I'll Get.' " *Southern Exposure*, vol. 7, Spring 1979, 55–63.

Cunningham, Cheryl V. "The Desegregation of Tulane University." M.A. Thesis, University of New Orleans, 1982.

Dent, Tom. *Magnolia Street*. New Orleans: Tom Dent, 1976.

——— . "Mardi Gras Eve/1968." *Exquisite Corpse*, vol. 6, nos. 1–4, January–April 1988, 14–16.

——— . "New Orleans versus Atlanta: Power to the Parade." *Southern Exposure*, vol. 7, Spring 1979, 64–68.

——— . "St. Joseph's Day Celebrations or the Origins of Super Sunday." *New Orleans Tribune*, March 1986, pp. 14–15.

Dominguez, Virginia, R. *White by Definition: Social Classification in Creole Louisiana*. New Brunswick, N.J.: Rutgers University Press, 1986.

Donze, Frank. "Second-Liners March Dutch Morial Home." *Times- Picayune*, December 27, 1989, pp. A-1, 8.

Dykeman, Wilma, and Stokley, James. *Seeds of Southern Change: The Life of Will Alexander*. Chicago: University of Chicago Press, 1962.

Elie, Lolis E. "Niggertown Memories." *Black River Journal*, New Orleans, 1977, 8.

Erikson, Erik H. *Identity, Youth and Crisis*. New York: Norton, 1968.

——— . *The Life Cycle Completed: A Review*, New York: Norton, 1982.

Evans, Sara. *Personal Politics: The Roots of Women's Liberation in the Civil Rights Movement and the New Left*. New York: Knopf, 1980.

Farmer, James. *Lay Bare the Heart: An Autobiography of the Civil Rights Movement.* New York: Arbor House, 1985.

Fitzgerald, Joseph M. "Autobiographical Memory: A Developmental Perspective." *In Autobiographical Memory.* David C. Rubin, ed., Cambridge, Mass.: Harvard University Press, 1986, 123–33.

Foner, Laura. "The Free People of Color in Louisiana and St. Dominque: A Comparative Portrait of Two Three-Caste Societies." *Journal of Social History*, vol. 3, Summer 1970, 406–30.

Fraser, Ronald, et al. *1968: A Student Generation in Revolt.* New York: Pantheon, 1988.

Gergen, Kenneth, and Gergen, Mary. "The Self in Temporal Perspective." In Ronald P. Abeles, ed., *Life-Span Perspectives and Social Psychology*. Hillsdale, N.J.: Lawrence Erlbaum, 1987, 126–32.

Goodman, Ernest. "The NLG, the FBI, and the Civil Rights Movement: 1964—A Year of Decision." *Guild Practitioner*, vol. 38, no. 1, Winter 1987, 1–17.

Haas, Edward F. *DeLesseps S. Morrison and the Image of Reform: New Orleans Politics, 1946–1961.* Baton Rouge: Louisiana State University Press, 1974.

Hankiss, Agnes. "Ontologies of the Self: On the Mythological Rearranging of One's Life-History." In Daniel Bertaux, ed., *Biography and Society: The Life-History Approach in the Social Sciences.* London and Beverly Hills: Sage, 1981, 203–9.

Hays, Charlotte. "The Life and Times of Dutch Morial." *Figaro*, November 16, 1977.

Inger, Morton. *Politics and Reality in an American City: The New Orleans School Crisis of 1960.* New York: Center for Urban Education, 1969.

Jacoway, Elizabeth, and Colburn, David R eds. *Southern Businessmen and Desegregation.* Baton Rouge: Louisiana State University Press, 1982.

Jupiter, Clare. "New Orleans, 1979: 'It Was Worth It.'" *Southern Exposure*, vol. 7, Spring 1979, 55–63.

Katz, Alan. "Bleak Picture." *Times-Picayune*, May 4, 1986, p. 27.

Kelso, Iris. "Wild Card in the Mayor's Race." *Times-Picayune- States Item*, September 12, 1985, p. 31.

Kinoy, Arthur. *Rights on Trial: The Odyssey of a People's Lawyer.* Cambridge, Mass.: Harvard University Press, 1983.

Klandermans, Bert, and Tarrow, Sidney. "Mobilization into Social Movements: Synthesizing European and American Approaches." In Bert Klandermans, Hanspeter Kriesi, and Sidney Tarrow, eds., *From Structure to Action: Comparing Movement Participation across Cultures.* Greenwich, Conn.: JAI Press, 1988, 3–20.

Klibaner, Irving. *Conscience of a Troubled South: The Southern Conference Educational Fund.* New York: Carlson, 1989.

Ladner, Joyce A. "A Sociology of the Civil Rights Movement: An Insider's Perspective." Paper presented at the annual meeting of the American Sociological Association, Atlanta, Georgia, August 27, 1988.

Lawson, Steven E. *Black Ballots: Voting Rights in the South, 1944–1969.* New York: Columbia University Press, 1976.

Lewis, Pierce. *New Orleans: The Making of an Urban Landscape.* Cambridge, Mass.: Ballinger, 1976.

Liebling, A. J. *The Earl of Louisiana.* Baton Rouge: Louisiana State University Press, 1970.

Lipsitz, George. *A Life in the Struggle; Ivory Perry and the Culture of Opposition.* Philadelphia: Temple University Press, 1988.

Mahoney, Martha Ruth. "The Changing Nature of Public Housing in New Orleans, 1930–1974." M.A. Thesis, Tulane University, 1985.

Mannheim, Karl. "The Problem of Generations" In Karl Mannheim, *Essays on the Sociology of Knowledge,* edited by Paul Kecskemeti. New York: Oxford University Press, 1952.

McAdam, Doug. *Freedom Summer,* New York: Oxford University Press, 1988.

——— . *The Political Process and the Development of Black Insurgency, 1930–1970.* Chicago: University of Chicago Press, 1982.

McCarrick, Earlean Mary. "Louisiana's Official Resistance to Desegregation." Ph.D. Dissertation, Vanderbilt University, 1964.

McMahan, Eva M. *Elite Oral History Discourse: A Study of Cooperation and Coherence.* Tuscaloosa: University of Alabama Press, 1989.

McMillen, Neil R. *The Citizens' Council: Organized Resistance to the Second Reconstruction, 1954–1964.* Urbana: University of Illinois Press, 1971.

Meier, August, and Rudwick, Eliott. *CORE: A Study in the Civil Rights Movement, 1942–1968.* New York: Oxford University Press, 1973.

Merriam, Sharan. "The Concept and Function of Reminiscence: A Review of the Research." *Geronlogist,* vol. 20, no. 5, 1980, 604–8.

Mills, Gary B. *The Forgotten People: Cane River's Creoles of Color.* Baton Rouge: Louisiana State University Press, 1977.

Morris, Aldon. *The Origins of the Civil Rights Movement: Black Communities Organizing for Change.* New York: Free Press, 1984.

Munk, Erika. "The New Orleans Scene." *Reed,* vol. 4, no. 1, December 5, 1963, pp. 3–4.

Neisser, Ulrich. "Nested Structure in Autobiographical Memory." In David C. Rubin, ed., *Autobiographical Memory.* Cambridge, Mass.: Harvard University Press, 1986, 71–81.

Oren, Michel. "The Umbra Poets' Workshop, 1962–1965: Some Socio- literary Puzzles." In Joe Weixlmann and Chester Fontenot, eds., *Studies in Black American Literature,* vol. 2, *Belief v. Theory in Black Literary Criticism.* Greenwood, Fla.: Penkeville, 1986, 177–235.

Parker, Joseph B. *The Morrison Era: Reform Politics in New Orleans.* Gretna, La.: Pelican Press, 1974.

Peebles, Jack. "Subversion and the Southern Conference Educational Fund." M.A. Thesis, Louisiana State University of New Orleans, 1970.

Perry, Huey L. and Stokes, Alfred. "Politics and Power in the Sunbelt: Mayor Morial of New Orleans." In Michael B. Preston, Lenneal Henderson, Jr., and

Paul L. Puryear, eds., *The New Black Politics: The Search for Political Power*. New York: Longman, 1987, 222–55.

Piliawsky, Monte and Stekler, Paul, J. "From Black Politics to Blacks in the Mainstream: The 1986 New Orleans Mayoral Election," *Western Journal of Black Studies* Vol. 15, No. 2, 1991, 114–21.

Piven, Frances Fox, and Cloward, Richard A. *Poor Peoples' Movements: Why They Succeed, How They Fail*. New York: Pantheon, 1977.

Polkinghorne, Donald. *Narrative Knowing and the Human Sciences*. Albany, N.Y.: SUNY Press, 1988.

Polster, Erving. *Every Person's Life Is Worth a Novel*. New York: Norton, 1987.

Pope, John. "Albert Walter Dent Dies Sunday at 79." *Times- Picayune*, February 13, 1984, pp. 1, 4.

Portelli, Alessandro. " 'The Time of My Life': Functions of Time in Oral History." *International Journal of Oral History*, vol. 2, no. 3, November 1981, 162–80.

Post, Jerrold M. "The Seasons of a Leader's Life: Influences of the Life Cycle on Political Behavior." *Political Psychology*, Vol. 2, nos. 3–4, Fall–Winter 1980, 35–49.

Read, Frank, and McGough, Lucy S. *Let Them Be Judged: The Judicial Integration of the Deep South*. Metuchen, N.J.: Scarecrow Press, 1978.

Rogers, Kim Lacy. "Humanity and Desire: Civil Rights Leaders and the Desegregation of New Orleans, 1954–1966." Ph.D. Dissertation, University of Minnesota, 1982.

———. "Lawyers' Stories: White Attorneys and the Black Civil Rights Movement." Unpublished ms.

———. "Organizational Experience and Personal Narrative: Stories of New Orleans' Civil Rights Leaders." *Oral History Review*, vol. 13, 1985, 23–54.

———. " 'You Came Away with Some Courage': Three Lives in the Civil Rights Movement." *Mid-America*, vol. 71, no. 3, October 1989, 175–94.

Rohrer, John H., and Edmonson, Monroe S., eds. *The Eighth Generation Grows Up: Cultures and Personalities of New Orleans' Negroes*. New York: Harper & Brothers, 1960.

Romaniuk, Michael. "Review: Reminiscence and the Second Half of Life." *Experimental Aging Research*, vol. 7, no. 3, 1981, 320.

Rubin, David C., ed. *Autobiographical Memory*. Cambridge, Mass.: Harvard University Press, 1986.

Scheingold, Stuart. *The Politics of Rights: Lawyers, Public Policy, and Political Change*. New Haven: Yale University Press, 1974.

Sosna, Morton. *In Search of the Silent South: Southern Liberals and the Race Issue*. New York: Columbia University Press, 1977.

Spence, Donald R. *Narrative Truth and Historical Truth: Meaning and Interpretation in Psychoanalysis*. New York: Norton, 1982.

———. "Some Contributions of Symbolic Interaction to the Study of Growing Old." In V. W. Marshall, ed., *Later Life: The Social Psychology of Aging*. Beverly Hills and London: Sage, 1986, 107–23.

Spence, Donald R., and Lonner, Thomas D. "Career Set: A Resource Through

Transitions and Crises." *International Journal of Aging and Human Development*, vol. 9, no. 1, 1978–1979, 51–65.

Stuckey, Sterling. *Slave Culture: Nationalist Theory and the Foundations of Black America*. New York: Oxford University Press, 1987.

Tarman, Vera Ingrid. "Autobiography: The Negotiation of a Lifetime." *International Journal of Aging and Human Development*, vol. 27, no. 3, 1988, 184.

Tarrow, Sidney. *Struggling to Reform: Social Movements and Policy Change During Cycles of Protest*. Ithaca, N.Y.: Center for International Studies, Cornell University, 1983.

Thompson, Daniel C. *The Negro Leadership Class*. Englewood Cliffs, N.J.: Prentice-Hall, 1963.

Warren, Robert Penn. *Who Speaks for the Negro?* New York: Random House, 1965.

Wisdom, Betty. "Letter from a New Orleans Mother." *Nation*, November 4, 1961, p. 353.

WWOZ, New Orleans, "The Civil Rights Movement Remembered," 16 January 1989.

Interviews

Kim Lacy Rogers-Glenda B. Stevens Collection, Amistad Research Center, Tulane University

Interviews by Author

Dr. Leonard Burns, 14 May 1979; 8 July 1988; 13 July 1988.

Judge Robert Collins, 8 June 1988.

Virginia Young Collins, 11 July 1988.

Walter Collins, 17 May 1979.

Oralean Davis, and Joyce Davis, 19 May 1979.

Albert Dent, 12 November 1978.

Tom Dent, 10 May 1979; 31 October 1987; 25 June 1988; 20 July 1988.

Ann Dlugos, 12 November 1978; 30 June 1988.

Dr. James Dombrowski, 24 April 1979.

Rev. Albert D'Orlando, 27 July 1988.

Lolis E. Elie, 10 November 1978; 24 April 1979; 22 May 1979; 15 November 1980; 23 June, 1988; 12 July 1988.

Oretha Castle Haley, 27 November 1978.

Richard Haley, 25 April 1979; 9 May 1979.

Harry B. Kelleher, 8 May 1979; 9 June 1988.

Rosa Freeman Keller, 9 November 1978; 28 November 1978; 7 May 1979, 8 April 1988.

Moon Landrieu, 11 November 1978; 13 June 1988.

Dr. Rudy Lombard, 9 May 1979; 7 June 1988.

Mrs. Leontine Goins Luke, 22 May 1979.

Helen Mervis, 18 November 1978; 7 May 1979; 1 July 1988.

Ernest "Dutch" Morial, 30 October 1987; 30 July 1988.

Peggy Murison, 1 May 1979.

John P. Nelson, Jr., 23 April 1979; 22 June 1988; 28 July 1988.
Judge Revius O. Ortique, 9 November 1978; 28 November 1978; 1 July 1988; 26 July 1988.
Doris Jean Castle Scott, 19 January 1989.
Jerome Smith, 8 July 1988; 26 July 1988.
Doratha Smith-Simmons, 27 July 1988.
Llewellyn Soniat, 1 June 1988.
Matt Suarez, 20 June 1988.
Alice Thompson, 25 July 1988.
Daniel C. Thompson, 23 May 1979.
Betty Wisdom, 16 November 1978.
Judge John Minor Wisdom, 10 June 1988.

Interviews by Glenda B. Stevens
Virginia Y. Collins, 31 August 1979.
Albert W. Dent, 15 September 1979.
Revius O. Ortique, 21 November 1979.
J. Skelly Wright, 9 December 1978.

Thomas C. Dent Papers, 1969–1984, Amistad Research Center, Tulane University
Interviews by Tom Dent
Jerome Smith, 23 September 1983.
Matt Suarez, 31 July 1977.

Civil Rights Documentation Project, Moorland-Springarn Research Center, Howard University
Lolis Elie, Interview by James Mosby, 26 May 1970.
Oretha Castle Haley, Interview by James Mosby, 26 May 1970.
Richard Haley, Interview by Robert Wright, 12 August 1969.
Matteo Suarez, Interview by Robert Wright, 11 August 1969.

Manuscript Collections
Amistad Research Center, Tulane University
Clippings Files, Amistad Research Center.
Albert Walter and Jessie Covington Dent Papers, 1908–1985.
Thomas C. Dent Papers, 1969–1984.
Giles Hubert Papers, 1881–1977, n.d.
Rosa [Freeman] Keller Collection, 1955–ca. 1977.
Louisiana Weekly, New Orleans, Louisiana, Photographs, 1973–1979.
John P. Nelson, Jr., Papers, 1957–1977, n.d.
Save Our Schools (SOS) Papers, 1957–1963.
A. P. Tureaud Papers, 1783–1981, n.d.

Tulane University Archives
Tulane Hullaballoo, 1960–1963.

Reed, 1961 . . . 1964.

The State Historical Society of Wisconsin, Madison
The Carl and Ann Braden Papers.
Papers of the Congress of Racial Equality (CORE).
Southern Patriot, 1953–1971.

Earl K. Long Memorial Library, University of New Orleans
NAACP Papers.

Index

Aaron, Julia, 124, 129–30
ACLU. *See* American Civil Liberties Union
Actionist (for CORE), 13, 88, 197
Activism, 8–16, 25–27, 30, 38, 39, 50, 109, 118, 128, 135, 144, 145, 147–50, 152, 156–57, 159–62, 173, 190, 192, 195–201, 203–5, 207, 209, 212
Activist careers, 14, 192, 199, 205, 206
Activists, 2, 6, 8–11, 13–16, 17–18, 26, 27 37, 44, 49, 59, 60, 94, 104, 105, 109, 110, 112, 118, 123, 124, 129, 130, 136, 143, 144, 145, 147–49, 153, 159, 161–62, 165, 174, 175, 176, 178, 180, 181, 182, 183, 186, 189, 190–95, 198, 199, 200, 201, 205, 206–12; black activists, 2, 9, 17, 18, 36, 37, 44, 107, 135, 150, 186, 204, 206; intimidation and violence against activists, 5, 9, 17–18, 32, 33, 36–37 44, 51, 71–73, 83–84, 85, 89, 90–91, 99–100, 115, 118, 124, 125, 129, 130, 132, 133–34, 140, 142, 143, 148, 150, 154, 157, 159, 162, 166–67, 168, 182–83, 199, 206, 210; timing of activism, 11, 13, 196, 200, 203; white activists, 2,

6, 9, 13, 18, 26, 27, 37, 44, 77, 133, 149–50, 204, 206
Addison, Lloyd, 122
Africa, 4, 112; back-to-Africa movement, 20; Republic of New Africa, 156; South Africa, 53; West African culture, 4
African beliefs, 2
African-Afro-American Conference, 146
African-Americans, 1–5, 7; musicians, 1; slave culture, 3
African diaspora, 186
Agrarian Southern Right, 36
Alexander, Rev. Avery, 67, 70, 78, 90, 109, 144, 155; Consumers' League and Dryades Street Boycotts, 67; march on City Hall, 92, 93
Alexander, Will, 23, 200
Alienation, 143, 172, 189
Allen, Mary, 61, 202, 203
American Civil Liberties Union (ACLU), 68, 69, 104, 105, 126, 159, 172, 204
American Jewish Congress, 105
American Legion, 32, 102
American Student Union, 31, 47
Anti-poll tax movements, 20

School desegregation cases, 33, 34, 167
School integration, 50, 61–63, 66, 70, 73, 75, 91, 157
SCHW. *See* Southern Conference for Human Welfare
Schwerner, Mickey, 135, 141, 179
SCLC. *See* Southern Christian Leadership Conference
Scott, Doris Jean Castle, 174, 175, 177–78. *See also* Castle, Doris Jean
Second Reconstruction, 140, 192
Segregation, 2, 9, 13, 20, 22–27, 31, 33, 35–37, 39, 43–48, 50–53, 56, 57, 59–61, 63, 65, 68, 70, 75–77, 93, 94, 97, 101, 104, 110, 112, 114–16, 118, 123, 127, 133, 142, 153, 160, 161, 162, 165, 175, 177, 178, 181, 183, 191, 198, 202, 205, 206, 209
Segregationists, 8, 14, 18, 26, 31, 32, 34, 36, 37, 40, 41, 44, 48, 50, 57, 58, 60, 61, 62, 63, 64, 65, 66, 68, 70, 72, 73, 75, 85, 87, 90, 92, 96, 107, 148, 157, 161, 203
Self-development, 140, 189
Selma, Alabama, 132, 142, 156
Selma to Montgomery March, 142
Senate Internal Security Subcommittee (SISS), 40, 102, 208
Seventh Ward (New Orleans), 5, 108, 115, 116, 167
Shakespeare Park, 40, 91
SISS. *See* Senate Internal Security Subcommittee
Sit-ins, 52, 59, 67, 68, 69, 70, 86, 111, 115, 118–19, 124, 126–27, 144, 151, 159, 211; F. W. Woolworth's on Canal Street, 69, 86, 118, 126; *Lombard vs. Louisiana*, 52, 59, 70, 127, 170, 209, 210; McCrory's lunch counter, 59, 69–70, 86, 119, 126–27
Smith, Ben, 58, 79, 80; Louisiana Joint Legislative Committee on Un-American Activities (LUAC) and the raid on the Southern Conference Educational Fund (SCEF), 101–4; membership in the American Civil Liberties Union, 104
Smith, Carleen, 126, 144
Smith, Doratha, 126, 138, 144, 145
Smith, Jerome, 10, 68, 111–12, 113, 124–

26, 129–30, 135–36, 138, 140, 142, 143, 146, 149, 174, 184–86, 195, 205, 206; Consumers' League and the Dryades Street Boycotts, 68, 110, 112; meeting with Attorney General Robert F. Kennedy, 143; membership in the Congress of Racial Equality (CORE), 90, 123, 124, 125, 126, 129–30, 135, 145, 185, 205; participation in the Freedom Rides, 124, 129–30, 211; Tamburine and Fan, 184
Smith County, 135
Smith vs. Allwright, 19
SNCC. *See* Student Non-Violent Coordinating Committee
Social change, 9, 11, 13, 14, 61, 69, 110, 119, 123, 140, 160, 175, 191, 194, 198, 202, 206
Socialization, 173, 200, 203
Social mobility, 82, 199
Soniat, Llewellyn, 78
Sophie Newcomb College (women's division of Tulane University), 61, 97, 202
SOS. *See* Save Our Schools
SOUL. *See* Southern Organization for United Leadership
South (the), 2, 5, 6, 8, 9, 17, 20, 23, 27, 29, 32–34, 41, 51, 52, 54, 60, 62, 63, 74, 80, 83, 84, 86, 90, 105, 108, 109, 123, 124, 125, 139, 145, 158, 160, 162, 168, 187, 189, 202, 203
Southern Christian Leadership Conference (SCLC), 22, 35, 84, 149, 155; launches "Project C" in Birmingham, Alabama, 84
Southern Conference Educational Fund (SCEF), 20, 21, 27, 32, 33, 35, 36, 44, 47, 79, 101–5, 156, 157, 160, 161, 200, 201, 208, 214 n. 1; *Dombrowski vs. Pfister*, 103–4; investigation by U.S. Senate Internal Security Subcommittee (SISS), 40–41; offices raided by Louisiana Joint Legislative Committee on Un-American Activities (LUAC), 32. *See also* Southern Conference for Human Welfare
Southern Conference for Human Welfare (SCHW), 20–21, 33, 199–200. *See also* Collins, Virginia Young; Dombrowski, Dr. James; Southern Conference Educational Fund